William Henry Stevenson

The Crawford Collection of Early Charters and Documents Now in

the Bodleian Library

William Henry Stevenson

The Crawford Collection of Early Charters and Documents Now in the Bodleian Library

ISBN/EAN: 9783337218041

Printed in Europe, USA, Canada, Australia, Japan

Cover: Foto ©ninafisch / pixelio.de

More available books at **www.hansebooks.com**

London
HENRY FROWDE
OXFORD UNIVERSITY PRESS WAREHOUSE
AMEN CORNER, E.C.

New York
MACMILLAN & CO., 66 FIFTH AVENUE

CONTENTS

PREFACE .	v
CHARTERS AND DOCUMENTS	1
NOTES . .	37
INDEX .	153

PREFACE

THE collection of MSS. of which these charters form a part was purchased by the Curators of the Bodleian Library at the sale of the library of W. H. Crawford, of Lakelands, county Cork, by Messrs. Sotheby, Wilkinson, and Hodge, on March 14, 1891. The charters are inserted in a large oblong scrap book, bound in Russia leather, now numbered '*MS. Eng. hist.* a. 2,' kept as '*Arch. F.* a. 3.' The remainder of the collection, which has been removed from this volume and transferred to other classes in the Bodleian, comprises fifty-one later charters, thirty-six of which relate to Surrey, from c. 1230 to 1537; a fragment of a Walsingham abbey chartulary (*MS. Top. Norf.* b. 1); an early-eleventh cent. fragment of St. John's Gospel ii. 6–iii. 34 and vi. 19–vii. 10 in Old English (*MS. Eng. Bib.* c. 2), printed by A. S. Napier in the *Archiv für das Studium der neueren Sprachen*, vol. 87, p. 255; and fragments of Persius, the *Achilleis* of Statius, Avianus, and the *Carmen Paschale* of Sedulius (*MS. Lat. class.* d. 7). Other fragments, mainly Latin, have the following Press Marks: *Gr. liturg.* c. 2; *Lat. Bib.* c. 1; *Lat. liturg.* d. 3; *Lat. th.* c. 3; *Lat. misc.* c. 7; *Eng. poet.* f. 1 (fragment of a seventeenth century transcript of an English chronicle); *Fr.* b. 1.

Little is known of the history of this collection. The volume containing them bears no owner's name except that of Mr. Crawford, to whom the collection was sold by Mr. Quaritch some twenty years ago. The binding appears to be about a hundred years old, and as No. VI was in possession of Robert Austen, F.S.A., of Shalford Hall, co. Surrey, in 1791, it is probable that the collection was made or completed by him. This suggestion will account for the number of Surrey deeds in the collection. Austen, who died at his house in Gower Street, London, on

November 3, 1797 (*Gentleman's Magazine*, vol. 67, p. 987), was a considerable collector of coins, medals, and MSS., &c. These were bequeathed by him as heir-looms in the family, and, in certain contingencies, to the Trustees of the British Museum. By 1812 the conditions under which the collection might revert to the Museum had become impossible, and, by virtue of a private act (52 Geo. III., c. 156), the collection of coins and medals was sold by Austen's son to the Bank of England. It is now in the British Museum, amongst the coins and medals given to the Museum in 1877 by the Governor and Directors of the Bank of England[1]. It was probably about this time that Austen's collection of MSS. was disposed of, but we have been unable to trace their fate, or to obtain a list of them.

It is possible that Austen purchased the whole or part of this collection at the sale of the books and MSS. of Thomas Martin (1697–1771), a well-known antiquary, in May 1774, for the fragment of St. John's Gospel included in the collection bears the following note: 'This Saxon Fragment of St. John's Gospell was us'd as the Cover to a Court Book at Flixton Hall in Suffolk, A° 1722. Tho: Martin.' The same hand has also written: 'Shewn to ye Society of Antiquaries at London June ye 18. 1730 and the word Se hælynd (for Jesus) entred in their book.' The catalogue of Martin's sale does not enable us to identify the deeds, which are very roughly described, as e.g. Lot 306, 'Twenty very ancient and curious deeds.' It is sometimes stated that a lot was 'collected by Mr. Le Neve.' Martin married Le Neve's widow, and Nichols, *Literary Anecdotes of the 18th Century*, i. 415, records that, at Le Neve's sale in February, 1731, 'a considerable part of them [Le Neve's MSS. and records] came into the hands of Mr. Martin, who before came into the possession of many of them at the time of his marriage.' Peter le Neve, the well-known herald, died on September 29, 1729. One of the charters printed in the following pages (No. IX.) was certainly in Le Neve's hands, for it is endorsed by him with a note of its price and purchase in 1727. This MS. was in possession of the Dean and Chapter of Westminster in 1702, when it was printed by Thomas Madox. Another charter (No. VI) was added to this collection some time between 1705, when it was still in the

---

[1] For this information, we are indebted to Mr. H. A. Grueber, of the Coin Department, British Museum.

possession of the Dean and Chapter of Westminster, and 1791, when it was in Austen's hands. It is possible that this, like the other Westminster charter, was acquired by Le Neve, although it has no endorsement to this effect [1]. We are unable to prove Le Neve's ownership of the remainder of the collection, as the catalogue of his sale does not describe his MSS. sufficiently. It is certain that Nos. V and XIV were added to the collection after Le Neve's death, as the former was in possession of Dr. Mason in 1773, and the latter in that of Francis Blomfield (1705-1752), the historian of Norfolk, in 1740. Probably, the collection was commenced by Le Neve, and was augmented by Martin and Austen.

The nucleus of the collection is a valuable set of documents relating to Crediton monastery, which restore to us a large portion of the forgotten history of that foundation. These Crediton muniments (Nos. I, II, III, IV, VII, X, XIII) have been, no doubt, kept together from the time of the dissolution of the monastery, for they probably remained at Crediton after the bishop's see was transferred thence to Exeter, since Crediton retained its chapter until the dissolution of the monasteries [2]. Certainly No. XIII, Bishop Warelwast's confirmation of the liberties of the canons, must have come from Crediton long after the transfer of the see. Possibly these charters came from Crediton Free School, upon which Edward VI conferred the church and some of the lands of this old foundation. To these Crediton documents have been added two Westminster charters (Nos. VI, IX), which, as we have said, were in possession of the Dean and Chapter in 1705 and 1702; a charter (No. XI) that formerly belonged to the great monastery of St. Albans, where it passed under the eyes of Matthew of Paris; a charter (No. XII) from the monastery of St. Augustine, Canterbury; another (No. VIII) that probably owes its preservation to the monks of Coventry; and one (No. V) whose earlier home we are unable to trace. The few twelfth-century charters (Nos. XIV to XVII) have obviously no relationship to any of the foundations above named, and they were,

[1] It may be noted that Le Neve did not endorse the Harley Charters, 83 A. 2 and 83 A. 3, in the British Museum, which, according to Wanley's endorsement, were bought from him.
[2] One of the Crediton charters (Ordnance Survey *Facsimiles of Anglo-Saxon MSS.*, part ii; *Cart. Sax.*, iii. 623) was given to the Public Record Office in 1870 by Mr. Hy. Garling, of Southborough Hall, Kent. See 3 *2nd Report of the Deputy-Keeper of the Public Records*, p. iv. Nothing is known of the earlier history of this charter.

no doubt, acquired at separate times, like the later deeds in the collection.

The importance of the documents printed in the following pages is evinced by the fact that eight of them are inedited and unknown[1]. These inedited texts are of singular interest. They include an early copy of an apparently genuine charter of King Æðelheard of Wessex, a monarch who has been hitherto represented by one charter; an original charter of King Æðelstan, an important addition to the very brief list of original charters of this great king; an almost contemporary copy of a letter of St. Dunstan in Old-English; an original charter of King Æðelred 'the Unready'; the will of a bishop of Crediton; and the rules made for the canons of Crediton by the bishop of Exeter in the early years of the twelfth century. The collection is hardly less important in regard to documents of which printed texts exist, since it comprises the originals of the following: a charter of King Eadwig, printed by Kemble and Birch from an eighteenth century transcript; the famous forged charter of Edgar to Westminster, hitherto printed from corrupt copies in chartularies; the will of Leofwine Wulfstan's son, reprinted by Kemble and Thorpe from Madox's text, the original having disappeared; King Æðelred's charter to St. Alban's, printed, without the O. E. boundaries, by Kemble from a thirteenth century copy.

We have proceeded upon very conservative lines in editing the texts, reproducing, so far as type will permit, the abbreviations of the MSS. The abbreviations in O. E. charters are few and simple, and the reader may solve any difficulty connected with them by reference to the table of *compendia* given by Kemble, *Codex Diplomaticus*, i. p. cxvi (reprinted by Earle, *Land Charters*, p. cxi).

In the annotation we have allowed ourselves very wide limits, as it has been our endeavour to illustrate the diplomatic, historical, and philological points of interest. In all these provinces very much remains to be done, for it cannot be said that the O. E. charters have yet been edited. Kemble gives very little real help towards deciding the question of the authenticity of the charters printed by him, whilst Mr. Birch does not attempt to distinguish genuine from forged charters. He is, indeed, sometimes misleading, as when he speaks of an 'Original

---

[1] Since our notes were in type, the first five have been printed from our text in Mr. Birch's *Cartularium Saxonicum*.

charter in the British Museum,' meaning occasionally a much later copy on a single sheet of parchment. Owing to these causes our progress has been constantly delayed by the necessity of carefully examining the texts of the numerous documents cited by us. We have been enabled, as the result of our examination, to correct the dates of many deeds, some of which bear wrong dates in the chartularies wherein they are preserved, whilst others have been incorrectly dated by Kemble and Birch. Some of these corrections appear in the notes, but there are naturally many others that we have not cited. It has not been at all an uncommon experience for us to find that the date assigned by Kemble and Birch has been rendered impossible by the dates of office of the archbishops or of the bishops who witness the particular charter. This is a very easy way of testing the date of a document, but the application of it to scores of charters involves a great expenditure of time and considerably delays one's progress. In addition to this, we have had to compile our own *apparatus* for dealing with questions of the *formulae* and stiles of the different kings, as next to nothing has been done in this important branch of the study of O. E. charters. The labour involved in this has been considerably increased by the necessity of examining and eliminating charters containing *formulae* inconsistent with the usages of the compilers of the charters of the kings to whom they are assigned [1]. We have also found it necessary to make lists of the dates of the attestations of the Ealdormen who witness the O. E. royal charters. This has enabled us to fix the dates of several documents, to authenticate many doubtful ones, and to correct and add to what has been written upon the lives of some of these Ealdormen. Our results are embodied in the notes on the Ealdormen, in which our object has been not to write biographies, but to deal mainly with the fixing of the dates of office, the determination of the provinces, and the kinship of the Ealdormen who come within our view. Although we frequently differ from Mr. Robertson, the principal worker in this field, it will be seen that we repeat much of the information given by him. This arises from the fact that our notes were compiled by ourselves

---

[1] In our notes we have occasionally, for the sake of convenience, spoken of the 'chancery' of a particular king. As no such office existed under this name under the OE. kings, it is perhaps necessary to explain that we use this word to express the *formulae*, stile, usages, &c., of the clerks who drew up the charters of the respective kings.

before reading his articles; thus they have the merit of being independent compilations. It will be found that they have the greater merit of giving the authorities for important statements for which Mr. Robertson frequently cites no reference. Some of these Ealdormen are very briefly dealt with by Robertson, whilst some are not even mentioned by him. In the case of Yric, Cnut's earl of Northumberland, we have given a sketch of the life of a great hero of the Norse sagas, who flits across the pages of our histories as a mere name. We have also given a life of his contemporary Eglaf, of whose relationship and history Freeman knew nothing. The lives of these two *duces* are necessarily drawn mainly from the Scandinavian sagas, and our notes will, we hope, show that the sagas are worthy of a more patient study than Freeman gave to them as sources illustrative of English history.

In compiling our notes, we have carefully examined every text cited by us as the authority for any statement in the departments of history and *formulae*, and have generally noted the dubious or spurious texts conflicting with our conclusions. We have not, however, pointed out dubious charters that do not conflict with our assertions or whose evidence is supported by genuine deeds of the same, or earlier or later date, as the case may be. We are not prepared to assert that every one of the charters that has passed our examination is authentic, since in many cases it is very difficult to decide the question of authenticity. But it may be taken that the texts not stigmatized by us present no very obvious proofs of being forgeries. Sometimes a genuine charter is ascribed by the scribes of the chartularies to a wrong king, and is liable under such circumstances to be regarded as spurious[1]. We have not gone so fully into the question of authenticity of the charters cited in the philological notes, since it frequently happens that a late copy or a spurious charter is a sufficient authority for the statement it is intended to support.

Regarding the division of the editors' labours, it may suffice to say that both are responsible for the text, and that, roughly speaking, Prof. Napier has supplied the philological and Mr. Stevenson the historical

[1] As there are several charters in Kemble and Birch of which the wrong ascriptions have escaped the editors, we may refer, as examples of this process, to the two charters of King Æðelred of Wessex, King Alfred's brother, which are ascribed to King Edgar and King Eadred (*CS*. iii. 24, 488). See *Academy*, June 30, 1894, pp. 536, 537.

PREFACE xi

and diplomatic notes. But there has been throughout a constant overlapping of the functions of the two editors, so that in some cases it would be impossible to determine each editor's share in a note. The whole of the notes have, of course, been independently revised, both in MS. and in type, by both editors.

We cannot take leave of the work without recording our most sincere thanks to the Bishop of Oxford, who has not only shown the kindest interest in this volume throughout its tardy preparation, but has found time to read through the proofs of the notes and has favoured us with very valuable additions and corrections. We have had not only the benefit of his counsel and revision, but also the encouragement afforded us by finding that so many of our notes passed his review without change or criticism. This, of course, does not entitle us to vouch his great authority for any particular statement.

Our thanks are also due to Bodley's Librarian, to whose vigilance the acquisition of this collection is due, for his interest in the work and for numerous kindly attentions during its progress, and to Mr. Falconer Madan for palaeographical help.

A. S. N.

W. H. S.

March 25, 1895.

CHARTERS AND DOCUMENTS.

I.

739, 4 Id. April (=April 10.)—*King Æðilhard to Forðhere, bishop (of Sherborne).—Grant of land for the foundation of Crediton monastery, co. Devon.*

✠ IN NOMINE DŇI NR̄I IH̄U XP̄I SALUATORIS. Om̄a quę uidentur secundum apłm temporalia sunt . & quę non uidentur aeterna sunt. Idcirco terrenis ac caducis rebus perpetua & mansura dō patrocinium prestante mercanda sunt. Quam ob rem ego AETHELHARDUS rex aliquam terram ad construendum monasterium id est .XX. cassatos 5 in loco ubi dicitur CRIDIE pontifici nr̄o forthhero ppetualiter impendere curaui cum commoditatibus cunctis in ea consistentibus . han[c]q; donationē coram idoneis testibus corroboraui . ut nemo sine piculo animę suę infringere ualeat . quod coram tam egregiis consiliariis pactum est. Territoria autem hęc sunt. Ærest of cridian brycge on herpað . 10 andlanges herpaðes on sulhford to exan . þonne andlang eaxan oð focgan igeðas . of focgan igeðum on landsceare hricg . of landsceare hricge on luhan treow . of luhan treowe on hagan get . of hagan gate on doddan hrycg . of doddan hrycge on grendeles pyt . of grendeles pytte on ifigbearo . of ifigbeara on hrucgan cumbes ford . of hrucgan 15 cumbes forda on fearnburh . of fearnbyrig on earnes hricg . of earnes hrycge on wealdan cumbes ford . of wealdan cumbe on tettan burnan . of tettan burnan up on stream oð lyllan broc . of lyllan broce on middelhrycg . of middelhrycge on herepaðford . of herepaðforda on cyrtlan geat . of cyrtlan gate on suran apuldre . of suran apuldran on grenan 20

CHARTERS AND DOCUMENTS.

weg . of grenan wege on wulfpyt . of wulfpytte on stream oð þa laca tolycgaþ . þonne up on hrycg myddewcardne andlang hrycges oð þone pað . of þam paðc sceaftrihte on alr suð ofer on hlypan . of hlypan on byrccumbes heafod . of byrccumbes heafode on hanan forda . þanon on
25 bradan æsc . of bradan æsce on foxcumbes heafod . þanon on stanford on eowan . of stanforda on arlscagan . of alrscagan on eorðgeberst . þanon on grenan dune . of grenan dune on herepað on puttan stapul . þanon on beornwunne treow . þanon on bucgan ford . of bucgan forda on brunwoldes treow . þanon on æsccumb . þoñ on won broc . ⁊langes
30 streames on teng upon stream on teng oð paðford . þanon on francan cumb of fran[can] cumbe on drosncūbes heafod . þanon on deormere . of deormere on langan stan . þanon on hurran cumbes heafod . of hurran cumbes heafde on riscford on nimed . þanon on healre dunæ . of healre dune on wærnan fæsten . þanon on cyddan ford . of cyddan
35 forda on cæfcan græfan . þanon on caines æcer . of caines æcere on wulfcumbes heafod . þanon on stanbeorg . of stanbeorge on cærswille . of cærswille on diðford . þanon on dices get . of dices gate on unnan beorh . þanon on swincumb . of swincumbe on egesan treow.

On nymed oð doflisc up oð wiðigslæd . of wyþigslade on eahta
40 æc . þanon on hafoccumb . of hafoccumbe on hagan get . þanon ut on hlypan . þanon on beonnan ford on crydian . þonne on stream oð hafoccumb . þonne on hagan get . þonne on ðone ealdan herepað oð þa eastran crydian . þonne andlang streames to cridian brycge.

Huic autem terrę hanc libertatem augebo & firmiter constituo . ut
45 oṁium causarum fiscaliū . & rerum regalium ac seculariū operum sit inmunis . sempiternaliterq; secura . nisi tantum expeditionaliū rerum. Qui augeat augeantur bona illius . & qui minuat seu transmutet . conuertatur gaudium illius in luctum . pęnasq; infernales perpetualiter luat. Acta est autem hęc donatio anno ab incarnatione dñi nŕi iħu xp̄i
50 DCCXXXVIIII . Indictione VII . die . IIII . iduum aprilium :—

       + Signum manus   AÐILHARDI regis.
       + Signum manus   cuthredi.
       + Signum manus   frythogythę.
       + Ego danihel ep̄s   canonice subscripsi.
55   + Ego forthhere ep̄s   consensi & subscripsi.

26. *arlscagan*] so in MS. The *l* of the following *alrs-* is altered from *r*.

CHARTERS AND DOCUMENTS. 3

+ Signum manus   hercfrythi prefecti.
+ Signū manus   duddi abbatis.
+ Signū manus   ccgfrithi p̄fecti.
+ Signū manus   puttoc p̄fecti.

Endorsed in same hand: boc .xx. hyda to crydian. 60
„ *in a* 12*th cent. hand:* æðelardi Reḡ. de .xx. hidis de cridia.
„ *in a* 14*th cent. hand:* vł Criditonia.

II.
Boundaries of above land.

✠ Þis sint þa landgemæro cridian landes . ærest of cridian brycge on herepaþ andlang herepaþes on sulhford to eaxan . þoñ andlang eaxan oþ focgan igeþas . of focgan igeþum on landscare hrycg . of landscare hrycge on luhan treow . of luhan treowe on hagan get . of haga`n' gate on doddan hrycg . of doddan hrycge on grendeles pyt . of grendeles 5 pytte on ifigbearo . of ifigbeara on hrucgan cumbes ford . of hrucgan cumbes forda on fearnburg . of fearnbyrig on earnes hrycg . of earnes hrycge on wealdan cumbes ford . of wealdan cūbe on tettan burnan . of tettan burnan up on streā oþ lillan broc . of lillan broce on middelhrycg . of middelhryge on herepaðford . of herepaðforda on cyrtlan geat . 10 of cyrtlan gate on suran apuldre . of suran apuldran on grenan weg . of grenan wege on wulfpyt . of wulfpytte on stream oþ þa laca tolicgaþ . þoñ up on hrycg middeweardne 7lang hrycges oþ þone paþ . of þæm paþe sceaftrihte on alr suþ ofer on hlypan . of hlypan on byrccumbes heafod . of byrccumbes heafde on hanan ford . þanon [on] bradan æsc . 15 of bradan æsce on foxcumbes heafod . þanon on stanford on eowan . of stanforda on alrscagan . of alrscagan on eorþgeberst . þanon on grenan dune . of grenan dune on herepaþ on puttan stapul . þanon on beor`n'wynne treow . of beor`n'wynne treowe on stanford on eowan . þanon on bucgan ford . of bucgan forda on brunwoldes treow . þanon on æsccumb . 20 of æsccumbe on won broc 7langes streames on teng . up on stream on teng oþ paþford . þanon on francan cumb . of francan cumbe on drosncumbes heafod . þanon on deormere . of deormere on langan stan . þanon on hurran cumbes heafod . of hurran cumbes heafde on riscford

10. *hrygc*] so in MS.

25 on nymed . þanon on healre dune . of healre dune on wærnan fæsten .
þanon on ciddan ford . of ciddan forda on cæfcan græfan . þanon on
caines æcer . of caines æccre on wulfcumbes heafod . þanon on stanbeorg . of stanbeorge on cærswille . of cærswille on dyðford . þanon
on dices get . of dices gate on unnan beorg . þanon on swincumb . of
30 swincumbe on egesan treow . þanon on riscbroc mid streame oþ scipbroc .
on scipbroc mid streame oþ nymed . On nymed mid streame oþ
doflisc . of doflisc up on stream oþ wiþigslæd . of wiþigslade on
eahta æc . þanon on hafoccumb . of hafoccumbe on hagan get . þanon ut
on hlypan . þanon on beonnan ford on cridian . þonne on stream oþ
35 hafoccumb . þoñ on hagan geat . þoñ on þone caldan herepaþ oþ þa
easteran cridian . þoñ 7lang streames to cridian brycge ;

Endorsed in contemporary hand: Cridian landes lan[dgemæro].
„ „ *late 13th cent. hand:* Cridiam land ys land ȝemere.
„ „ *late 14th cent. hand:* Cridiam londes land ȝemere .
Angl[ice].

III.

Late fifteenth century version of boundaries of No. I.

Cridyton.

Fyrst fram Crydian brugge to herpaþ and ewn langys herpath
to Sulford 'to' Exe and þan ewn lang Exe anonto fogan flodys fram
fogan flode to landsceare rygge fram landscear rygge to luhan tre .
fram luantre luhan tre to hagan yate fram hagan yeate to doddan
5 rygge fram doddan rygge to gryndelys pytte fram gryndelys pytte
to yfigbearo fram yfigbeara to herl hurgan cumbes ford fram hurgan
cumbes ford to fearnburgh fram fearnburgh to yearnys rygge fram
yearnys rugge to Weldecomys rugge forde fro Weldecome to
Tettanburna fram Tettanburna vp by the stream to lyllan broke and
10 fram lyllan broke to myddelrugge fram myddelrugge to herpaþ ford
fram herpaþ ford to Kyrtelane yeate fram Kyrtelane yeate to Suran
apuldre fram Suran apuldre to grene way fram grene way to Wolfpytte
fram Wolfpytte by þe streame þat þe lake tolythe Than vp on the
rugge mydway langryggys anon to þe paþ fram þe paþ ewnryght south

4. *luantre*] cancelled. 6. *herl*] cancelled.
8. Second *rugge* cancelled.

wardys ouerto lypan fram lypan to brygcombes heauyd fram bryg- 15
combys heauyd to hanonford fram thans to bradanaysch fram Bradanaysch to foxecombys heade fram thans to Stanford on ewyn fram
Stanford to Arlschag fram Arlschag to yeorþberst fram that to grene
downe fram grene downe to herpaþ on puttanstapyl fram thens to
bernwone tree fram thens to bugganford fram Bugganford to Brym- 20
woldys tree fram thens to Aysch'comb' fram thens to Wonbroke ewne
langes stremys of Teynge and apon the stream on Teynge anon to
Paþford fram thens to Fra[n]cancumbe fram Francancumbe to Dros-
com'b'yshede fram thens to Deremere fram Deremere to langestone fram
thens to Hurrancombysheade fram Hurrancombysheade to ryschforde 25
on nímed fram thens to Alre down fram alre downe to warnan fasten
fram thans to Kyddanford fram Kyddanford to cafcan grefa fram thens
to Kaynys aker fram Kaynys aker to Wolfcombysheade fram thans
to Stansbrygg fram Stanbrugge to Carswyll fram Carswyll to Dyþford
fram thens to Dychys yeate fram Dychys yeate to Vnnan burgh fram 30
thens to Swyncomb fram Swyncomb to egesan tree fram nymed to
Doflysch vp anonto þe Wydeslade fram þe Wydeslade to viii. oke fram
thens to Haffoccomb fram Haffoccomb to hagon yeate fram thens out
to lypan fram thens to beannanford on crydyan þan by þe stream
anon to Haffoccomb þanne to hagan yeate þan to þe olde herpaþ anon 35
to þe yester crydyan þan ewnlang þe stremys to Crydyan brugge.

IV.

930, III. Kal. Maii (= April 29).—*King Æðelstan to Eadulf, bishop
(of Crediton) and the monastery at Crediton.—Grant of three hides
at Sandford, near Crediton, co. Devon.*

[1018].—*Endorsed with note of grant by Eadnoð, bishop (of Crediton),
to Beorhtnoð of a yardland at Creedy for his lifetime, in consideration of 30 gold mancuses lent to the bishop for the redemption
of his land (from the Danegeld?).*

✠ Regnante perpetualiter atque omnem humanç inbecillitatis
sensum . benignitate transce[n]dente . largiflua tonantis iduma . que

33. Second *Haffoccomb* altered from *Haffac*.

mirando inęffabiliq; pprii arbitrii priuilegio . alta media infima . iusta
inuicte fortitudinis lance trutinata gubernat . et ea que infra sunt . non
5 motata sed sempiternaliter manenti elucubratione uoluntatis . inestimab-
iliter luce inaccessibili rimatur . que massam humane conditionis
generalem . olim fraude falsitatis decoeptam . patria naturalis sinceritatis
pulsam . merito piaculi heu pro dolor commissi iustę trusam . cyrographum ęterne seruitutis seu damnationis subituram . temporibus
10 labilis uite uoluentibus nouissimis . precepto pantacratoris miseri-
co`r´diter reformauit . cuiusque foedata flumine ęternarum lacrimarum
timpora . orario adsumpte mortalitatis tergens . eam dolores cruciatusq;
sempiternos euadentem . ad optabilia ęternorum gaudiorum deduxit
limina . quorum atria . pars eiusdem recuperate masse . terreni incolatus
15 ęrumnas . operibus examinatis transuolans . inter ca`n´dentia beatorum
angelorum agmina . feliciter exultando congaudet . altero uero aliena
gemende peregrinationis diuturnitate exulans . splendida meritis adhuc
nutantibus regione orbatur . Huius siquidem exose peregrinationis
merore pressus . gaudio longeue beatitudinis illectus . ad demenda scele-
20 rum commissorum peccamina . et ad nanciscendam iam antefatę glorię
coronam . ego æthelstanus rex anglorum . anno dominice incarnationis
.DCCCC . $\overset{o}{XXX}$. regni uero gratis mihi commisi . $\overset{o}{VI}$. indictione . $I\overset{a}{II}$.
epacta . .$XV\overset{a}{III}$. concurrente .IIII. kalendis maii tertiis . luna rotigere
uagationis .$\overset{o}{XXVI}$. per eiusdem omni patrantis dexteram . totius brytt-
25 annię regni soľi´o sublimatus . quandam mihi ab ea telluris particulam .
mirabiliter concessam me[o fi]deli episcopo eadulfo . id est trium cassat-
arum . in loco quem solicolę æt sandforda uocitant . que sub episcopali
dicione fuit . sed tamen mihi census iniquorum actuum prius reddebatur .
familięq; æt cridiantune tribuo . ut illa eam sine expeditionis ꝓfectione .
30 arcis pontis constructione . omniq; regaliū uel seculariū tributorum
seruitutis exactione . liberaliter ac ęternaliter in perpetuū habeat . si
autem quod absit . feruente tumide superbię cocabo . aliqui ex familia .
quod libet iniquitatis facinus commisserint ꝵ Hoc in eis iudicialiter atque
regulariter uindicetur . predictus agellus in sua stabilitate . semper
35 fratribus ad mensam . qui in antefato ergasterio ꝵ .dō . ęclesię . domno
prelato . humiliter fideliterq; obtemperare uoluerint . firmus et in-

6. *inaccessibili*] the second *i* altered from another letter.
10. *pantacratoris*] alt. from *pantacreatoris*.
15. *transuolans*] two letters erased before *u*.
16. *altero*] for *altera*.
19-20. *scelerum*] *u* on erasure.
27. After *que* a letter has been erased.
32. *cocabo*] for *cacabo*.

CHARTERS AND DOCUMENTS.

auferabilis pduret . nec habeant fratres licentiam . illum foras dandi .
regi . episcopo . uel cuilibet homini . nisi alium maiorem atq; meliorem .
p eius uicissitudinis commotatione . alia similiter cum cartula . perpetualiter hereditaria recipiant . tellus siquidem predicta . his terminis circum- 40
cincta clarescit . ærest of fintes leage west on herepaþ oþ holan cumbes
heafod . norþ þanon on díc . sceaftryht on cuddan cnoll easteweardne .
þær west on herepaþ oþ þornisces weg . on þornisces weg þoñ norð on
scipbroc . úp on stream oð herepaþ . þoñ sceaftryht oð lilles forda .
þonne on cealdan hlinc westeweardne . þoñ on wyrtrum oþ cealdan hlinc 45
easteweardne . on wyrtrum þoñ git norð oþ brocheardes hámm . þoñ of
dune on hagan on bromleage niþewearde . þoñ sceaftryht oþ pideres
leage . þoñ sceaftryht oþ hlosleage nioþewearde . þoñ on stream oþ
fileðleage . norþ on herepaþ oþ ðelbrycge . þoñ úp on stream oþ æsculfes
weorðig . norð þanon sceaftryht oþ efes . þonne on wyrtrum oþ lucan 50
                                                 on stream . of dune on cridian
weorðig . norð on hagan oþ cyneferðes broc . þoñ of dune . oþ cridian .
oþ þone broc þe scyt from fileðleage . úp on stream oþ stanford . suþ þonne
on wyrtrum oþ henne stigele eastewearde . þonne sceaftryht oþ hroces ford .
þoñ on weardsetl suð þonne on wyrtrum oþ fintes leag[e .] Si uero quod
non optamus . aliquis pteruię atque arrogantię flammiuoma administrante . 55
inuidia . afflatis spu . euenerit . [qui] hanc meę compositionis ac confirmationis breuiculam . demere infringere . ad nihilum deducere temptauerit ꝛ
sciat se nouissima ac magna examinationis die . tuba perstrepente
archangeli . bustis sponte dehiscentibus . somata diu fessa amittentibus .
elimentis omnium creaturarum pauefactis . cum iuda pditore . qui á 60
satoris pio sato . filius pditionis dicitur . eterna confusione . edacibus
innumerabilium tormentorum flammis . perituru; huius namq; á dō
dñoq ; ihū xpo . inspirate atq; inuente uoluntatis ꝛ scedula . in uilla
omnib; notissima que cyppan hamm nuncupatur . episcopis . abbatib;
ducib; patrię pcuratoribus . regia dapsilitate ouantib; . uirgineo áterrimi 65
lacrimas liquoris forcipe . in planitiem tetragoni campuli albentem .
destillante pscripta est . cuius etiam inconcusse firmitatis soliditas .
hi's' testib; roborata constat . quorum nomina subtus caracterib; depicta
annotantur :⸺

51-52. *oþ cridian . oþ þone broc* is written, by the same hand as the rest of the charter, on an erasure.
56. *afflatis*] for *afflatus*.
56. [*qui*] omitted in MS.
61. MS. *pdititionis* ; over the second *ti* are dots indicating deletion.

70 + Ego æthelstanus singularis priuilegii monarchia prꝫditus rex . huius indiculi firmitatem . cum signo s̄c̄e sempꝗ; amande crucis . corroboraui et subscripsi ;
+ Ego wulfhelmus dorobernensis eccłe archiepiscopus . consensi et subscripsi ; + Ego hroðwardus eboracensis eccłe eps̄. ɔs̄ et subs̄.
75 + Ego ælfwine eps̄ consensi et subscripsi.
+ Ego eadulf epīsc cons̄ et subs̄.
+ Ego sighelm epīsc cons̄ et subs̄.
+ Ego ælfheah epīsc cons̄ et subs̄.
+ Ego oda epīsc cons̄ et subs̄.
80 + Ego cenwald epīsc cons̄ et subs̄.
+ Ego eadgær epīsc cons̄ et subs̄.
+ Ego cyneferð epīsc cons̄ et subs.
+ Ego friþestan epīsc cons̄ et subs.
+ Ego þeodred epīsc cons̄ et subs.
85 + Ego eadweard epīsc cons̄ et subs̄.

[Col. 2.]

+ Ego osferð dux cons̄ et subs̄.
+ Ego ælfwald dux cons̄ et subs̄.
+ Ego æscbriht dux cons̄ et subs̄.
+ Ego ælfstan dux cons̄ et subs̄.
90 + Ego uhtred dux cons̄ et subs̄.
+ Ego styrcær dux cons̄ et subs̄.
+ Ego guþrum dux cons̄ et subs̄.
+ Ego þurferð dux cons̄ et subs̄.
+ Ego fræna dux cons̄ et subs̄.
95 + Ego grim dux cons̄ et subs̄.

[Col. 3.]

+ Ego odda minister cons̄ et subs̄.
+ Ego buga mīn cons̄ et subs̄.
+ Ego wulfgær mīn cons̄ et subs̄.
+ Ego sigered mīn cons̄ et subs̄.
100 + Ego wulfhelm mīn cons̄ et subs̄.
+ Ego ælfheah mīn cons̄ et subs̄.
+ Ego æþelstan mīn cons̄ et subs̄.
+ Ego æþelhelm mīn cons̄ et subs̄.

CHARTERS AND DOCUMENTS.

+ Ego wulfgar mīn consˉ et subsˉ.
+ Ego æþelstan mīn consˉ et subsˉ.

[Col. 4.]

+ Ego ælfred mīn consˉ et subsˉ.
+ Ego eadric mīn consˉ et subsˉ.
+ Ego æþelweard mīn consˉ et subsˉ.
+ Ego wulfmær mīn consˉ et subsˉ.
+ Ego wulfnoþ mīn consˉ et subsˉ.
+ Ego æþelhelm mīn consˉ et subsˉ.
+ Ego ælfred mīn consˉ et subsˉ.
+ Ego wihtgar mīn consˉ et subsˉ.
+ Ego cadric mīn consˉ et subsˉ.
+ Ego wulfsige mīn consˉ et subsˉ.

Endorsed in hand of 11*th cent.*: ✠ In nomine dñi nr̄i iħu xp̄i. Ic cadnoð bisceop cyðe on þisson gewriton . þ ic onborgede .xxx. mancsa goldes be leadgewihte to minre landhreddinge æt beorhnoðe. 7 ic gesealde hym ane gyrde landes to underwedde be cridian to þam forewerdon. þ he hæbbe his dæg. 7 ofer his dæg becweðe þone sceat þam þe him leofost beo þe on þam lande stent. Ðis sind þa landgemæro þære gyrde be cridian. Ærest on sceocabroces ford. Þonne east on herpað on þone lytlan garan easteweardne . suð on þa deadan lace on cridian. up ongean stream on þone ænlypan æcer. Þonne east on herpað eft on sceocabroces ford. Ðisses ys to gewitnisse. cnút cyning. 7 wulstan arcebisceop 7 lifing arcebisceop. 7 birhtwold bisceop 7 eadnoð bisceop. 7 burewold bisceop. 7 æðelwine bisceop 7 birihtwine bisceop. 7 æðelwerd ealdorman. 7 aðelwold abbud. 7 call se hired on exan cestre 7 se hired on cridian tune . 7 þis cydde se bisceop þam burhwiton on exan ceastre 7 to tottanesse. 7 to hlidaforda 7 to beardastapole . Pax sit hoc scruantibus & infernus sit hoc frangentibus.

Endorsed in early 14*th cent. hand:* Carta Regis Etllthelstan de Est Samford in diebus eaddulfi episcopi huius loci sub anno domini DCCCC 'nongentesi[mo]' xxx[mo] apud Chippenham confecta.

126. The first *arcebisceop* on an erasure.   127. The first *bisceop* on an erasure.

V.

957, VII. Id. Maii (=May 9).—*King Eadwig to Archbishop Oda [of Canterbury].—Grant of land 'æt Helig.'*

✠ IN NOMINE DÑI NR̄I IHV̄ XP̄I. Diuina gratia largiente et originali prosapia ante cessorum meorum . . . . EADWIG . rex totius brittannię fidelissimo meo archi episcopo meoq: patrono toto mentis affectu cum consensu meorum obtimatum .XL. MANSAS . perpetualiter
5 concedo . ODONO . vbi ab antiquis ruricolis uocatum est . ÆT HELIG . Quatínus possideat et cuicumq; uoluerit heredi derelinquat in æterna POSSESSIONE . sit uero hoc rús pr̨e dictum absolutum ab omni mundiali obstaculo exceptis his tribus que omnib; communia sunt ID EST EXPEDITIONIS ET ARCIS PONTISUE CONSTRUCTIONE HÆC DONATIO FACTA
10 EST ANNO DÑIC̨E INCARNATIONIS DCCCLVII INDICTIONE XV. regni mei SECUNDO in uilla q; dicit^r EÐAN DVN .VII. IDVS MAĪ . coram IDONEIS TESTIB; quorum nomina infra collecta sunt . Siquis ħ augere uoluerit tribuat illi dŝ in hóc scĺo uitam longeuam et in futuro sempiternam . SIN autē minuere satagerit nr̄am liberam largitionē sit sotius
15 eorum quibus dicet ÆQUISSIMUS libripens in die iudicii ite maledicti in ignem æternum . qui pre paratus EST DIABOLO et angelis eius . si non híc prius emendare maluerit.

    + Ego Eadwig rex anglorum cum consensu doctorum meorum con signo sc̄ę crucis roboraui.
20 + Ego Eadgar eiusdem regis frater consensi celeriter.
    + Ego Oda archi episcopus dorouernsis æcclęsię xp̄i possedi et subscripsi.
    + Ego ælfsinus pręsul sigillum agię crucis impressi.
    + Ego byrhtelm epŝ confirmaui.
25 + Ego cenwald   epŝ consignaui.
    + Ego oscytel   epŝ conroboraui.
    + Ego osulf   epŝ adquieui.
    + Ego byrhtelm epŝ non rennui.

2. After *meorum* a hole in the MS.   6. The *i* of *uoluerit* covered in repairing MS.
19. *con*] for *cum*.

CHARTERS AND DOCUMENTS.

[Col. 2.]

+ Ego alfwold eps̄.
+ Ego wulfsige eps̄.
+ Ego aþulf eps̄.
+ Ego cynesige eps̄.
+ Ego daniel eps̄.

[Col. 3.]

+ æðelstan dvx
+ eadmund dvx
+ ælfhere dvx
+ æþelsige dvx
+ æþelwold dvx

[Col. 4.]

+ byrhtnoð dvx
+ ælfheah mīs
+ ælfsige mīs
+ ælfred mīs
+ æþelgeard mīs

[Col. 5.]

+ ælfsige mīs
+ æþelferþ mīs
+ ælfwine mīs
+ ælfric mīs
+ ælfgar mīs
+ byrhtferþ mīs
+ wulfgar mīs

[Col. 6.]

+ wulfstan mīs t̄.
+ ælfweard mīs t̄.
+ wynsige mīs t̄.
+ wulfric mīs t̄.
+ ælfsige mīs t̄.
+ eadric mīs t̄.
+ alfwold mīs t̄.

Endorsed in same hand: ✠ þis is þæs landes boc æt helig ðe eadwig cing gebocode odan arcebiscope on ęce yrfe.

Endorsed in somewhat later but pre-conquest hand: De Eðandune.

Endorsed in late 13th cent. hand: Eadredus.

VI.

969, Id. Maii (= May 15).—*King Eadgar to the monastery of Torneie (i. e. Westminster).—Confirmation of lands and liberties, reciting bull of Pope John.*

Regnante dño nro ihū xp̄o inppetuū . · Λ · ω · EGO EADGARVS dei gra anglo⁊ rex ⁊ om̄ib⁹ epīs . abbatib⁹ . comitib⁹ . uicecomitib⁹ . centenariís . cęterisq; agentibus nostris . pręsentibus scilicet et fut'is ⁊ salutem. Dignū et conueniens est clementię
5 p̄ncipali inter cęteras actiones illud quod ad salutem animę pertinet . et quod p̄ diuino amore postulat' . pio auditu suscipere . et studiose ad effectum perducere . quatinus de caducis rebus presentis sęculi quę nunquam sine inquinamento et erumpna possidentur . peccatorum emundatio . et uitę ęterne sęcuritas adquiratur ⁊ iuxta preceptum
10 dñi dicentis . date elemosinam ⁊ et om̄ia munda sunt uobis . Ergo dando elemosinam iuxta hoc ipsius dictum . oportet nos mercari peccatorum nostrorum emundationem . ut dū ęccliis xp̄i imptim' . ęgrua beneficia . et iustas bono⁊ uiro⁊ petitiones efficacit audim⁹ ⁊ retributorē dm̄ ex hoc habc meream' . IGITVR postqᵃm dono dei et patna
15 successione in regnū anglo⁊ intronizat⁹ 7 c̄firmat⁹ fui . ubi uidi ęccl̄as dei tam peccatis exigentib⁹ Qᵃm crebris barbarorū irruptionib⁹ dírutas . . et maximę sc̄am et apl̄icā uitā id . ē . monachicū ordinē p̄ om̄s regni mei p̱uincias fundit⁹ deperisse ⁊ grauit dolens . et consilium a sc̄o sp̄u accipiens . DVNSTANO archiep̄o . et aþelwoldo wintoniensi ep̄o . hoc
20 negotium indixi . ut om̄ia monasteria que intra t̄minū toti⁹ anglię sita sī supᵃ uel infra circūirent ác réédificarent . et possessiones que ad fiscū redacte erant de ipsis monasteriís . uel ab aliís scl̄arib⁹ potestatib⁹ p̱uasę . ubicunq; chartis uel testimoniís recognoscerent ⁊ mea auctoritate freti ⁊ ad integrū restituerent . Et tanqᵃm dicente m̄ dño á capite
25 incipe ⁊ inþmis eccl̄am domni et specialis patroni ác p̱tectoris nr̄i Petri . que sita . ē . in loco t̄ribili q̧ ab íncolis Torneie nuncupat' ab occidente scilicet urbis Lundonię . quę olim id . ē . dn̄ice incarnationis anno . DC. IIĪI. beati Ædelberti hortatu þmi anglo⁊ regis xp̄iani . destructo þ⁹

---
1. *R* of *Regnante, A* and Ω in red, with traces of gilding.
14. *I* of *Igitur* in red, with traces of gilding.

CHARTERS AND DOCUMENTS. 13

'ibidem' abhominationis templo regū paganoꝫ . á sæberhto prediuite ꝙdā subregulo lundoniensi nepóte uidelicet ipsi⁹ regis constructa . c̄ ꝛ 7 30 ñ ab alio sed ab ipso sc̄o Petro apl̄oꝫ p̂cicipe in suū ipsi⁹ ꝑp̄ū honorē dedicata . dehinc ab Offa et Kenulſo regib⁹ cęleberrimis possessionū priuilegíſs et uaríís ornam̄toꝫ specieb⁹ uchem̄ter fuerat ditata ꝛ et in qᵃ sedes regia . et locus etiā consecrationis regum antiquit⁹ erat ꝛ hanc p̄cepi ut studiosi⁹ restruerent . 7 om̄s possessiones ei⁹ readunárent ꝛ 35 7 ipse de meis indominicatis t̄ris- aliqᵃnta addidi . 7 carthis atq; legitimis testib⁹ corroboraui . Deinde succedente tēpore concilio habito intra ipsā basilicā p̄sidente me cū filio meo EADWARDO . 7 eodē archiep̄o uenerabili DUNSTANO ꝛ 7 uniuersis ep̄is . et baronib⁹ meis . sęcut⁹ exemplū maiorū meoꝫ renouaui . addidi . 7 corroboraui carthas 7 40 p̂uilegia ei⁹dē loci . 7 ad apl̄icam sedē legenda et c̄firmanda tᵃnsmisi ꝛ atq; legitima c̄cessione in hc̄ modū astipulata recepi . IOHANNES ep̄s . urbis rome seruu⁹ seruoꝫ dei . domno excellentissimo EADGARO filio suo regi angloꝫ salutē . 7 apl̄icā benedictionē. Quia literis tuę celsitudinis fili km̄e nobis innotuisti de monasterio sc̄i Petri specialis patᵒni 45 tui . qᵒd ab antiꝙs anglię regib⁹ á potestate lundonicę sedis ep̄i cū c̄silio pontificū ei⁹dē patrię fuerit ereptū ꝛ 7 ab hinc sub regiminę regū uel clarissimoꝫ abbatū sēp dispositū . 7 postulasti á nobis ut pⁱuilegiū ep̄oꝫ de eodem monasterio factū . nr̄o p̂uilegio immo magis apl̄oꝫ p̂ncipis roborarem⁹ auctoritate ꝛ libentissime scd̄m tuę beniuolentię petitionē 50 facim⁹. Auctoritate siꝙdē beati Petri apl̄oꝫ pⁱncipis qⁱ potestatē ligandi atq; soluendi á dño accepit . cui⁹q; nos uicaríí existim⁹ ꝛ stabilim⁹ . ut ipse locᵒ regū p̄ceptis et p̂uilegíís apl̄icis fult⁹ . p om̄ia tēpora sine repetione cui⁹cunq; lundónicę urbis ep̄i . aut alicui⁹ iudiciarię potestatis . uel cui⁹cūq; prepotentis hominis . cui⁹q; ordinis ꝛ uel dignitatis sit ꝛ 55 sed semp sicut p̄optat et éxpetit beniuolentia tua rat⁹ futʳo tēpore pmaneat . Venerabiles igitʳ ei⁹dē loci fr̄es ꝛ idóneos ex sé ꝛ uel ex qua uoluerint c̄gregatione ab̄bes síue decános sibi p successiones eligendi . ex auctoritate h⁹ sc̄ę romanę sedis et nr̄a . sic̄ postulasti amplius habeant potestatem . et ne impediantʳ ꝛ apl̄ica auctoritate p̂hibemus . neq; 60 p uiolentiā extᵃnea psona intd̄ucatʳ . ñ qᵃm om̄is c̄cors c̄gregatio elegerit . Pretea illi loco ꝙcꝙd c̄tuleris . uel collatū . c̄. ut c̄feretʳ . diuina 7 nr̄a

31. *p̂cicipe*] so in MS.
42. *I* of *Iohannes* in red, with traces of gilding.
43. *seruu⁹*] so in MS.
51. *A* of *Auctoritate* in red, with traces of gilding.
54. *repetione*] for *repetitione*.

auctoritate roboram⁹ ⁊ p̄uilegia ū possessionū et dignitatū km̄i fr̄is nr̄i uenerabilis DUNSTANI alioɻq; fideliū ibidē indulta . necn̄ et p̄uilegia ūra ad honorē dei p̱tinentia q̨ ibi instituere uolueris gᵃtanti affectu annuim⁹ . c̄firmam⁹ . ⁊ c̄firmando inp̱petuū rata īuiolataq; stare decernim⁹ . ⁊ īfractores eoɻ ⁊ ætīna maledictione dāpnam⁹ . Obseruatores aū h⁹ firmitatis ⁊ grām ⁊ miscd̄iā á dño c̄seqⁱ mereantʳ . Causa ǥ infractionis nr̄i p̄uilegíí ⁊ ad posteros nr̄os p̱ueniat. Datʳ rauenne ⁊ īx̄. kl. febr̄. Cognoscat g̊ magnitudo seu utilitas ūra qm̄ decnim⁹ ⁊ inp̱petuo mansurū iubem⁹ . atq; c̄stituim⁹ ⁊ ut p̱ reuerentia reliq̨arū gt̄osissimi apt̄i Petri . ⁊ p̱ q̨ete monachoɻ ibidē dō famulantiū honor . ⁊ laus eidē ęcct̄ę habeatʳ ⁊ observetʳ ⁊ id . ē . ut q̨sq̨s fugitiuoɻ p̱ q̨libet scélere ad p̄fatā basilicā beati apt̄i fugiens p̱cinctū eí⁹ intᵃuerit . siue pedes . siue eques . siue de curia regáli . siue de ciuitate . séu de uilla . seu cui⁹cūq; c̄ditionis sit ⁊ q̨cūq; delicto facínoris c̄tᵃ nos ⁓ uel succedentes reges angloɻ uel c̄tᵃ aliū quēlibet fidelē . sc̄e ęcct̄ę dī forisfact⁹ sit ⁊ relaxetʳ . ⁊ lib̄etʳ . ⁊ uitā atq; m̄bra absq; ulla c̄tᵃdictione optineat . Pręt̄ea intīminamʳ diu'i'na auctoritate ⁊ nr̄a . ut neq; nos . neq; successores nr̄i . neq; q̨libet ep̄s . uel archiep̄s . nec q̨cūq; de iudiciaria potestate in ipsā scām basilicā ⁓ uel immanentes in ipsa . ut in hōes q̨ cū sua substantia ut rcb⁹ ad ipsam tᵃdere ⁓ uel deuouére sé uoluerint ⁊ nisi p̱ uoluntatē ab̄bis ⁊ suoɻ monachoɻ ullā unqᵃm hab̄āt potestatē . sed sit hęc sc̄a mat̄ ęcct̄a pęculiaris pat̄ni nr̄i beati Petri apt̄i ⁓ lib̄a . ⁊ absoluta ab ōi inuasione ut ̄inq̨etudine ōium hominū cui⁹cūq; ordinis ⁊ uel potestatis .c̄e. uideantʳ . In mañria ū ut curtes p̄fatę basilicę ubi ⁊ ubi ī qᵃscūq; regiones ut pagos ī regno nr̄o ⁓ q̨cq̨d á die p̄senti ipsū monasteriū possidere ⁊ dñari uidetʳ . ut q̨d á dm̄ timentib⁹ hōib⁹ p̱ legitima cartharū īstrum̄ta ibidē fuit c̄cessū . ut ī antea er'i't additū ut delegatū . nec ad c: usas audiendū . nec ad fideiussores tollendos . nec ad freda ut bannos exigendū . ⁊ ad mansiones ut paratas faciendū . nec ullas redibitiones req̨rendū ⁊ infra immunitatē scī Petri íngredi ut req̨rere q̨q̨ tēpore p̄sumu: ⁊ sed q̨cq̨d éxinde fiscus nr̄ exauctare pot̄at ⁊ oīa ⁊ ex ōib⁹ p̱ mercedis nr̄ę augm̄to . sub ītegᵃ ⁊ firmissima immunitate c̄cedim⁹ ad ip̄m sc̄m locū . ⁊ inp̱petuo c̄firmam⁹ . Concedo etiā ⁊ c̄firmo om̄s lib̄tates ⁊ donatiōes īrarū q̨ a p̄dictis regib⁹ séu alíís sic̄ legitʳ ī antiq̨ telligᵃpho lib̄tatis ante me donate st̄ ⁊ scit̄ . hāme . p̄inintune . mordúne .

70. C of *Cognoscat* in red, with traces of gilding.
90. a of *c[a]usas* worn away by fold.
93. p̄sum̄u::ʳ] the letters after *mu* worn away.

CHARTERS AND DOCUMENTS. 15

fentúne . aldenhā . bleccenhā . loþereslége . qˢ tam ueñabit DVNSTAN⁹
á me uná cū p̄dicto loco emerat . necñ 7 libtates atq; emptiones qˢs
idē DVNSTAN⁹ me ccedente ab optimatib⁹ meis m̄cat⁹ .ē. 7 qˢs etiā corā 100
legitimis testib⁹ sigillo suo 7 ánulo ep̄ali ibídē ī usū ſrm p̄fatę ęccłę
ī ppetuā p̱stⁱnxit possessiōem . Nos itaq; ad laudē nōis dn̄i 7 ad honorē
scī Pet . īras ɋ hic karaxantʳ ibidē donauim⁹ . holewelle . dęcewrthe .
wattúne . cillingtúne . Héc ʝ supᵃdicta rúra cū oīb⁹ ad sé ptinentib⁹ . et
cū cęnobio ɋd stána uocatʳ ⸱⸱ 7 oīb⁹ sibi ptinentib⁹ scił . tudintún . 105
halgeford . felthā . ecelesford . p̱scis tēporib⁹ ad eandē p̱hibētʳ ęccłam
scī Petⁱ ptinére . sic̄ legitʳ ut dixim⁹ ī antiɋ telligᵃpho libtatis . qᵃm
rex offa illi monastio ctulit . qᵃndo eccłís p uniūsas regiōes anglo⸺ recup-
atiua þuilegia a wlfiredo archiep̄o hortante scribe iussit . Ǫd cenobiū
stanense . iā olī regłari monacho⸺ examine pollebat . þea ū hostili 110
qᵃdā expeditiōe frib⁹ disp̱sis . solotén⁹ .e. díruta . Hāc itaq; eādē libtatē
p̄fatę ęccłę scī pet þncipis apło⸺ ccessi . cui loc⁹ p̄dict⁹ . ɋ tēplū fuerat
dudū apollinis ⸱⸱ dī ꝑuidentia `ñc' mirabilit̄ ab ipso clauigo .ē. csecᵃt⁹ . ac
dedicat⁹ ⸱⸱ qᵃtin⁹ ab ōi scłari sit lib . īppetuū seruitute . Et ne ɋs
p̱sentiū uł magis futʳo⸺ ābiget ɋ sit illa libtas qᵃm amabilit̄ 7 firmit̄ 115
ccedo . ōimodis cūcta illi⁹ monastīí possessio nullis sit unqᵃm gᵃuata
honerib⁹ . nec expeditiōis . nec pontis 7 arcis edificamīe . nec iuris
regalis fragmine . nec furis apþhensiōe . 7 ut oīa simul cōphendā ⸱⸱ nil
debet exsolui . nec regi . nec regis p̄posito . uł ep̄o . uł duci . uł ulli
hōi . sed oīa debita exsoluāt iugit̄ ɋ ī ipsa dn̄atiōe fuerīt ad supᵃdictū 120
scm locū . scdm ɋd ordinauerīt frs eī⁹dē cenobíí . Obsecᵃm⁹ etiā ōs successores nr̄os reges . 7 þncipes . p scam 7 īdiuiduā trinitatē . 7 p aduentū
i⁹ti iudicis . ut ɋm ex munificentia añcesso⸺ nr̄o⸺ ipse loc⁹ uidetʳ .ēe.
ditat⁹⸱⸱ nullus ep̄o⸺ . uł abbm aut eo⸺ ordinatores . uł ɋlibet p̱sona possit
ɋɋ ordine de loco ipso aliɋd auferre . aut aliqᵃm potestatē sibi ī ipso 125
monastio usurpáre . uł aliɋd `qᵃsi' p cōmutatiōis titulū absq; uoluntate
ipsi⁹ cgregatiōis ⸱⸱ uł nr̄m p̱missū minuere . aut cálices . aut crúces .
seu indumta altaris . uł sac̄s códices . aurū . argentū . uł qᵃlēcūq;
specīem ibidē collatā auferre ⸱⸱ uł aliás deferre p̱sumat . Sed liceat ipsi
cgregatiōi ɋd sibi p rectā delegatiōem collatū .c̄. ppetī possidere ⸱⸱ 7 130
p stabilitate regni nr̄i iugit̄ exorare . ɋa nos p dī amore 7 reucrentia scī
apłi 7 adipiscenda uita ętna . hoc beneficiū ad locū ipsū tribilē 7 scm cū

129. *specīem*] so in MS.

16   CHARTERS AND DOCUMENTS.

csilio pontificū 7 ill⁹triū uiroʒ nr̄oʒ pcerū gᵃtissimo animo 7 īteg* uoluntate
uisi fuim⁹ prestitisse . eo uidelicet ordine . ut sic tēpore p̄decessoʒ meoʒ
135 ibidē chor⁹ psallentiū p tʳmas fuit īstitutᵒ ⁘ ita die noctuq; ī loco ipso cęle-
bretʳ . Si aū q̇spiā hāc nr̄am auctoritatē ul immunitatē īfring̃e uoluerit ⁘
7 alios ad hoc c̄duxerit ⁘ un⁹q̇sq; p sé ipso libras .v. partib⁹ sc̄i Pet psol-
uat . 7 ut dictū .ē ⁘ q̇cq̇d éxinde fiscus n̄r ad partē nr̄am spare potat ⁘
in luminarib⁹ ⁘ ul stipendíís monachoʒ . séu 7 elemosinas paupū ipsi⁹
140 monastíí phēnīt p nr̄a oracla ad ītegrū sit c̄cessū ⁘ atq; īdultū . Et ut
hęc auctoritas nr̄is 7 futʳis tēporib⁹ circa ipsū sēm locū pennīt firma 7
īuiolata pmaneat ⁘ ul p oīa tēpora illésa cᵒtodiatʳ atq; c̄seruetʳ ⁘ 7 ab
oīb⁹ optimatib⁹ nr̄is 7 iudicib⁹ publicis 7 puatis meli⁹ ác certiu⁹ credatʳ
man⁹ nrę substptiōib⁹ subī eā decreuim⁹ roborare . 7 de sigillo nro ⁘
145 iussim⁹ sigillare.

    SIGNVM ✠ EADGARI incliti 7 serenissimi angloʒ reḡ. SIGNV̄
✠ EADWARDI ei⁹dē reḡ filíí. Signū ✠ æþelrédi fratris eius.

    + In xp̄i noīe ego DVNSTAN ácsi peccator doroƀnensis ęcclę
archieps . hāc liƀtatē sc̄ę crucis agalmate c̄signaui . ác deinde scdm
150 aplici Ioħis p̄ceptū . obseruatores h' liƀtatis auctoritate qᵃ p̄fruor a
peccatis suis absolui . infractores ū p̄petī maledixi . ħ resipiscāt ⁘
7 .III.b.⁹ annis á liminibus sc̄ę ęcclę sequestrati . penitentiā agant.

    + Ego ospoldus eboracensis archieps.   IMPOSVI.
    + Ego elfstan⁹ lundoniensis ęcclę ep̄s.   ADQVIEVI.
155   + Ego athelþold⁹ wintoniensis ęcclę ep̄s.   CORROBORAVI.
    + Ego ælfstan⁹ rofensis ęcclę ep̄s.   SVPPOSVI.
    + Ego æscẃíus Dor`c′censis ęcclę ep̄s.   IMPRESSI.
    + Ego ælfeag⁹ Licedfeldensis ęcclę ep̄s.   CONSOLIDAVI.
    + Ego æþelsín⁹ scireburnensis ęcclę ep̄s.   COMMODVM DVXI.
160   + Ego þulgar⁹ piltuniensis ęcclę ep̄s.   CONFIRMAVI.
    + Ego aþulfus herefordensis ęcclę ep̄s.   OVANTER DIVVLGAVI.
    + Ego æþelgar⁹ cisseniensis ęcclę ep̄s.   ADNOTAVI.
    + Ego Sigar⁹ willensis ęcclę ep̄s.   GAVDENTER C̄CLVSI.
    + Ego æluricus cridiensis ęcclę ep̄s.   AMEN DIXI.
165   + Ego Sigar⁹ ællmhamensis ecclę ep̄s . CONSIGILLAVI. atq; cū
p̄scriptis archep̄is . 7 ep̄is . aƀƀib⁹ . luminib⁹ accensis ⁘ uiolatores h'

---

146. *S* of *Signum* in both cases and cross in red, originally gilt.
147. Crosses and *S* of *Signum* in red, originally gilt.
148–184. Crosses in red, originally gilt.
155. athelþoldus] for athelpoldus.

CHARTERS AND DOCUMENTS. 17

munificentię dignitatis . immo apŕici tⁿnsgressores h⁹ decti ī ppetuū excōnic . h̀ p̄titulatā penitētiā resipiscēdo p̄agāt.

[Col. 2.]
+ Ego folcmǣrus. abƀ.
+ Ego ælfric. abƀ.
+ Ego Kineward. abƀ.
+ Ego osgar. abƀ.
+ Ego æþelgar. abƀ.
+ Ego Sideman. abƀ.
+ Ego foldbriht. : bƀ.
+ Ego Godwi : : :: ƀ.
+ Ego Leofl : : : abƀ.
+ Ego þimer. abƀ.
+ Ego ældréd abƀs ɔsensi . 7 rege suisq; p̄cipientib⁹ hāc ʾliƀtatis singᵃphā scripsi . anno dn̄ice īcarn̄. D. CCCC. LXVIIIĪ. Indicī .XĪI. Id⁹ mai. Anno .XIII. regni reḡ eadgari.

[Col. 3.]
+ Ego ælfere . dux.
+ Ego Marchere . dux.
+ Ego oslác . dux.
+ Ego byrhtnod . dux.
+ Ego osred . dux.
+ Ego fo'r'dwine . dux.
+ Ego friðelaf . dux.
+ Ego ænulf . dux.
+ Ego ælfeg . dux.
+

[Col. 4.]
+ Ego þúred . pƀr.
+ Ego leoffa . pƀr.
+ Ego Wlstán . pƀr.
+ Ego æþelbeald . pƀr.
+ Ego Wlfgeat . pƀr.
+ Ego beremund . pƀr.

175-177. Hole in MS.
178. þimer] for þimer.
182-190. Small red crosses, not gilt.

191. blank line.
192-200. Crosses gilt.

+ Ego æþelsige.   pbr.
+ Ego Wineman .   pbr.
200 + Ego oswárdus pbr cū sup⁴ dictis . 7 cū alíís ⫶Ϲ̄⫶ Ⅶ̈. pbris ꝶ ífractores h⁹ firmitatis excōmunīc.

[Col. 5.]

Ad ultimū itaq; uná cū rege et fillís ei⁹ . nos ōs c̄f̄rs . 7 coepī . 7 cū tota hac popłosa 7 scā sínodo . ei⁹dē loci ōs fut͛os abbes . decános . atq ꝶ p̄positos c̄testam͛ . uerētiā ī nōe pats . 7 filĺĺ . 7 sp̄s sc̄ī phibem⁹ .
205 qᵘtin⁹ saɛ̄s illi⁹ ęcc̀tę thesauros ñ distraāt . neq; īras . seú reddit⁹ . ut bñficia ī suis ut parētū suoƺ usib⁹ stolide expēdāt . neq; á seruis dī ɋ p illis ibidē habet͛ substātiā ꝶ subtᵃhendo minuāt . Q°dsi aliɋs p̄sūpserit ꝶ illū sīc uiolatorē atq; tᵃnsḡssorē h⁹ nr̄i deɛ̄ti īmo apłici . añ sūmū iudicē c̄ uenerit sc̀m iudicare p igne . respōsurū sup hac ré inuitam⁹ .
210   SIGNVM . . . . GIS

Endorsed in late 12*th cent. hand:* Edgari.

„ *in early* 14*th cent. hand:* Prima carta Regis Edgari de libertatibus et quibusdam possess[ionibus] confirmat͛ a summis pontif[icibus] Iohanne . Paschali . Eugenio .III. bis Alexandro III. et
215 multis aliis.

Endorsed in late 14*th cent. hand:* Dat. anno Domini D.CCCC.ᵐᵒ LXIXⁿᵒ. Bona. ƀn . circa medium cum bulla Iohannis pape inserta.

Endorsed in late 13*th cent. hand:* Edgarus Rex.

VII.

[980 × 988.]—*Archbishop* (*Dunstan*) *to King Æðelred.—Letter concerning certain estates belonging to the diocese of Cornwall.*

✠ Þís géwrit sendeþ sé arcebisceop hís hlaforde æþelrede cynge . hit gelamp þæt westwealas ónhofon hí óngean ecgbriht cyng . þá ferde sé cyng þyder 7 gewylde hí . 7 géteoþude þone erd 7 áteh swa him

202. *A* gilt.   210. Strip of parchment several inches in length cut out.

CHARTERS AND DOCUMENTS. 19

þuhte . Scalde þá inn tó scireburnan . þreo land . polltún . cællwic .
landwiþan . 7 þæt swa þa stod wintra þrage . oþ hæþene herias þysne 5
eard ofor eodun 7 gésætun ; þá wearþ oþer tid æfter þan þæt lariowas
afeollun . 7 ut gewitun of angla lande . for þære geleafleste þé him þá
ónsæge gewearþ . 7 stod eall westsexena rice .VII. gear buton bisceope .
þá sénde formosus sé papa óf rome byrig . 7 gemyngude eadweard
cyng 7 plegmund arcebisceop þæt hí þæt gebetun . 7 hí swa dydun . 10
mid geþeahte þæs papan 7 eall angelcynnes witena . gesettun .V.
bisccopas þær ǽr wærun twegen . anne æt wi[n]tancestre þæt wæs fryþestan . oþerne tó hremnes byrig þæt wæs æþelstan . þriddun tó scireburnan þæt wæs wærstan . feorþan tó wyllun . ' þæt wæs æþelm' . fiftan
tó cridian tune þæt wæs eadulf . 7 him mon betæhte þá þreo land ón 15
wealan . tó innstinge inn tó defenun forþam þe hí ǽr þam . unhyrsume
wærun buton westsexena ege . 7 eadulf bisceop þyssa landa breac his
lifes tida . æþelgar bisð æfter him eall swa . þa gelamp hit þ æþestan
cing ' sealde cunune bisceoprice ealswa tamur scæt' . þa gelamp þæt
eadræd cyng het hadian daniel 7 betæhte þá land swa him witan 20
ræddun . inn to sēę germane tó þam bisceopstole . æfter þám þá eadgar
cyng me het . þæt ic wulfsige hadude . þá cwæþ hé . 7 ealle ure
bisceopas . þæt hí nystun hwa rihtlucur þá land ahte þonne þære scire
bisceop . þá he innhold wæs . 7 godes geleafan ón riht bodude . 7 hís
hlaford lufude . gyf þonne þes bisceop nu swa deþ. ic nat hwy hé né sy . 25
þara landa wyrþe . gyf him heora gód ann . 7 ure hlaford for þan us ne
þing þ hi ænig man rihtlicor age þonne he 7 gif hi ænig man him to teo
hæbbe hi butan godes bletsunge 7 ure.

VIII.

*998.—King Æðelred to Ealdorman Leofwine.—Grant of land at
Southam, Ladbroke, and Radburn, co. Warwick.*

☩ IN nomine dī excelsi qui quadrifida mundi moderamina moder-
ando gubernat Nobis ergo karissimi in xp̄o illius egregii predicatoris

13. *hremnes*] altered from *hremmes*.
14. *þæt wǽs æþelm*] in a different hand.
17. *eadulf*] written on an erasure.
18-19. *þa gelamp hit þ æþestan cing*] written
in a third hand on an erasure.
19. *sealde—scæt*] above the line by same hand
that wrote *þa gelamp*, etc. in line 18.
26-28. *for þan—ure*] added in same hand as
þa gelamp—scæt.

sententia diligenter consideranda est frs nihil intulimus in hunc mundū
uerū nec auferri quid possumus . Sed sicut illa generalis mater de qua
5 dicitur . terra es et in terrā ibis . nos nudos ueraciter procreauit . Sic
iterum nos nudos excipere debet . nisi aliquis diuino inpunctus amore
ad hoc idoneus sit ut adeptas res . pro omnipotenti dō et expiatione
peccaminum . suorum pauperibus et dī seruis . beniuola mente . distribuere uoluerit et suum thesaurum thesaurizare in altis caelorū culmini-
10 bus.   Hinc ego .ÆÞELRED. altithrono amminiculante anglorum cetera-
rūque gentiū in circuitu triuiatim persistentiū basileus aliquā terre
particulam ad donandum curaui leofwino meo fidelissimo duce id est
.VII. tributariorū et dimidium non tamen in uno loco sed in tribus
uillulis in suþham .III. mansas et in hlodbroce hreodburnanque .IIII.
15 manentes et inter illos dimidium unius manse ut habeat et perfruat cū
omnibus bonis ad illam terram rite pertinentibus in perpetuam hereditatē
et quamdiu lux fulgebit super terrā et hanc donationē dabo cū omni
libertate nisi arcis et pontis instructione et expeditione et ab homnibus
aliis notis ignotisque causis perpetualiter in libertatem compono. Si quis
20 uero tam epylempticus phyrargirie seductus amentia qđ non optamus
hanc nr̄e munificentiae dapsilitatē ausu temerario infringere temptauerit . sit ipse alienatus a consortio sc̄e dī aeclesie necnon et a participat-
ione sacrosc̄i corporis et sanguinis ihū xp̄i filii dī per quem totus
terrarū orbis ab antiquo humani generis inimico liberatus est . et cum
25 iuda xp̄i proditore sinistra in partæ deputatus . ni prius hic digna satis-
factione humilis penituerit . þis syn þara .X. hida longemæra to suþhā
þe þa .III. hida binnan synd þe wistan forworhte wið þone cyning
æþelred mid unrihtū monslihte 7 fifte healf hid æt hlodbroce 7 æt
hreodburnan þe mid þā oþrū lande forworhte wæron 7 he hyra ealra
30 geuþe his ealdormen leofwine a in ece yrfe . ꝥ is þonne þær hlodbroc
fealþ on ycænan æfter streame ꝥ to þǣ hyærde wycan fram þā hyerde
wycan up to þā ællenstubbe to þā mærstanæ of þā mærstane to þæm
gemyþan . 7 æfter streame ꝥ to beornewæaldes hlawe of þā hlawe to þā
pytte up on þā beanhlande . 7 to þǣ pytte ʽ7 swa of þē pytte to cocce-
35 byle ʼ 7 to yppescelfe of yppescelfe æfter þæm heafdan to hæahhewellan
of þam wyllan to hlodbroce . æfter þǣ broce þæt æft on ycenan . þis syn
þa hlandgemære into hlodbroce 7 to hreodburnan ꝥ is þonne to wylman

8. *distribuere*] the first *i* altered from *e*.   32. After *þæm* a letter erased and the *m*
18. *homnibus*] for *omnibus*.   itself on an erasure.

forda 7 of þā forda efter sealtstrete to þā grenan wege of þā wege ꝥ æft on wylman broce æfter streame ꝥ on hreodbroce of þā broce ꝥ up to þā hlangan þorne of þā þorne æfter þā heafdan ꝥ on þa wyllan æt hlodbroce æfter streame ꝥ þōn up æfter þā heafdan to þā mere of þā mere to þā hlawe on yppescelfe . of þā hlawe to grenan hylle of þā hlawe to cocgebyll of cocgebyll æfter heafdan to þā wætergefeal æfter streame ꝥ on stanhemeforde of þā fordæ ꝥ æft on wylman forde.

Hæc kartula karaxata est anno dñicæ incarnationis .DCCCC .L. XXXXVIII. huius munificentię singrapha his testibus . consentibus quorū inferius nomina secundū u[n]ius cuiusque dignitatē caraxantur.

+ ego æþelred britannię rex anglorū monarchus preformatas ꝑpinquarū sed et regū donationes hoc taumate agie crucis roboraui.

+ ego ælfric dorobernensis eclesie archiepṡ eiusdē regis beniuolentiā subscripsi.

+ ego aldulf eboracensis basilice primas hoc eulogiū agie crucis taumate confirmaui.

+ ego ælfheah licetfeldensis coenobii antistes iubente rege tropheū scǣ crucis impressi.

+ ego ælfheah wintoniensis æclesię presul canonica subscriptione hoc donū coroboraui.

+ ego wulfstan epṡ lundoniensis testudinem scāe crucis huic regali dapsilitati libens adposui.

+ ego wulfsige scireburnensis æclesie catascopus donū eiusdem regis confirmaui.

+ ego aþulf herefordensis æclesie pontifex consensum prebui.

+ ego alfwold epṡ hoc eulogiū manu ꝑpria apicibus depinxi.

+ ego ælfsige   abb.
+ ego ælfweard   abb.
+ ego wulfgar   abb.
+ ego leofric   abb.
+ ego æþelweard   dux.
+ ego ælfric.   dux.
+ ego ælfelm   dux.
+ ego leofwine   dux.
+ ego ordulf   m̄

38. Between the *e* and the *g* of the second *wege* a letter erased.

46. *consentibus*] for *consentientibus*.
49. *ꝑpinquarū*] so in MS. for *ꝑpinquorū*.

CHARTERS AND DOCUMENTS.

+ ego æþelmær m̄
+ ego wulfheah m̄
75 + ego wulfgeat m̄.

· *Contemporary endorsement in capitals:* Ðis is þæra landda boc to Suþham 7 to Hlodbroce ` 7 to Hreodburnan ' þe Æþelred cyning sealde Leofwine ealdormen on ece yrfe.

IX.

998, XVII. Kal. Mai (= April 15).—*Will of Leofwine Wulfstan's son, in favour of Westminster Abbey.*

✠ CHIROGRAPHUM.

✠ In nomine dn̄i nr̄i ihū xp̄i . þys is leofwines cwide wulfstanes suna . þæt is þonne ærest þæt ic gean criste 7 sc̄e petre for minre saule in to westmynster ealra þara þinga þe me crist to gefultumian wyle æt þam lande æt cynlaue dyne . 7 æt mearcyncg seollan on wuda 7 on 5 felda . 7 ic gean of purlea in to hnutlea healfere hide landes on eastheaIf stræte for mine sawle þam godes þeowan . 7 minre faþan leofware þæs heafodbotles on purlea . 7 ealles þæs þe me þær to locaþ . 7 gif eadwold længe libbe hire suna þonne heo . fo he þærto . gif heo þonne læng beo 7 ꝥ god wille sylle hit on þa hand þe hire æfre betst gehyre 10 on uncer bega cynne . 7 ic gean minum hlaforde wulfstane bisceope þæs landes æt bærlingum. Þys wæs gedon þæs geares fram ures drihtnes
gebyrdtide. _{anni dn̄i} DCCCXCVIII _{indic̄} XI _{epac} XX _{c̄cur̄} V _{ciclos} VIII _{dies . xiiii . luñ} XVII kł mai _{dies pasce} XV kł mai
_{luñ ipsius}
XVI.

Endorsed in contemporary hand: þis is leofwines cwide wulfstanes
15 suna.

Endorsed in slightly later hand: Cynlæuedene . ✠ .

Endorsed in early 14th cent. hand: Killauedene uersus ecclesiam.

Endorsed in last century hand: 1727, 25th Augusti. Petri le Neve Norrey pretium 1*li*. 11*s*. 6*d*.

The top half of ✠ CHIROGRAPHUM cut off.

X.

[1008-1012.]—*Will of Alfwold, bishop (of Crediton).*

✠ Þis is alfwoldes bisceopes cwyde þ̄ is ðæt he geann þæs landes æt sandforda in tó þam mynstre in tó crydian tune him tó saulsceatte mid mete 7 mid mannum swa hit stent butan wíteþeowum mannum. 7 ánes hiwscypes he geann godrice þærof 7 án sylhðe oxna. 7 hé geann his hlaforde feower horsa. twa gesadelode 7 twa unsadelode. 7 feower scyldas 7 .IIII. spera 7 twegen helmas 7 twa byrnan. 7 .L. mancsa goldes þé ælfnoþ him sceal æt wudeleage 7 ænne scegð .LXIIII.ǽre he is eall gearo butan þam hánon he hine wolde ful gearwian his hlaforde to gerisnum gif him god úðe. 7 ordulfe twegra bóca hrabanum 7 martyrlogiū. 7 þam æþelinge .XL. mancsa goldes 7 þæra wildra worfa æt æscburnan lande 7 twegra getelda. 7 alfwolde munuce .XX. mancsa goldes 7 ánes horses. 7 ánes geteldes. 7 byrhtmære preoste .XX. mancsa goldes 7 ánes horses. 7 his þrim magon eadwolde 7 æþelnoðe 7 grimkytele hira ælcon .XX. manc̄ goldes 7 hira ælcon ánes horses. 7 wulfgare his mæge twegra wahryfta 7 twegra setlhrægla 7 þreo byrnan. 7 godrice his aðume twegra byrnena. 7 eadwine mæsse-preoste .V. manc̄ goldes 7 his kæppan. 7 leofsige mæssepreoste þæs mannes þe he him ǽr tólét wunstan hatte. 7 kenwolde helm 7 byrnan. 7 boian ánes horses. 7 mælpatrike .V. manc̄ goldes 7 leofwine polgan .V. manc̄ goldes 7 ælfgare writere án pund penega he lǽnde tune 7 his geswysternon gehealdon hi hine. 7 eadgyfe his swyster án strichrǣgl. 7 .I. hrigchrægl. 7 .I. sethrægl. 7 ælflæde offestran .V. manc̄. pē. 7 spilan .III. manc̄ goldes. 7 LX. pē. 7 leofwine ʼpolgan'. 7 mælpatrike. 7 byrhsige hira þreora ælcon án hors. 7 ælcon hiredmen his onrid þe he álǣned hæfde. 7 his hiredcnihton eallon .V. pund tó gedále ælcon be þam þe his mǣð wære. 7 in tó crydian túne þreo þeningbéc mæssebóc. 7 bletsungbóc. 7 pistelbóc. 7 án mæsseréaf. 7 on ælcon bisceopháme ælcon men freot þé witeþeow wære. oðþe he mid his féo gebohte. 7 in tó wiltune calic 7 disc on .CXX. manc̄ goldes butan þrim manc̄. 7 búrþenon his beddréaf. 7 þises ís tó gewitnesse

wulfgar ælfgares sunu . 7 godric be crydian . 7 eadwine mæssepreost .
7 alfwold munuc . 7 byrhtmær preost.

Endorsed in early 14th cent. hand: Ealwold Bisscopes biquide at
samforde to Cridihamtones minstre.

XI.

1007.—*King Æðelred to St. Alban's monastery.—Grant of land at
Norton, 'æt Rodanhangron,' and at Oxhey, co. Hertford.*

☧ Regnante in perpetuum d[ō] & dño nr̄o ihū xp̄o ⁊ Quamuis
ubiq; per uniuersū mundū merita beatorū martyrum diuinis celebranda
sint preconiis ⁊ eorumq; suffragia qui pro xp̄i nomine sanguinem suū
fuderunt totis nisibus amplectenda ⁊ anglorū tamen populis intra
5 ambitum britanniae constitutis ⁊ specialiter est honoranda beati martyris
ALBANI gloriosa uictoria ⁊ qui & ipse pro xp̄o martyrium subiit ⁊ &
hanc gentem rosei sanguinis effusione consecrauit; Qua propter ego
ÆÐELRED totius al[b]ionis superna largicn[te] gratia basileus . ut in
tremendo magni iudicii die scōrum patrociniis interuenientibus superni
10 regni coheres existere merear ⁊ trium possessionem terrarum dō
omnipotenti ad monasterium prefati martyris aeternaliter possiden-
dam concedo ⁊ quarum duae simul adiac[e]nt ⁊ hoc est æt norðtune .
& una mansa æt RODANHANGRON ⁊ Tertia uero seorsum sita ⁊ usitato
uocabulo ÆT OXANGEHÆGE nominatur ⁊ Harum quidem terrarum
15 portionem OFFA rex merciorum quondam regali iure possedit ⁊ eamq;
ad predictum monasterium . pro amore t[anti] martyris qui inibi
r[e]quiescit . aeterna l[e]ge lib[erat]am con[cessit] . sed [eo] postmodum
def[unc]to p[er] potentiā quorundā iniquorum uiolenter abstracta est .
& tamdiu ab ipso loco iniuste exclusa [d]onec tandem f[ie]r& a
20 Leof[s]ino duce possessa . Qui dum culpa sua exigente patria pulsus
exularet ⁊ ÆLFRIC mihi fidelis archiepiscopus & LEOFRIC abbas frater
eius ⁊ eandem portionem dato pretio [me] concedente emerunt & ut
dō quae dī erant restituerem ⁊ rogatu humillimae deuotionis obtin-

uerunt ⁊ Post obitum uero nominati super[iu]s archiepi . interpellante
fratre ipsius hanc cartam meae donationis & renouationis scribere iussi ⁊
in qua pr̨cipio tam mea quam dī omnipotentis auctoritate ⁊ ut nulla
altior inferiorue persona cuiuscumq; sit dign[i]tatis ⁊ hanc portionem
s[c̄o] martyri subtrahere qualibet occasione presumat ⁊ siue in meis ⁊
siue successorū meorū temporibus ⁊ sed permanente iugiter & pre-
ualen[t]e restitutionis huiusce priuilegio ⁊ omnia contrariorū molimina
adnullentur ⁊ Sitq; predicta terrarū possessio perpetualiter ea libertate
donata ⁊ qua memoratus rex merciorum tam coen[obi]um Sc̄ī ALBANI ⁊
quam omnes quas illuc intromisit possessiones omni deuotione ditauit ⁊
tribus exceptis ⁊ rata expeditione ⁊ pontis arcisue restauratione ⁊
ceterum cuncta ad se per[tine]ntia ⁊ campi ⁊ pascua ⁊ prata ⁊ silų &
reliqua ⁊ libera permaneant ; Si quis igitur h̨c decreta uiolare presumpserit ⁊ omnipotentis dī & omniū sc̄orum ⁊ meaq; & omniū xp̄ianorum
ben[e]dictione careat ⁊ & aeterna maledictione damnatus intereat ⁊ nisi
digne citius emendauerit ⁊ quod contra dm̄ & sc̄m martyrem eius
ALBANUM deliquit ; Hi sunt fines quibus earundem possessio terrarū
gyratur ; + Þis synt þa landgemæro to norðtune ; Ærest of readan
wylles heafdan to wil[i]gbyrig ; Fram wiligbyrig andlang stodfald dices ;
Swa andlang stodfald gemær[es] . þæt hit cymð to stocc gemære ; swa in to
þære ea ; Andlang ea oþ þæt hit cymð eft to readan wylles h[ea]fdon ;·
+ Ðis synt þære hide landgemæro æt rodan [ha]ng[r]on ; Ærest
æt bradan wætere of smeðan hleawe to þære stræt ; Andlang stræte
þæt hit cymð to :y: an lege ; Of þære l[e]ge ⁊ þæt hit cymð to frobirig
stocce ; Of þa[m] stocce ⁊ to ::þingham gete ; Of þam gete . to
eadw[i]nes gemære ; þanone on gerihte æfter gemære ⁊ út to wiþigho .
þanone eft to smeþan h[le]awe ;· + Þis synt þa landgemæro to oxan-
g[e]hæge ⁊ 7 to bæcces wyrðe ; Ær[est] of watforda ⁊ in[to] puda
wyrðe ; Of puda wyrðe ⁊ in ON mapuldorg[eat]. Of þam gate ⁊
to east heale to þam þrym gemæron ; Of þam gem[ær]on . to
þam cyrstelmæle ; Of þam cyrstelmæle ⁊ to þære smalan æc ; Of þære
æc . to haran þorne ; Of þam þorne . to þære defe ; Of þære defe ⁊ to
beorclege ; of þære lege ⁊ in to cuðhelming beam ; Of þam beame ⁊ in
on þa stigele ; Of þære stigele ⁊ on r :: ding[w]ylle . Of þære wylle . in
on colen ::: ge ; Anno dominicae incarnationis millesimo septimo ⁊ indic̄
.V. scripta est huius munificentiae scedula ⁊ his testibus consciis ⁊
q[uor]um h[e]c n[o]mina sunt ;
[IV. 7.]

+ Ego ÆÐELRED anglorum rex . pro amore dī & sc̄i ma[rt]yris ALBANI . hanc donationem gratulabundo corde renouaui ŕ & renouatā huic stilo commendare precepi ;
+ Ego ÆLFHEAH dorobernensis ecclesiae archiepiscopus . huic donationi regiae signaculum scāe crucis im[po]sui.
+ Ego ÆLFGIFU regina mente deuota consensi ;
+ Ego Uulfstan eboracensis ecclesiae archiepiscopus . huic diffinitioni consentaneus extiti :
+ Ego ÆÐELSTAN filius regis cū fratribus meis clitonibus . adplaudens consensi.
+ Ego Aþeluuold uuintoniensis eccte modernus episcopus . assensum prebui .
+ Ego Ordbyrht australium saxonum episcopus corroboraui.
+ Ego Adulf episcopus . consignaui.
+ Ego Lyuing episcopus . consolidaui.
+ Ego Goduuine episcopus . consygillaui.
+ Ego Ælfhun episcopus . confirmaui.
+ Ego Ælfgar cū reliquis coepis . conclusi.

[Col. 2.]

+ Ego ælfweard   aƀƀ.
+ Ego ælfsige   aƀƀ.
+ Ego wulfgar   aƀƀ.
+ Ego ælfsige   aƀƀ.
+ Ego ælfsige   aƀƀ.

[Col. 3.]

+ Ego Germanus   aƀƀ.
+ Ego ælfere   aƀƀ.
+ Ego birhtwold   aƀƀ.
+ Ego ælfmær   aƀƀ.
+ Ego eadnoð   aƀƀ.
+ Ego godeman   aƀƀ.

[Col. 4.]

+ Ego ælfric   dux.
+ Ego leofwine   dux.
+ Ego eadric   miñ.
+ Ego ælfgar   miñ.
+ Ego æþelmær   miñ.

+ Ego aþelwold   miñ.
+ Ego leofwine   miñ.
+ Ego godric   miñ.
+ Ego æþelwine   miñ.

[Col. 5.]

+ Ego byrhsige   miñ.
+ Ego ulfkytel   miñ.
+ Ego æþelric   miñ.
+ Ego ælfgar   miñ.
+ Ego oswig   miñ.
+ Ego leofwine   miñ.
+ Ego ælfwig   miñ.
+ Ego æþelwine   miñ.
+ Ego aþelwold   miñ.

Endorsed in same hand: + þis is þæra þreora landa boc to norðtune 7 to rodan hangron . 7 to oxan gehæge mid bæcces wyrðe . þe ælfric arce bisceop 7 his broðor leofric abbod gebohtoɴ . 7 æþelræd cynincg þa gebocode gode ælmihtigon into sc̄e albanes stowe on ece yrfe.

Endorsed in 12*th cent. hand:* Eþelred⁹ rex . No[rþt]one . Rodenhan[gre]n . O:::aghen . Baceswrþe.

XII.

1023.—*King Cnut to Christ Church, Canterbury.—Grant of the port of Sandwich, &c.*

✠ In nomine dei summi & saluatoris nr̄i iħu xp̄i . Certis adstipulationibus nos sc̄i & iusti patres frequentatiuis ortationibus admonent . vt dm̄ quē diligimus & credimus intima mentis affectione cum bonorum operum diligentia incessanter eum timeamus & amemus . Quia retri-

2. First *t* of *or/ationil us* partly erased.

28 CHARTERS AND DOCUMENTS.

5 butionem omniū actuum nr̄orum in die examinationis iuxta unius cuiusq;
meritum reddet . Ideoq; subtilissima mentis certatione illū imitari
satagamus . licet mortalis uite pondere pressi & labentibus huius scti
possessionibus simus infoecati . tamen miserationis ei⁹ largitate caducis
opib⁹ ęterna celestis uite premia mercari queamus . Qua propter ego
10 CNVT . diuina fauente gr̄a . anglorum ceterarumq: adiacentiū insularum
basileus . propriis manibus meis capitis mei auream coronam pono
super altare xp̄i in dorobernia ad opus ei⁹dem ęccłę . & concedo eidem
ęccłę ad uictum monachorum portum de sanduuic . & omnes exitus
ei⁹dem aquę ab utraq; parte fluminis cui⁹cumq: terra sit . a pipneasse
15 usq; ad mearcesflcote . ita ut natante naue in flumine cum plenum fuerit .
quam longius de naui potest securis paruula quā angli uocant tapereax
sup terrā proici . ministri xp̄i rectitudines accipiant . Nullusq; omnino
homo habet aliquā consuetudinē in eodem portu . exceptis monachis
ęccłę xp̄i . Eorum autē est nauicula & transfretatio portus . & thelo-
20 neum omniū nauiū cui⁹cumq: sit & undecumq; ueniat quę ad predictū
portū & ad sanduuic uenerint . siquid autē in magno mari extra portu
quantū mare plus se retraxerit & adhuc statura unius hominis tenentis
lignū quod angli nominant spreot & tendentis ante se quantum potest ꝛ
monachorum est ꝛ Quicquid etiā ex hac parte medietatis maris inuentū
25 & delatū ad sanduuic fuerit ꝛ siue sit uestimentū siue rete . arma .
ferrū . aurū . argentum ꝛ medietas monachorum erit . alia pars remane-
bit inuentoribus . Quod si alt̄ deinceps quilibet codicellulus emerserit .
qui priscę tempestatis stilo digestus . huic nostrę confirmationi uisus
fuerit aliquatenus refragari illi⁹ modi litteraturę membranula . siricum
30 morsibus conrodenda aut certe potius igniuomi uaporis incendio com-
burenda adnichiletur . eiusq; pręsentator cuiuscumq; extiterit psonę ꝛ
ꝑ purgamento fauille deputetur . & ignominiosissima confusione sub-
sannetur . & ab omnibus in circuitu pręsentibus unianimo detestetur .
huiusq: priuilegii rata confirmatio semp inposterum preualeat . & tam
35 dei omnipotentis auctoritate . quam mea . simul & omnium concorditer
optimatum corroboratione confirmata . contra uniuersa refragatorum
cogitamenta . cunctis succedentibus aeui temporibus . stabilis & inconcussa columnaris status similitudine . pseuerantissimo iure consolidetur .
Si autem quod non optamus . aliquis tumulo supcilio inflatus . hanc

21. Erasure over *u* of *portu*.   29. *siricum*] the top of the second *i* gone.

nr̃am corroborationem infringere uel minuere temptauerit . nouerit se 40
anathematizatum . esse á deo & scīs eius . ni ante mortem digna satis-
factione emendauerit . quod˙iniuste deliquit . Scripta est hęc scedula
anno ab incarnatione dn̄i nr̄i ih̄u xp̄i . millesimo .xxiłi his testibus con-
cordantibus quorum onomata inferius lucide karaxantur. + Ego .CNVT.
rex anglorum hanc litteraturę confirmationē indeclinabiliter confirmo 45
+ Ego . æþelnoðus dorobernicus archi presul hanc prerogatiuā uexillo
sc̄o confirmaui. + Ego ælfricus . eboracensis ęccłę archieps eiusdem
regis beniuolentiam cum sc̄ę crucis signo corroboro. + Ego ælfwius .
lundoniensis ęccłę pontifex . consensi. + Ego ælfsinus . wentonie ēps
assensum prebui. + Ego byrhtwoldus . coruiniensis ęccłę eps . con- 50
donaui. + Ego æþericus . dorccensis ęccłę eps . consolidaui. + Ego
ælmær b. + Ego godwine b. + Ego brihtwine b. + Ego æþestan
b. + ælmær abb. + Ego brihtmær abb. + Ego brihtwig abb.
+ Ego wulfnoð ab. + Ego Godwine dux. + Ego :laf dux. + Ego
Iric dux. + Ego þorð .m̄. + Ego þrym m̄. + Ego agmund m̄. 55
+ Ego æþelric m̄. + Ego ælfwine m̄. + Ego byrhtric m̄. + Ego
leofric m̄. + Ego Sired m̄. + Ego godwine .m̄. Ego eadmær m.

Endorsed in 12*th cent. hand :* P^{l}uilegiū regis Cnut de donatiōe
Sandwicc 7 c̄suetudinū ei^9 7 coronę capitis sui.
Endorsed in 12*th cent. hand:* latine. 60
Endorsed in late 14*th cent. hand:* Cum codicello Edgari regis et
inquisitione habita in villa de Sandwico.
Endorsed in 13*th cent. hand :* Registratur.

XIII.

[1107 × 1137.]—*William of Warelwast, bishop of Exeter. Confirmation to the Canons of Crediton of their liberties.*

✠ Witł d̄i grā Exoniensis eps. omnib; suis parrochianis . clericis
& laicis tam p̄sentib; quā futuris . salutes r & d̄i benedictionē . & suā .

2. *salutes*] so in MS.

Qm ecc̄la d̄i sponsa mat nr̄a liba est ꝭ dignū siquidē & iustū est . ut
ei⁹ libertatē tanquā boni filii conseruare & restituere nr̄is temporib;
quantū fas est ꝭ d̄i adiutorio ad nr̄am & succedentiū nr̄oꝫ utilitatē
satagamus . Proinde sciatis om̄s tā futuri quam p̄sentes . qᵒd ego Will
d̄i gr̄a Exoniensis ep̄s concessi . & carta mea confirmaui d̄i ꝑ amore
Ecc̄le de Cridiatona & ei⁹dē canonicis pręsentib; & futuris . talē libtatē
in reb; & p̄positura ecc̄le p̄dictę . qualē unquā meli⁹ & honorabili⁹
habuit ipsa & canonici ei⁹ . tēpore p̄decessoris mei uidelicet domni
Osbti ep̄i beatę memorię uiri. Est autē hęc libtas hui⁹modi . scilicet
concessi q̄d canonici simul habeant in manu sua p̄positurā ecc̄lę . &
q̄d ei ꝑtinet . & canonici ex se ipsis unū qualē uoluerint eligant int se
in p̄positū . & electū ꝭ m̄ p̄sentabunt . & meo consilio & mea laude &
meo dono . elect⁹ & p̄sentat⁹ fiet p̄posit⁹ ꝭ absq; omni exactione &
recognitione inde reqsita. Volo enī & confirmo ut nulla in posterū ab
aliq̄ exigatur consuetudo ꝑinde aut exactio . Qd̄ 'si forte p̄posit⁹ iste in
p̄positura p̄p̄t forisfactū suū canonicis n̄ placuerit ꝭ m̄ monstrabunt . &
hoc ostenso ꝭ m̄ em̄dabit. & canonici aliū ex se ipsis eligent ꝭ similit meo
dono constituendū. Idem q̄q; meis successorib; sup hoc fieri constituo .
Preīca ad augm̄tū substantię canonicoꝫ . & ad seruitiū ei⁹dē ecc̄lę corro-
borandū ꝭ de decē & octo p̄bendis ei⁹dē ecc̄lę q̄a admodū paupes st ꝭ
ēsilio & assensu capituli mei matris ecc̄lę exoniensis . concessi & in
ppetuū confirmaui ꝭ q̄d redigantʳ in duodecī p̄bendas . ad usū duodecī
canonicoꝫ d̄o ibidem seruientiū. Et his ita libe sic p̄fatū est concessis ꝭ
canonici p̄dicti loci debent eccl̄am suā & officinas ecc̄lę canonicales
pficere & manutenere ad honorē d̄i & ecc̄lę suę. Verū ut de cętʰo rata
& inconcussa hęc ēcessio pmaneat ꝭ carta & sigillo meo confirmaui . &
ecc̄lę meę capituli ēsilio confirmatū ꝭ p̄sentib; & futuris contradidi .
Quicunq; ğ hui⁹ concessionis & confirmationis auctoritatē inrefregabilit
manutenuerit ꝭ a d̄o retributionē accipiat . & orationū & beneficioꝫ
ecc̄lę p̄nominatę . particeps & consors effici mereatʳ. Qui autē hui⁹
statuti libtatē n̄ quę ih̄u xp̄i sed que sua st querens uiolare ꝑtemp-
tauerit ꝭ tanquā reus diuinę subiaceat ultioni . A M E N ; .+. Porro
hui⁹ libtatis ēcessionē . & capitulū nrm̄ & sc̄i Petri attestʳ & confirmat .
& sigillo suo simul assignat . In p̄mis . Robtus de Waręlwast . Will

16, 17. *ab aliquo*] partially erased. 27. Erasure of letter after *verum*.
26. Erasure of letter (*f*?) after *canonici*. 34. *ultioni*] the *tio* partly decayed.

CHARTERS AND DOCUMENTS. 31

de augo . Odo . Ernaldus . archidiaconi . Magist'h Leowin⁹. Witt de normanuile . thesaurari⁹ . Rađ medic⁹ . Walt'h fr ei⁹ . Witt lotoringensis . Osbt⁹ capett . Radulf⁹ uitat . Gauf'h de s'h. laudo . Philipp⁹ de furn'h. Deiñ totū capit'h . & extra . Rađ de leu . Alured⁹ . subarchidiaconi . Rob 40 de rothom'h . Hemmin⁹ . Rob de normanuile . & quā plures clerici & laici . Testes libtatis supi⁹ ptaxatę.

Endorsed in early 14th cent. hand: [De] libtate eccte C'ditoñ & canōicis ei⁹dm̄ ecce [conc]esse p dñm̄ Wittm Ep̄m Exoñ.

XIV.

[C. 1150.]—*William (de Albini) earl of Chichester, to the church of St. Lazarus of Jerusalem (Burton Lazars).—Grant of 120 acres in Wymondham, co. Norfolk.*

W. comes cicestrię . W. đi gr'ha ep'ho norwici . & om̄ib; fidelib; sc'hę ęcctię . 7 om̄ib; hominib; 7 amicis suis francis & anglis de Norfulch & suffulch r sat . Noscat dilectio u'hra me concessisse & dedisse đo 7 Scę Marię 7 ęcctię Sci Lazari ierosolimitani . & fr'hib; ibidę d'ho seruientib; sexies viginti acras in villa Wimundehamię . scilicet int'h meā dñicā 5 mansurā & t'hras cāpestres in ppetuā elemosinā. Videlicet p rege Stepho 7 regina Mathildi . 7 filíis eo⁊ . p me ipso & p regina Adelide . 7 filiis nr'his 7 p animab; patris 7 matris meę 7 filiis eo⁊ . 7 p uniuersis xp'hianis uiuis atq; defunctis. Quā u° terrā uolo 7 firmit'h p̄cipio ut bene & in pace 7 honorifice . libere 7 ꝗete cū om̄ib⁹ libtatib; 7 sine om̄i 10 exactione sctari teneant. Test'h Rogero de albineio . Hub de monte chañ . Morett de mert . Rađ cap'h de chen'h . 7 Witto cap'h . 7 Ric filio hac. Herueo de Ing. Witt uat . Warino masc'h . Rog'ho cam̄ . 7 Ric filio Ailwardi.

7. Erasure between *me* and *ipso*. 9. Erasure between *ut* and *bene*.

XV.

[C. 1150.]—*Nigel de Moubrai to the Canons of St. Mary's Southwark. Grant of an orchard, etc., at Banstead (co. Surrey).*

Nigell de moubrai omīb3 hominib3 suis francis 7 anglis 7 vniuⁱsis sc̄e matⁱs eccl̄e filiis tā p̄sentib3 qᵃ fut⁻is ꝶ sal̄. Not sit om̄ib3 uobis me concessisse 7 dedisse 7 hac mea carta confirmasse dᵗo 7 beate MARIE 7 Canonicis eccl̄e sc̄e Marie de sudwurcħ in libᵗam 7 ppetuā elemosinā .
5 pomᵗiū qđ est apđ aqⁱlonē intʰ eccl̄am de benested 7 uiā qᵃ gᵃditʳ apđ domū vital de sutt̄ . 7 intʰ uiā q̄ ducit ad curiā meā 7 semitā q̄ in occidente ducit ad eccl̄am. Et .v. acᵉs in hāma . habendū 7 possidendū sic libᵗam 7 p̄petuā 7 qⁱetā elcmosinā ex om̄i seclari sʰuitio 7 exactione tenendū de me 7 de hᵗedib3 meis etʰnaᵗr . hanc u° elemosinā optuli suꝑ
10 altare sc̄e MARIE in eccl̄a de sudwʰcħ ꝓ salute mea 7 vxoris mee 7 om̄iū ꝑipinq°r̄ meoƺ. His test̄. Ric̄ de Hastīg . Witt̄. capett̄. Rogʰ de moubrai . Ric̄ de aluers. Rob de buci Rob filio Rog. Vital de Suttʰ. Witt de coueħ. Goc̄ uinator̄. Rađ uinator̄. Rađ bucett̄. Walt de Wett. Michæl filio Rađ de cornħ. Pet° p̄posito . 7 aliis qᵃ plurib;.

XVI.

[C. 1150.]—*Bartholomew de Glanville.—Confirmation of his father's grants to Bactun or Bromholme monastery (co. Norfolk).*

Notū sit oīb3 tā futuris qᵃ presentib3 qđ ego bartoloms de glāuilla c̄cedo & p̄senti carta c̄firmo oīa que patʰ m̄s Witlm⁹ de glāuilt concessit & dedit dō & sc̄e marie 7 sc̄o andree apl̄o 7 monachis apud baketuniā dō seruientib3 uⁱ patʰ m̄s reqⁱescit . Scit . tʰrā stanardi p̄sbitʰi de casewic .
5 Et eccl̄iā ei⁹dē uille cū ptinentiis. Et brōholm uⁱ manēt. Et eccl̄iam de dilhā cū apendiciis . Decimā q°q; manerioƺ meoƺ . Scil . de baketunia

11. *ꝑipinq°r̄*] for *propinquorum*.

totā . 7 .ii⁽ᵃˢ⁾. partes decime de haninges . 7 similitʰ de horhā . 7 de alretunʰ . 7 dalīgeho . 7 de burg de dñiis mīs . 7 similitʰ de sueftlinges . Decimā qᵒq; molendinoʒ meoʒ de baketunʰ . 7 de wileford totā . 7 ii⁽ᵃˢ⁾. partes molendini decime de haninges. Et unū molendinū ī mulesle ī dñio. Et tʰrā herefridi p̄sbitʰi in dñio. Et qᵃndā partē mee silue a uia molendini usq; tochesgate. Et .ii⁽ᵃˢ⁾. partes decimarū meoʒ hoīū. Scit. Rogʰi auuncti mei de bertune 7 galfridi p̄sbitʰi de haninges . 7 turstani dispensatoris . 7 warini de torp . 7 Ricardi hurel . 7 walteri utlage . 7 Robti de Ruskeuile . 7 totā decimā ricardi filii ketel . 7 totā decimā de pannagio de baketunʰ . 7 de horhā . 7 de tʰbagio de suathefeld .ii⁽ᵃˢ⁾. partes . 7 Isr̄ increm̄tū qd̄ ad finē suū delegaū . Scit . Geilholm . 7 oīa qᵉ ibi habuit ī agⁱs . ī hōibʒ . Scit . wistan cem̄tariū . 7 ōs alios qˡ ibidē sui iuris erāt . sole 7 qⁱte ab oībʒ c̄suetudinibʒ p̄tʰ denegeld regis. Et Isr̄ qᵉ ego barthot dedi ī elemosina . Scit . eccliā de pastunʰ cū p̄tinentiis . Et tʰrā silue . 7 tʰrā pastunʰ . 7 tʰrā de greneho . 7 tʰrā ad cap̄ briges . 7 tʰrā ad aldehithe . 7 lākeland . 7 tʰrā toche de briges qᵉ ipse toche dedit in elemosina quarū sūma ē qⁱnqᵃginta due acre . Et p̄tʰea dedi eis .xxx. acras iuxta mare . Et meū pᵃtū de brakeholm p̄ptʰ decimā p̄curatioīs dom⁹ mee . 7 mariscū meū iuxta broholm. Et p̄tʰea dedi eis .x. acᵃs iuxta mare . 7 decimā Ricardi p̄sbitʰi de baketunʰ 'ī honore dī 7 sc̄e marie 7 sc̄i andree apli p salute aīe mee 7 aīe p̄ris mei 7 oīu amicoʒ meoʒ uiuoʒ ac defunctoʒ.' Teste Ricardo p̄sbitʰo de bachetuñ . 7 baldewino decano de caresfeld . 7 Radulfo capellano . 7 gocelino p̄sbitʰo . 7 jurdano de sacheuit. Rodbto de ualeinʰ . Heruico de glāuit . 7 Randulfo de glāuit filio ei⁹. Rogʰo de glāuʰ . 7 Rodbto filio ei⁹ . 7 witt de glāuʰ . Odone de wrthested 7 Ricardo 7 ebrardo filiis ei⁹ . Hosbto de glāuit . Reginaldo de glāuit . 7 witt filio petˡ . 7 hūfrido frē suo . Rogʰo taleuaz . 7 michet filio ei⁹ . 7 Ricardo p̄posito . 7 witt de gisnei . 7 witt filio ulf . 7 Alexa[n]dro filio odonis de wrthested . 7 Reginaldo frē ei⁹ . 7 Rodbto de bonesboz . 7 Gamel sacriste . & Ædrico palmʰ . 7 Gilebto 7 witt auunculo ei⁹ de gᵃndgāp . 7 Gocelino nepote pⁱoris . 7 dña basit mr̄e dñi bartholomʰ 7 matilde uxore dñi . 7 leticia filia ei .

The deed has CHIROGRAPVM on one side. It is cut through, not indented.   16. *Suathefeld*] altered from *suathefeld*.

XVII.

[C. 1150.]—*Thomas son of Hugh de Horton. Grant to St. Mary's, Woodkirk, a cell of St. Oswald's, Nostell* [*co. York*].

Sciant tam p̄sentes q̊ fuīi q̊d̄ ego thomas fili⁹ hugonis de hortona dedi 7 ɔcessi 7 hac mā karta c̄firmaui d̊o 7 sc̄e Marie de wudekyrcæ 7 canonicis de sc̄o oswaldo ibidem d̊o 7 sc̄e Marie seruientib; ꝑ aīa pat¹s mei 7 mat¹s méé . 7 ꝑ aīa mea . 7 vxoris méé . 7 parentū meoꝫ 7 an̄ces-
5 soꝫ in purā 7 ꝑpetuā elemosinam 7 de oī exactione quietam . dimidie-tatē unius bouate īre in aldewrþa . cū ꝑtinentíís scilicet occidentalem partem illi⁹ bouate q̊ ricard⁹ filius ede tenet de me . suꝑ q̊ idem Ricardus manet . 7 cōmunem in oīb; aisiamentis . in bosco . in plano . in pascuis . in pasturis . in aq¹s . in ulís . in semitis . q̊ ad illam uillam ꝑtinent . 7
10 Ego 7 heredes mei warentizabim⁹ p̄dictis canonicis īrā p̄noīatam. His testib; Witło f⁷ roḃti de sicclinhala . witło clerico de trescs . Sansone de wrīslesfordia . hugone de swinlentona . witło de bolling . witło [de] tlorrentona . Iohe de thorrentona . Rog⁴o de thorrentona . Gaufrido Kardinal . Thome Kardinal . henrico f⁷ Nigelli de thankerleia . Rog⁴o
15 de oustona . Gaufrido filio ingolfi . 7 M V L T I S   A L I I S ;

12. *wrīslesfordia*] *a* altered from *e*.
13. *Tlorrentona*] so in MS.
14. erasure (of *e* ?) after *Kardinal* in both cases.
thankerleia] *r* altered from *l*.

XVIII.

[C. 1150.]—*B. de Balliol to St. Mary's Abbey, York.—Grant of Gainford church and the chapel of Barnard's Castle, co. Durham.*

B⁴ . de balliolo . Oīb⁹ suis ꝓ hōib⁹ francis 7 angt . 7 oīb⁹ sc̄e eccłe fidelib⁹ ⁓ sał; Sciatis me concessisse 7 hac mea carta confirmasse dō 7 sc̄e marie ebor⁴ . 7 monach ibidē dō seruiētib⁹ eccłam de Gainesforď c⁷ capella de castello Bern⁷ 7 aliis ꝑtinentiis suis . I purā 7 ꝑpetuā elemosinā .
5 q̊ ecctiā Wid⁴ de balliol me⁹ auūcul⁹ de q̊ hereditatē habeo p̄fato monast⁴io ded⁴ 7 sua carta ɔfirmauit . ꝑ sał; aīe ipsi⁹ Wid̊ . 7 ꝑ sał; aīe mee 7 pat¹s 7 mat¹s mee . necnō 7 filioꝫ meoꝫ uiuoꝫ 7 defunctoꝫ .

CHARTERS AND DOCUMENTS. 35

Test{h} . Ingelra{h}no de balt . Walt{h} . de hedig Herebt{h} de doura clerico
bnard{h} de balt . Rainer{h} de stocchest. Elsi de neutun{h} . Walt{h} de abbeuill.
Daniel fil Walt{h}. Paulino Medico. 10

XIX.

[C. 1150.]—*Ralph Lestrange to St. Katherine's, Blackburgh.—Grant of his land in Wormgay, co. Norfolk.*

Sciant oms tam psentes quā futuri quod ego Radulfus lestrange concessi 7 donaui & hac carta mea presenti confirmaui deo 7 sce MARIE 7 sce Katerine 7 domui sue de blakeberge . 7 omibȝ ibidē dō 7 sce katerine seruientib{s} atq; seruituris r totā terrā qm teneo de feudo wirmegeie in marisco iux{a} blakebergiā in liberā 7 ppetuā elemosinā ꝑ 5 animab{s} omniū parentū meoȥ tenendā de me 7 heredib{s} meis pacifice 7 honorifice . libere . 7 quiete . ex omi exactiōe & interrogatiōe . reddendo annuatim unā marcā argenti r ꝑ omi sclari seruicio 7 consuetudine r ad quatuor t{er}minos . scilicet ad IIII{or}. tēpora anni . ad qdlibet quatuor tempoȥ .XL. denarios. His testib{s} . Galfrido decano de 10 finchehā . Odone presbit{er}o . Magistro Robto de nuiers. Randulfo de hunstanestun . 7 filiis ei{s}. Rodlando 7 Hamone . Iohe milite de nereburg . Galfrido pposito . Roberto de scal. Rog{h}o fre suo . Alano de mideltun . Rog{h}o de spannie . Rog{h}o 7 Willo frib{s} ei{s}. Widone lestrange . Alano de geitun . Ricardo pdume . Willo de cnaresburc . Odone clerico . 15 Edwardo lesire . Radulfo barat . Rog{h}o filio reiner de svildam . Godardo de mideltun . Herberto de acra . Willo talebot . Iohe lestrange . 7 multis aliis.

LIST OF ABBREVIATIONS.

AfdA. = *Anzeiger für deutsches Alterthum*, herausgegeben von E. Steinmeyer &c., Berlin, 1876, &c.

B.M.Fcs. = *Facsimiles of Ancient Charters in the British Museum*, 1873-1878.

CD. = *Codex Diplomaticus Aeui Saxonici*, opera Johannis M. Kemble, London, 1839-1848.

CS. = *Cartularium Saxonicum*, ed. by W. de Gray Birch, 1885-1893.

DB. = Domesday Book.

Munch, *N.F.H.* = P. A. Munch, *Det Norske Folks Historie*, Christiania, 1852, &c.

O.E.T. = *Oldest English Texts*, ed. by H. Sweet, London, 1885 (Early English Text Society).

PBB. = *Beiträge zur Geschichte der deutschen Sprache und Literatur*, herausgegeben von Paul und Braune, Halle, 1874, &c.

Schmid = Reinhold Schmid, *Die Gesetze der Angelsachsen*, Leipzig, 1858.

Sievers = *Angelsächsische Grammatik*, von Eduard Sievers, 2nd edition, Halle, 1886.

Steenstrup = J. C. H. R. Steenstrup, *Normannerne*, Copenhagen, 1876-1882.

Freeman, *N.C.* = E. A. Freeman, *History of the Norman Conquest* (the references are to the third edition of vol. i, Oxford, 1877).

Thorpe, *Diplom.* = Benjamin Thorpe, *Diplomatarium Anglicum Aeui Saxonici*, 1865.

OS. Fcs. = *Facsimiles of Anglo-Saxon MSS.* Ordnance Survey Office, Southampton, 1878-1884.

Earle, *L.C.* = John Earle, *Hand-Book to the Land-Charters and other Saxonic Documents*, Oxford, 1888.

NED. = *A New English Dictionary*, ed. by J. A. H. Murray and H. Bradley, Oxford, 1888, &c.

ZfdA. = *Zeitschrift für deutsches Alterthum*, herausgegeben von Moriz Haupt, K. Müllenhoff, &c., Leipzig und Berlin, 1841, &c.

NOTES.

I.

THE text of this charter, which is now printed for the first time, is derived from a copy written in the square handwriting in use about the middle of the eleventh century. A somewhat older and more accurate text of the boundaries is given in No. II.

In the absence of the original charter, it is difficult to decide whether the copy represents a genuine document of Æðelheard's or is merely a later fabrication. Very little assistance in deciding this question can be drawn from the study of *formulae*, owing to the exceedingly small number of eighth century charters preserved in contemporary handwriting. No original charter of this king's is known to be in existence, and there is only one charter, preserved in a later copy, that is ascribed to him[1] (*CS.* i. 228). The proem of the present charter suggests comparison with later charters, but much stress cannot be laid upon this, as the text and the reflection it contains are common ones. On the whole, there seems to be nothing in the charter to justify its being labelled as spurious. The contention that it is a genuine charter is supported by its brevity (except in the boundaries), the fewness of the witnesses, the repeated use of *signum manus* in the attestations, the clearness and simplicity of its Latin, and the absence of Greek words. All these are characteristics that it shares with the undoubted charters of early date. It has, moreover, come down to us in copies older than the Norman Conquest, and it therefore occupies a position superior to charters dependent upon copies made after that event, as the great majority, if not all, of the spurious OE. charters were made in the century or so following the Conquest. It is not possible to found arguments for or against the charter upon the absence of the future tense in the granting clause[2], as the use of that tense is not invariable in the early charters. Indeed, the future is in no case used in the original charters prior to A.D. 740 in the *uerba*

[1] He also confirms a very dubious charter of King Æðelbald (*CS.* i. 224). See below, p. 117, note to l. 48.

[2] See Kemble, *CD.* i. p. xxviii; Heinrich Brunner, *Zur Rechtsgeschichte der römischen und germanischen Urkunde*, Berlin, 1880, p. 165.

NOTES.

dispositiua[1]. The absence of the future in this position in the early charters militates against Brunner's unsatisfactory explanation of its use in OE. charters. Offa is the first king who thus used the future with anything like consistency, and it is possible that most of the charters of secondary authority of earlier date than his reign wherein the future is used are really of later origin [2].

Another argument in favour of the authenticity of the charter is the form *Aðilhardi* in line 51. The retention of the *i* in the second syllable of *aðil* favours the view that the charter was copied directly from an original belonging to the first half of the eighth century. The charters up to 740 preserve the *i* in unaccented syllables, but after that date it is superseded by *e* (cp. Sievers, *Anglia*, xiii. p. 13). In the case of names beginning with *æðil*, the traditional spelling with *i* is occasionally met with in the second half of the eighth century, and even so late as the beginning of the ninth. As this spelling cannot well be later than the beginning of the ninth century, and as it is the only form to be expected in 739, we think it may fairly be adduced as an argument in favour of the authenticity of the charter.

There are thus several features that we should expect to find in a charter of this date, and nothing that distinctly suggests a later origin.

The Indiction is the correct one for 739, so that we may conclude that the eleventh century scribe copied the figures accurately, for we can hardly assume that he would take the trouble to alter the Indiction so as to agree with a wrongly-copied date. The year 739 is the date of King Æðelheard's death, according to the Northumbrian Chronicle [3], whose chronology is hereabouts superior to that of the OE. Chronicle. The Parker MS. of the latter records Æðelheard's death in 741, although it fixes the date of his successor Cuðred's death in 754, in contradiction of its statement that Cuðred reigned sixteen years. But the dates in the Chronicle are two years behind the real dates from 754 onwards, so that 754 means 756 [4]. Thus Cuðred's accession occurred in 740, the date

[1] The words used are as follow: Hloðhere of Kent, A. D. 679, *dono, conferimus, adiunxi* (*CS.* i. 70 [16], [22], 71 [7]); Æðelred of Mercia, A.D. 691-2, *tradidi* (*Ib.* i. 109 [16]); Hodilred, A. D. 692, *trado, transscribo* (*Ib.* i. 115 [12], [18]); Wihtred of Kent, A.D. 697, *decreui dare* (*Ib.* i. 141 [1*]): Nunna of the South Saxons, *circ.* 725, *conscribo, attribuo* (*Ib.* i. 211 [10], [14]); Æðelberht of Kent, A. D. 732, *tribuo et dono* (*Ib.* i. 215 [9]); Æðelbeald of Mercia, A. D. 734, *indico me dedisse* (*Ib.* i. 220 [14]), and A. D. 736, *trado* (*Ib.* i. 222 [26]).

[2] This is certainly true of the charter of Cædwalla of Wessex, A.D. 683 (*CS.* i. 99), which uses *dabo* (line 19), as it embodies a phrase (*praedicta siquidem tellus his terminis circumcincta clarescit*) that seems to have originated in the chancery of Æðelstan.

[3] See continuation of the brief chronicle at end of Bæda's *Historia* (ed. Mayor and Lumby, p. 374); Simeon of Durham, ed. Arnold, ii. 32 ; Roger of Howden, ed. Stubbs, i. 5.

[4] Ludwig Theopald, *Kritische Untersuchungen über die Quellen zur angelsächsischen Geschichte des achten Jahrhunderts*, Lemgo, 1872, p. 16 sqq.

CHARTER I.   39

given in Chronicles C, D, E, and F. This date is supported by the statement that the battle of Beorhford, in 752, was fought in the twelfth year of his reign. The present charter shows that Æðelheard was alive in April, 739, and the MSS. of the OE. Chronicle agree so closely upon the date 740 that we cannot assume that this is merely an instance of an annal for 739 being entered inadvertently under 740. Theopald has shown clearly that Æðelheard's successor, Cuðred, began his reign in the year 740, although, curiously enough, he decides that Æðelheard's death occurred in 739. There is a like discrepancy of a year between the date assigned for Ine's death and Æðelheard's accession in Bæda and in the OE. Chronicle. The date in Bæda can only be obtained inferentially[1]. It is 724 or 725. Chronicles A and B say that Æðelheard succeeded in 728[2], and the other MSS. give 726. They all agree in saying that he reigned fourteen years. Yet A and B record his death in 741, which only allows him thirteen years. We have seen above that this must be a mistake for 740, the year given by the other MSS. Thus we reach 726 as the true date of the OE. Chronicle.

The date of the present charter, 739, is an impossible one if the entry in the Chronicle recording that Queen Friðugyð and Bishop Forðhere, two of the witnesses, 'went to Rome' in 737, means that they abjured the world[3]. This is the meaning of the phrase *Romam pergere* in the *Recapitulatio Chronica* at the end of Bæda's *Historia Ecclesiastica*, V. c. 24, under the years 688 and 709. In Bæda the brevity of the phrase may be explained on the ground that he had already given full particulars of the two pilgrimages in the body of his work (III. c. 30; IV. c. 12; V. cc. 7, 19). In the earlier instance the Chronicle says that Ceadwalla went to Rome, was baptized by the pope, and died there, thus copying from Bæda, V. c. 7. In the latter instance three MSS. of the Chronicle simply use the phrase 'went to Rome,' whereas two others add that one of the pilgrims remained at Rome until the end of his life. Similarly, a later scribe has added to the notice in the Parker MS. of Ine's journey to Rome the statement that he died there[4]. In this case it may not have been considered necessary to

---

[1] Bæda, *Hist. Eccl.* V. c. 7, records the succession of the *iuueniores* [Æðelheard and Oswald] to Ine, when he went to Rome. Bæda states that Ine reigned thirty-seven years after Caedualla's abdication, which occurred, he says, in the third year of the reign of Aldfrid of Northumbria. Aldfrid succeeded (V. c. 1) his brother Ecgfrid, who was slain in 685 (IV. c. 26). Ine therefore succeeded in 687 or 688. Adding the length of his reign to this, we get 724 or 725 as the date of Æðelheard's accession.
[2] This is the date given by the Lindisfarne Annals; Pertz, *Scriptores*, xix. 505.
[3] Bishop Stubbs suggests that there may be a mistake in the date in the Chronicle.
[4] A.D. 728: 'Her Ine ferde to Rome [7 þær his feorh gesealde], 7 feng Æþelheard to Wesseaxna rice.' The source of the annal is Bæda, *H. E.*, V. 7.

mention his death, as the accession of his successor is immediately afterwards recorded. The notices in the Chronicle of pilgrimages subsequent to Bæda's death (735) by no means support the view that *faran to Rome* means the renunciation of the world[1]. There is only one instance that is not in direct conflict with this view. This is the annal of 797, in Chron. F, recording that Sigeric, king of the East Saxons, 'fared to Rome.' In this case we do not know whether he died or returned, as the date of the accession of his successor, Sigered[2], is not recorded. In 799 the Chronicle says that Æðelheard, Archbishop of Canterbury, and Cyneberht, Bishop of Winchester, 'went to Rome.' Both these prelates returned, Æðelheard dying in 805 and Cyneberht witnessing a charter in 801 (*CS.* i. 420[19]). A similar instance occurs in 812, when Archbishop Wulfred and Wigbryht, Bishop of Winchester, are said to 'fare to Rome.' The archbishop lived for twenty years after this date, whilst Wigbryht witnesses charters in 814 and 816 (*CS.* i. 480[33], 498[19]). Chronicles E and F record that Archbishop Wulfelm, who died in 942, went to Rome in 927. In each of these three cases an Archbishop of Canterbury is concerned, so that the journeys were probably for the purpose of receiving the *pallium* from the pope. Even if this was so, they may fairly be cited as instances to disprove that 'to fare to Rome' necessarily means the end of one's worldly career, the meaning that Henry of Huntingdon unhesitatingly gives to the annal of 737 recording Friðugyð's and Forðhere's journey to Rome. That the phrase had not this meaning in later times is proved by the additions to the annals of 709 and 728. It is also indirectly proved by the annals of 855 and 874, which record, in the first case, the return of the pilgrim and, in the other, his death at Rome. The entries under 884, 887, 888, and 890 simply relate to the sending of alms to Rome, and have, therefore, no bearing upon the question. We have thus seen that 'to fare to Rome' is equivalent in the entries derived from Bæda to renouncing the world, and that in the latter part of the ninth century it merely means to journey to Rome. The question that we are unable to decide is whether the annal of 737 has the earlier or the later meaning. In favour of the earlier meaning, it may be pleaded that the annal is so very near to Bæda's time; in favour of the later, it may be urged that it is not derived from Bæda's continuators, but is purely a West-Saxon entry. The evidence of the charter

[1] It should be remarked, however, that in the will of the Reeve Abba (*CS.* i. 575[27]), in A.D. 835, the expression *suð to faranne*, 'to fare south,' undoubtedly has this meaning; but, in this instance, the phrase may be conditioned by the immediately preceding alternative of entering a monastery.

[2] His name occurs as a witness in 811 (*CS.* i. 472[31], 474[20]), in 812 (*Ib.* i. 475[27]). The *dux* of this name, who witnesses in 814 (*Ib.* i. 481[11]), 816 (*Ib.* i. 498[25]), &c., is, no doubt, another person.

CHARTER I.

now under consideration may also be cited in favour of the later meaning, since the charter is otherwise deserving of credence. Queen Friðugyð occurs once only as a witness, in a charter of 737 (*CS.* i. 214[24]). Bishop Forðhere subscribes from 712 to 737 (*CS.* i. 189[11], 210[29], 214[26], 225[6], 229[16]). Stubbs states that Forðhere's successor, Herewald, was consecrated in 736, and that he subscribes from 737. The authority given for the consecration is Simeon of Durham, who states, under 736, that Archbishop Noðhelm, having received his pall from the pope, ordained three bishops, Cuðberht, Heordwald, and Ethelfrið. This date conflicts with the occurrence of Forðhere as a witness in 737 and, in the present charter, in 739. It is, moreover, difficult to believe that Simeon or the Northumbrian annalists can have written *Heordwald* for *Herewald*. The former can only mean *Heardwald*[1]. Yet there can be no doubt that Herewald was the name of Forðhere's successor, as he occurs in the early ninth century list in Sweet, *O. E. T.*, p. 168[24], and in Florence of Worcester's list. Sweet's list precludes the suggestion that might otherwise have been made—that Heardwald was Bishop of Dunwich[2]. We have been unable to find an earlier subscription of Herewald's than 742 (*CS.* i. 234[24]), although Stubbs states that he signs in 737, on the authority of *CD.* i. 99[37], for which Kemble cites Heming (Tib. A. xiii, fo. 25). But this name does not appear in the MS., and it is clearly derived by Kemble from the Old *Monasticon*, i. 121 (= i. 585 of the new edition). As Dugdale only cites Heming, no MS. authority for the signature is known.

The boundaries in the present charter are given at greater length than we should expect in a charter of this date, and they are written in English of the tenth and eleventh centuries, not in West-Saxon of the eighth. They may, however, be original despite their length, for the original charters of this period are sadly too few to justify our drawing hard and fast conclusions from them upon such points as this. As for the language in which they are written, it was, no doubt, modernized when our copies were made. Similar instances of modernization in the eleventh and twelfth centuries are common. Possibly a few additional features may have been introduced into the boundaries when the tenth century copy (No. II) was written. Some of the localities mentioned in these boundaries and in No. IV also occur in a grant by King Edgar of

---

[1] The *Liber Vitae Dunelmensis* writes in two cases *Uulfheord* (Sweet, *O. E. T.*, p. 165[iii]), but always writes *Heard* when it forms the first syllable.

[2] It is possible that the Cuðberht and Heordwald of Simeon may have been evolved by some blunder from the *Fruidbertus* and *Fruiduualdus*, who were consecrated bishops by Archbishop Ecgberht of York in 735, according to the continuation of the brief chronicle at the end of Bæda's *Historia* (ed. Mayor and Lumby, p. 174), which probably represents the oldest form of the Northumbrian Annals.

land at Nymed near Copplestone, A.D. 974 (*CS.* iii. 623), and in one by King Æðelred of land at Sandford, A.D. 997 (*OS. Fcs.*, Pt. III, pl. 35)[1]. The boundaries as given by No. II, which is by a tenth-century scribe, are, as regards the form, better than those given in No. I, which has distinct traces of the eleventh-century copyist, e. g. *herpað*, I. 10, etc., compared with *herepað*, II. 2 ; the use of *i* for *y* in *hricg*, I. 12, and, conversely, the use of *y* for *i* in *Lyllan-broc*, I. 18, *Wypig-slade*, I. 39, *Crydian*, I. 43. In all these cases No. II preserves the older and correct forms. We have, therefore, taken No. II as the basis of our annotation of the boundaries.

The boundaries proceed from Creedy Bridge, Crediton, by the road through Lower Creedy to the Exe at Nether Exe. This road forms the boundary of the parishes of Crediton, Newton St. Cyres, Upton Pyne, and Brampford Speke[2]. The boundary then proceeds down the Exe to the junction of that river with the Creedy, and thence, probably along the southern boundaries of Newton St. Cyres and Crediton, to the junction of the Lilly Brook and the Tedburn near Harford. Hence it proceeds, partly or wholly along the southern boundary of Crediton, to the River Yeo, which it ascends to the source near Grendon, thus following in the main the boundary between Hittesleigh and Cheriton Bishop. From near Grendon it goes eastwards along the Oakhampton and Exeter road, probably to the crossing of the road by the brook running by Woodbrook into the Teign near Clifford Barton. It descends this brook into the Teign, and then proceeds up the latter along the southern boundary of Drewsteignton to the vicinity of the road from Easton to Parford, where it leaves the Teign and goes across country to Drascombe. From this point the line is not clear, but it seems to proceed by Hollycombe to the river Troney, up the latter to Nymet Wood, and thence, probably by the western boundary of Colebrooke or Clannaborough[3], to the Bow and Crediton road. It next proceeds to Copplestone, thence northward by the brook that joins the Ashbrook, and thence by the united stream of the two brooks (now called the Knighty Brook) until the stream runs into the (western) River Yeo. It follows the Yeo for a short distance up to the

---

[1] King Eadwig's grant of land at Æscford and Beohyll, A.D. 958 (*CS.* iii. 227), contains several names that occur in the Crediton boundaries, but their positions do not agree with those of the same names mentioned in the Crediton and Sandford boundaries. About this time the abbot of Abingdon granted 17 hides 'æt Crydan Brigce' to the Bishop of London in exchange (*CS.* iii. 162).

[2] It is probable that our identifications of the boundaries are more certain in cases where they agree with parish boundaries, but it is clear that they do not always follow the parish boundaries. The division into parishes may, moreover, be of later date.

[3] As Colebrooke is in Crediton Hundred, whilst Clannaborough is in North Tawton Hundred, it is probable that Clannaborough is not included in the boundaries.

CHARTER I. 43

junction of the latter with the River Dalch, which it ascends, following the boundary of Morchard Bishop. It then proceeds, probably by the northern boundary of Kennerleigh, to Binneford, and thence, probably by the boundary of Sandford, to Holly Water. Following the stream of Holly Water into the Creedy, it proceeds down stream back to Creedy Bridge.

In several instances the boundaries are not traceable for considerable distances; in such cases we have had to take the line *per saltum* to the first local name that we have been able to identify. We have made extensive use of the 6-inch Ordnance maps, whence most of the modern names mentioned in our notes are taken. It is possible that local research may recover some of the names that we have not identified, and may thus occasionally rectify the boundaries given by us. Our experience suggests that we may have sometimes wrongly identified an old name with a modern one of the same origin, as in Devonshire local nomenclature there are frequent cases where one and the same name occurs several times in different sites.

Assuming that our identifications are in the main correct, it will be seen that the land conveyed by this charter includes the parishes of Crediton, Newton St. Cyres, Upton Pyne, Brampford Speke, Hittesleigh, Drewsteignton, Colebrooke, Morchard Bishop, Sandford, Kennerleigh, and the modern parish of Sherwood, part of Cheriton Bishop, and possibly the whole of Clannaborough. It thus includes the whole of the Hundred of Crediton, but it is not co-extensive with the Hundred, for Upton Pyne, Brampford Speke, Hittesleigh, Drewsteignton, and Cheriton Bishop are in the Hundred of Wonford, whilst Clannaborough is in the Hundred of North Tawton [1].

If the twenty *cassati* conveyed by this charter include the whole of the land within these boundaries [2], it is curious that the whole of the land is not included in Crediton Hundred. If the Hundred was, as has been sometimes maintained [3], the local unit out of which the manors were subsequently carved, we should surely expect to find that the present estate formed a Hundred, for the grant was made soon after the English settlement of the district, the land almost abutted upon the wilds of Dartmoor, and it was seemingly not broken up into manors or townships. It is simply described, no doubt for lack of a compre-

[1] These are the modern Hundreds, but they appear to agree with the Hundreds in the *Nomina Villarum*, A.D. 1316. Neither the Domesday Survey nor the Exon Domesday gives us sufficient information to reconstruct the eleventh-century Hundreds.

[2] Nasse, *Ueber die mittelälterliche Feldgemeinschaft . . . in England*, Bonn, 1869, p. 18, maintains, 'dass die Grenzen in den Urkunden oft die der ganzen Ortschaft, nicht die der einzelnen concedirten Grundstücke sind.'

[3] H. Cabot Adams, in the *Essays on Anglo-Saxon Law*, Boston, U.S.A., 1876, p. 12. Cf. Maitland, *Archaeological Review*, iv. 233 sqq.

hensive name or names, as '20 hides in the place called Creedy,'—that is, the river-name[1]. Thus, if the charter does not support the theory that the Hundred was the unit, it certainly seems to favour the view that the manor or township was formed out of a larger *regio*[2]. The mistake seems to be in identifying the *regio* with the Hundred[3], although in many cases they corresponded. The word *hundred* itself does not occur in Old English until a late period. This lateness of the word is scarcely compatible with a very early origin of the Hundreds *eo nomine*. The history of the Gloucestershire Hundreds shows that the Hundreds in that county were permanent neither in name nor in area[4]. It is possible that the boundaries of Crediton Hundred may have been modified after the monastery had alienated part of the above estate. But if this was so, the modification must have occurred before the Domesday Survey, for when the Survey was taken the church of Exeter, the representative of Crediton, did not possess all the manors forming the Hundred of Crediton.

The local names mentioned in the boundaries, if they are faithfully copied from the original charter, prove that there was a considerable English settlement in this neighbourhood some time before the date of the charter. The numerous English words and English personal names occurring in the boundaries can be accounted for only upon this hypothesis. The founding of an English monastery at Crediton would hardly have occurred if Exeter was not already in English hands, as Crediton is only seven miles distant from that city. If Exeter was secure under English domination in 739, it is highly probable that it was captured by the English before the end of the seventh century. Freeman (*Exeter*, p. 16) was led to suggest that Exeter was captured by the West Saxons, advancing from the south-east, before the end of the seventh century. His grounds were simply that Willibald records that Winifrith (St. Boniface) was educated *Adescancastre*, which, as he says, no doubt means *æt Exanceastre*, Exeter[5]. The present charter confirms indirectly the accuracy of Willibald's assertion and of Freeman's deduction from it. If, as Freeman says, 'Damnonia was conquered from the north, we could hardly bring the West Saxons to Caerwisc [Exeter] in the seventh century, perhaps not in the eighth.' We have proof in this charter that the West Saxons

---

[1] The division into parishes can hardly be older than that into manors, although there are cases where a second manor was created in a parish. The diminutive manors of later times must be left out of the field of discussion. There is a case of the late creation of a parish in the charters relating to Downton, Wilts (*CS.* i. 47; iii. 3). In these charters the boundaries impinge upon those of Britford. There is now a (twelfth century?) parish of Nunton between them.

[2] Adams, ut supra.   [3] Adams, p. 13 sqq.

[4] C. S. Taylor, *Analysis of the Domesday Survey of Gloucestershire*, 1887, p. 33.

[5] *Escan-* (from *Isca*) is an older form than *Exan-*, which has arisen from the not uncommon OE. change of *sc* into *x*.

CHARTER I.

were in possession of Crediton in 739, and we may reasonably conclude from the local names in the boundaries that they had been there for some time.

1. **quę uidentur . . . aeterna sunt.** From 2 Corinth. iv. 18.

5. **ad construendum monasterium.** The uses of the gifts are similarly expressed in several early charters (*CS.* i. 108 ²⁶; 113 ¹³; 121 ¹; 222 ²¹; 225 ¹⁹). Lodge, in the American *Essays in Anglo-Saxon Law*, Boston, 1876, page 99, discusses the meaning of this declaration of uses.

6. **Cridie.** The River Creedy. The name is spelt in the same way in the Domesday Survey, i. 103, 114 b. It is *Cridia* in the Exon Domesday, p. 124.

7. **cum commoditatibus cunctis, &c.** Cf. Æõilbalt of Mercia, A.D. 736: *cum omnibus necessariis ad eam pertinentibus, cum campis siluisque, cum piscariis pratisque* (*CS.* i. 222).

49. Spelman, *Concilia*, i. 193, says that it is probable that the era of the Incarnation was seldom or never used in diplomas before Bæda's time. Kemble, *CD.* i. p. lxxi, has attempted to disprove this, maintaining that the era was introduced into England by Augustine. His arguments are exceedingly weak. It is certain that the era of the Incarnation was not used in papal records until a much later date[1], and it is therefore not likely that Augustine would introduce this era into England. Kemble, p. lxxvi, makes the loose assertion that 'the era of the Incarnation is found in those copies of Gregory's letters which Nõõhelm obtained for Bæda from the papal regesta.' He then proceeds to argue that we cannot 'attribute to Bæda the useless labour of attempting to illustrate *notum per ignotius*, a date that was, by a date that was not, familiar.' It will hardly be credited that the six letters of Gregory given by Bæda are not dated by the Incarnation, but, as we should expect, by the regnal and consular year of the Emperor and by the Indiction[2]. There are, in addition, three letters of Boniface, and one each of Honorius, John, and Vitalianus without dates[3]. The sole foundation for Kemble's assertion is the letter of Honorius (II. c. 18). This is dated by the triple imperial year, and by the Indiction, followed by *id est, anno Dominicae Incarnationis sexcentesimo tricesimo quarto*. Surely this is an explanation added by Bæda in his own phraseology to explain the complex date of the Pope's letter. The absence of the dating by this era from documents prior to Bæda's time is, in spite of Kemble's demurrer (p. lxxv), a good argument that it was not in use. As Earle has shown (*Land Charters*, p. xxxiii), this era is not used in genuine undoubted charters until after

---

[1] In fact not until the tenth century; Harry Bresslau, *Handbuch der Urkundenlehre für Deutschland u. Italien*, Leipzig, 1889, i. 839.
[2] *Historia Ecclesiastica*, I. cc. 23, 24, 28, 29, 30, 32.
[3] *Ib.* II. cc. 8, 10, 12, 17, 19; III. c. 29.

Bæda's death, and the present charter is rather an early example of its use [1]. There are plenty of early charters dated by this era that depend upon later copies, most of which are to be looked upon with suspicion. Ideler [2] is, no doubt, correct in his contention that this era was brought into use by Bæda.

52. **Cuthredi.** Cuðred succeeded Æðelheard as King of Wessex. He witnesses a Mercian Charter in 732-3 (*CS.* i. 218 [11]).

57. **Duddi abbatis.** No doubt the *Dud abbas* who witnesses a Glastonbury Charter in 744 (*CS.* i. 243 [18]).

II.

2 (=I. 10). **herepaþ.** This is probably the road proceeding from Creedy Bridge by Creedy to Nether Exe and Rewe; it forms the eastern boundary of the parish of Crediton and the northern boundaries of the parishes of Newton St. Cyres, Upton Pyne, and Brampford Speke.

As there is no reason to believe that this was a Roman road, it is evident that *herepað* does not necessarily mean a Roman road, as is frequently asserted. There are three different roads described by this name in these boundaries, and the word is exceedingly common in the charters [3]. Moreover, we meet with *herepað* in charters alongside of, and as something distinct from, the *strǣt* [4], rarely *here-strǣt* [5], which is the usual name for a Roman road. The meaning of *here* is

[1] There is an early example not mentioned by Earle in Baldred of Mercia's charter of 681 (*CS.* i. 96), which is preserved in a very early, if not contemporary, copy.

[2] *Handbuch der Chronologie*, Berlin, 1825, 1826, ii. 376.

[3] *Herepað* still survives as *harepath* in local names. See below, note to line 18. There is a *Harepath* (farm?) at Drewsteignton, near Crediton, and a *Harepath* near Burbage, Wilts. The latter is in the vicinity of Roman roads, but not on one. Cf. the surname *Heripath*. There is a *Hair Lane* at Gloucester, which is written *Herelone* about 1240 (Stevenson, *Calendar of the Gloucester Corporation Records*, 1893, Nos. 368, 429, &c.). This is a lane joining the Ermine Street by the north gate of the city. *Herpath* is the name of a road dividing the townships of Ray and Kirkwhelpington, co. Northumberland (Heslop, *Northumbrian Glossary*, E. D. S., p. 360). *Herepað* is sometimes strengthened by prefixing *þeod*, 'people' (*CS.* ii. 270 [7], 435 [1]; iii. 497 [1]). According to Baigent and Millard, *History of Basingstoke*, 1889, p. 195, the Ermine Street at Basingstoke is called 'le Herepathe' in a terrier of *circa* 1300. We are unable, for want of local knowledge, to check this assertion, but we think it is more probable that the 'Herepathe' was a road running into the Ermine Street. It is worthy of note that the *Liber de Hyda* translates *herepað* by *lawpathe, legalis semita* (*CS.* ii. 310 [26], 311 [10]). A *sealt-herpoð* is mentioned in 931 (*Ib.* ii. 354 [23]).

[4] See, for example, *CS.* i. 47 [13]; ii. 34 [71], 382 [22]; iii. 3 [26], 123 [16], 336 [16], 525 [18]; *CD.* iv. 49. See also No. XI, line 46.

[5] Cp. O.H.G. *heri-strāza*, O. Fries. *her-strēt*. There is a *Hare Street* (farm?) near Kennerleigh, probably within the present boundaries, and another near Great Hormead, co. Herts, on the road from Ware to Cambridge. In Edgar's charter to Westminster, A.D. 951 (?971, below, p. 90), the Roman road from Tyburn to St. Alban's Church, Holborn, which connects the Watling Street (Edgware Road) with London Bridge, is called 'the wide *here-strǣt*' (*CS.* iii. 261 [13]). The

CHARTER II.   47

'army, warlike band,' not simply 'crowd' as Sweet assumes[1]. The etymology of the word (see Kluge, *Etymologisches Wörterbuch*, s. v. 'Heer') shows that the fundamental idea was that of 'a fighting, warlike band,' and it is in this sense that the word is ordinarily used of an 'army.' The restriction in the Chronicle of this word to the Danish invaders is opposed to the view that it was felt as a synonym of *folc*. Even in Old Norse, where *herr* has the meaning of 'folk' as well as 'army,' there is evidence, in the statement in the *Edda* that a hundred persons constitute a *herr*, of an original restriction in meaning not possessed by *folk*. The Laws of Ine, § 13, define a band of more than thirty-five as a *here*. In early times there was very little travelling, and the inhabitants of a district were not so dependent upon made roads as we are, there being few enclosures. Hence the OE. conception of a 'road' or 'way' differed considerably from ours. But a large body of men like an army could not conveniently march across country by the roads that sufficed for local communication, and therefore an army naturally used the Roman roads in the first place, and, where they did not exist, other important roads, whose origin we cannot ascertain. Hence it is probable that *herepað* means a broad, well-established road, not necessarily Roman, upon which troops could march conveniently.

2 (= I. 11). **sulhford**. This is probably the ford on the Exe just below Fortescue on the boundary of the parish of Brampford Speke. It is, no doubt, the *sul-ford* mentioned in the boundaries of the adjoining parish of Stoke Canon or 'Hroca-stoc' in a charter dated 670 for 938 *CS*. ii. 431 [12, 20]). It is called 'Sulford' in No. III above. A *sulh-ford* on the Colne, co. Gloucester, occurs in a charter of 721–743 (*Ib*. i. 240 [21]). Cf. also the great Pershore charter (*Ib*. iii. 589 [11, 14, 17]): *ærest of sulanforda ... in suligcumb ... eft on sulan broc*. Cf. (?) also *syle ford* (*Ib*. ii. 246 [24]), *syl-weg* (*CD*. iii. 262 [20]).

The only recorded meaning of *sulh* in OE. is that of 'plough,' but 'ploughford' is not a very likely compound. *Sulh* is cognate with Latin *sulcus*, 'furrow.' This meaning is, apparently, preserved in the diminutive *sūlincel* in Wright-Wülcker, 348 [14], '*sulincela*, aratiuncula' (for *-culas*, 1 Kings xviii. 32; cf. *Anglia*, xiii. 324). Ducange gives the meaning of *aratiuncula* in late Latin as *fossa parua ad instar sulci aratri*. If *sūlincel* meant 'a small furrow,' it is probable that *sulh* meant 'furrow.' In that case, *Sulhford* would mean a ford approached on one or

road crossing the Icknield Way at Baldock, co. Herts, was evidently called *here-stræt*; see note to No. XI, line 46. Cf. *Laws of Henry I*, c. 10, § 2: *omnes herestrete omnino regis sunt*. The almost synonymous *fyrd-strǣt* occurs in *CS*. iii. 181 [25]; *CD*. vi. 214 [27], 221 [26]. This seems to be a road running from the Icknield Way near Bengeworth and Evesham, co. Worcester.

[1] *Gregory's Pastoral Care*, E. E. T. S., pp. 490, 491 : '*Here* originally implied nothing more than a crowd ... *herestræt* simply means a road for the *multitude*, without any reference to armies.'

both sides by a sunk road or gully. *Sulh* seems to denote such a sunk road (or a furrow) connecting two brooks in a Middlesex charter of 972: *æfter stanburnan on sulh, swa on yburnan ... on sulh eft to þæm ealdan tūnstealle* (*CS.* iii. 605 [13]). It is also referred to in 957: *andlang stræte on ða deopan fura, þonon inon sulh ... of hylfes hæcce innon sulc, up æftær sulue* [1] (*Ib.* iii. 188 [30]; 189 [2, 3]). A *sulgeat* is mentioned in a Berkshire charter of 944 (*Ib.* ii. 558 [6]), and a *sulig graf* at Lawern, co. Worcester, in 963 (*Ib.* iii. 341 [23]). Cf. *Sulwath*, the older form of Solway Firth? (Will. of Worcester, *Itinerarium*, p. 354).

3 (= I. 12). focgan igeþas. These seem to be the eyots at the junction of the Exe and the Creedy. The first part of the name is preserved in *Foghays* or *Voghays*, a hamlet adjoining Exwick Barton, in the parish of St. Thomas, Exeter. Foghays is close to the southern boundary of the parish of Upton Pyne, which is, probably, the line pursued by these boundaries. *Focgan igeþas* are called *Fogan flode* in No. III, line 3. Cf. *Foghanger* (farm) in Milton Abbott.

The same word appears in *focgan crundel* (*CD.* vi. 168 [27]) and *fogga crundel* (*CD.* vi. 186 [12]). The suggestion that *focge* means 'a she-fox' (cf. Leo, *Angels. Glossar*, p. 345, and Kluge, *PBB.*, ix. 161, Sievers, *ibid.* xx. 157 note), has but little to support it. One might be inclined to connect it with the ME. *fogge*, NE. (dial.) *fog* 'aftermath, winter grass,' if it were not for the forms *focginga byra* (*CS.* i. 480 [8]), *fucges flodan* (*CS.* ii. 358 [19]), and *fucces treow* (*CS.* iii. 344 [20]) which seem to point to a personal name.

on landscare hrycg. The word *landscearu* apparently means the line dividing one estate, or portion of an estate, from another, a boundary, a 'gemǣre.' As a rule it is applied, as here, to a portion of the boundary, but occasionally *sēo landscearu* is used collectively in the sense of *þā landgemǣru*. Cf. *CD.* iii. 338 [4] (co. Hants); *CS.* iii. 660 [1] (co. Devon); Earle, *L.C.* 296 (co. Cornwall); 301 (co. Cornwall).

Kemble (*CD.* iii. p. xii) asserts that the expression is only found in comparatively modern charters, and those principally belonging to the extreme South of England. The second part of this statement admits of still more precise formulation: although the word is of frequent occurrence in the charters—we have noted about forty instances of its use—it is only found in the South-Western counties. We have not met with any instance of it in South-Eastern boundaries. Only in one single case [2], viz. in a charter of Cnut, 1021–23 (*CD.* iv. 20 [1]) referring to land at Newnham, co. Northampton, have we found the word used outside the area mentioned.

[1] For *suluc*?
[2] The charter printed in *CS.* iii. 238 is there wrongly assigned to Berkshire. The estates referred to are in Dorsetshire.

CHARTER II.

With regard to the date of its occurrence, we have not met with it in documents written earlier than the tenth century. The few seventh to ninth century charters in which it is found (*CS.* i. 48[1]; ii. 14[12]; 143[3], 144[14]) are not originals, being only preserved in chartularies of the twelfth to fifteenth centuries, and it is not impossible that its use is there due to the later scribes. The tenth century charters in which the word is used are very numerous, but, with one exception (*CS.* iii. 3[40], A.D. 948), they are all later copies. In documents written in the eleventh century we have found three examples of the word (*CS.* iii. 660[1]; Earle, *L.C.* 296, 301). The great majority of instances of the use of *landscearu* occur, therefore, in quite late MSS. (twelfth to fifteenth century), and this would certainly seem to bear out Kemble's statement.

Of course the evidence here adduced is of a negative character, and it is quite possible that the non-occurrence of the word at an early date is merely the result of accident. In any case, no argument against the genuineness of our first charter can be founded on its use of this word, as its introduction may be due to the later copyist having substituted it for some other term.

In the tenth and eleventh centuries the word appears as *landscaru, -scearu*; in the later documents it assumes various forms: *land* (*lond-*)*scære, -schere, -share,* &c., and from the eleventh century onwards we meet with the spelling *landscore* (e.g. *CD.* iv. 20[4], A.D. 1021–3). The last mentioned form is noteworthy, as it cannot have been phonetically developed from *landscearu*, but is the result of the replacement of *-scearu* by another word, viz. *score* (NE. *score*), a word probably of Scandinavian origin.

According to Halliwell *landscearu* still survives in Devonshire in the form *landshare* 'the headland of a field,' and Elworthy, *West Somerset Word-Book*, gives *landsherd* as meaning 'a ridge or strip of land left unploughed or untilled, either between two crops or to mark a boundary where there is no fence[1].' This *landsherd* represents an older *landsher*, the *d* being excrescent, as in *millerd, scholard, liard* (='liar'), which occur in the same dialect.

The other form, *landscore*, has also survived. Halliwell cites an instance of *landscores*, and in the Devonshire Directory a *Landscore* occurs at Crediton and at Teignmouth.

4 (= I. 13). **luhan treow.** Cf. *Luhhan beorh* (MS. *luhhamb-*) in *CS.* iii. 227[22], a charter containing other boundaries of the same names as those of this charter (*Wonbroc, Stanford, Wiðigslæd*); see page 42 above, note 1. Cf. *Luhes ford, CS.* iii. 176[5]; *Luhhes geat, CS.* i. 515[18]; ii. 495[19], 529[27]; *Luhincwudu, CS.* iii. 589[4].

5 (= I. 14). **doddan hryeg.** There is a Doddridge about three miles to the north-east of Crediton; but the position does not suit, *doddan hrycg* should be to

---
[1] In other dialects *landmere*, from OE. *landgemǣre*, is still used with this same meaning.

the south-east of Crediton. The name *Dodda* occurs in other place-names, e. g. *Doddan ford* (*CD.* iii. 217 [10]; vi. 213 [20]), *Doddan læw* (*CD.* iv. 47 [1]) &c. The name *Dodda, Dudda* is elsewhere not unfrequent, and we find instances of its occurrence in Devonshire: a *Dodda* was one of Æðelred's moneyers at Totness, and under Cnut and Harðacnut there was a moneyer of that name in Exeter.

5 (= I. 14). **Grendeles pyt.** Possibly recorded in the name of *Pit Farm* (old 1-inch Ordnance map), near Whitestone Wood, near the boundary between the parishes of Newton St. Cyres and Whitestone. There is also a Tinpit Hill in Newton St. Cyres, near Shuttern Brook. It is possible that the name still existed in the fifteenth century, as it is called 'Gryndelys Pytte' in No. III.

Another *Grindeles pytt* is mentioned in Worcestershire (*CS.* i. 176 [27], 177 [1]). The same form occurs in *Gryndeles sylle* [1] at Battersea, co. Surrey (*Ib.* iii. 189 [25]), and in *Grindlesbec* at Beornoðes leah near the River Teme, co. Worcester (*Ib.* iii. 588 [22]). The form *Grendel* occurs in *Grendlesmere* [2], in Wilts (*Ib.* ii. 364 [11]) and in Staffordshire (*Ib.* iii. 223 [27]); and in *Grendeles gatan*, co. Middlesex (*Ib.* iii. 605 [14]). The *Grendel* in these names is generally identified with the monster in *Beowulf.* On the meaning of the word, see Jacob Grimm, *Deutsche Mythologie,* 4th ed. 1875, i. 201; Sarrazin, *Beowulf-Studien,* p. 65; and Paul's *Grundriss,* i. 1043. The *grendel* in a Devonshire charter of Edgar's (*CS.* iii. 336 [17, 19, 24]) *on grendel . . . anlang grendel . . . on grendel,* &c., is the Grindle Brook, which runs into the Clyst at Clyst St. Mary. There is a narrow street in Sheffield called 'Grindelgate.'

6 (= I. 15). **ífig-bearo,** 'ivy-grove.' This hitherto unrecorded compound probably means a grove of ivy-encircled trees. It is treated as an *u*-stem and forms the dat. in *-ra,* not *-rwe.*

hrucgan cumbes ford. This was probably on one of the branches of the Shuttern Brook, by Venny Cleave, that form the boundary of the parish of Newton St. Cyres. There is a *Northridge* close to Venny Cleave, and a *Rudge* about 1½ miles NW. But neither of these can well be derived from *Hrucgan,* as, in the absence of *umlaut* in that word, the *cg* should be represented by *g,* not by *dg.* A *ruggan broc* occurs in co. Warwick (*CS.* i. 179 [6]); but this may be miswritten for *rūgan.* There is a *Rug House* in Holcomb Burnel and a *Rug road* (farm or hamlet) in the parish of Spreyton, both near the boundaries of the present charter, but in positions far away from our *Hrucgan cumb.* Perhaps *Ruggins,* a hamlet of West Buckland, co. Somerset, may be compared.

[1] Corresponding to the *Gryddeles* (for *Gryndeles*?) *elrene* of *CS.* i. 117 [27].
[2] It might be thought that a *Grindles mere* is recorded in the *Grundeles-mare* in the Huntingdonshire Fens, A. D. 1146-1153, in the 14th cent. *Cartular. Monast. de Rameseia,* i. 161, but as the name is written *Grundlesemere* in an original charter of 1147 (Cott. Chart., vii. 3; *Monasticon,* v. 522), it is clear that it is derived from OE. *grundlēas,* 'bottomless' (cf. *on þone grundleasan pyt, CS.* iii. 395 [16]).

7 (= I. 16). earnes hrycg. Known as 'Yearnys Rygge' in the fifteenth century (No. III. 7). This may be from the personal name *Earn* or from *earn*, 'eagle.' The name of the bird seems to occur in *Earna dene* (*CD*. vi. 186²¹), *Earna leah* (*CS*. i. 331⁵; ii. 295³⁹, 349²⁹; *CD*. vi. 168²⁹). Cf. *Earna næs*, *Beowulf*, l. 3032. In all probability *Earn-hyll* (*CD*. iii. 279¹⁵) is derived from the bird. The following may be from the bird or from the personal name, the composition with the genitive favouring the latter derivation: *Earnes beam* (*CS*. ii. 114¹²); *Earnes beorh* (*Ib*. i. 47²³, 545⁵; ii. 382¹³, 444¹⁸; iii. 3³⁰, 12¹⁷); *Earnes dun* (*Ib*. iii. 174⁷, 257²¹); *Earnes hlewe* (*Ib*. iii. 126¹⁵); *Earnes hlinc* (*Ib*. i. 229¹²; ii. 437¹); *Earnes hyrst* (*Ib*. iii. 15¹⁰).

8 (= I. 17). Wealdan cumb. Probably the valley of the Kelland Brook, which is on the line of the Crediton parish boundary. *Wealdan cumb* was known as 'Weldecome' in the fifteenth century (No. III. 8).

Tettan burna. This is probably an older name of the Kelland Brook (recorded in the hamlet of Venny Tedburn, in the parish of Crediton?). It can hardly mean the River Culvery, the name borne by the stream formed by the junction of the Tedburn and Lilly Brook, as the boundary proceeds from *Tettan burna* up the stream (of the Culvery).

8 (= I. 18). stream. The River Culvery.

Lillan broc. The Lilly Brook. The present boundary proceeds up the Culvery to the point where the Lilly Brook and the Tedburn unite, thence proceeding for some little distance up the Tedburn. The boundary in the charter seems to vary slightly from this course. A *Lilles ford* is mentioned in our No. IV, line 44, but this was in the parish of Sandford, north of Crediton.

The name *Lilla* is not uncommon in the charters, which record a *Lillan hlæwes crundel* (*CS*. iii. 174⁶, 257²⁹), a *Lillan hrycg* (*Ib*. iii. 309¹⁶), a *Lilan mere* (*Ib*. ii. 118²⁶), and a *Lillan welle* (*Ib*. ii. 205⁶). This name is immortalized by the heroic devotion of the Northumbrian thegn of this name (Bæda, *Hist. Eccl. II*. c. 9). It belongs to an unexplained class of Germanic personal names, which are characterized by the initial consonant being doubled after an intermediate vowel. They usually end with the hypocoristic suffix -*a*. The vowels of the root-syllable are not regulated by the laws of *ablaut*. Instances of such names are: *Babba*, *Bebb*, *Bibba*, *Bobba*, *Bubba*; *Dodda*, *Didda*, *Dudda*; *Lilla*, *Lulla*; *Nunna*; *Pibba*, *Pippa*; *Tetta*, *Titta*, *Tot*, *Totta* (= *Torhthelm*?). As the great majority of these names occur only in hypocoristic forms, it is evident that they are not proper name-stems. Possibly some of them are formed by regressive assimilation, just as we form *Bob* from *Robert*.

Can the *y* in *Lilly Brook* represent the inflexional -*an*? Compare such Devonshire names as *Darniford* (OE. *dyrnan forda*), *Bradiford* (OE. *brādan forda*),

Babbicombe (OE. *Babban cumb), *Puddicombe* and *Shorticombe*. Or does it arise from the tendency of the South Western dialects to add an *i* or *y* at the end of certain classes of words, and especially between the two parts of compound place-names [1]?

9 (= I. 19). **middelhrycg.** This is probably the ridge of land between the Lilly Brook and the Tedburn.

10 (= I. 19). **herepaðford.** This ford was probably at the crossing of the Tedburn by the road along the 'middelhrycg' from St. Mary Tedburn to Crediton. The name is, no doubt, recorded in Lower and Higher *Harford*, hamlets in the immediate vicinity. The site here suggested is on the parish boundary of Crediton and St. Mary Tedburn.

cyrtlan geat. This must have been somewhere between the hamlets of Hembeer and Higher Berry. Higher Berry Camp, which might possibly be the *cyrtla or *cyrtle, is not on the modern boundary of Crediton, which hereabouts does not seem to correspond exactly with that of the charter.

Nothing is known of the meaning of *cyrtla or *cyrtle, which occurs, apparently, elsewhere in local names. Kirtlington, co. Oxford, is in Domesday *Chertelintone, Certelintone, Cherielintone, Cortelintone* (J. L. G. M., *Notes on the Oxfordshire Domesday*, Oxford, 1892). Kirtling, co. Cambridge, called *Chertelinge* in Domesday, and Kirklington, co. Notts, in Domesday *Cherlinton*, and Kirklington co. York, may perhaps be compared (Kirklinton, co. Cumberland is Kirk Linton). The Nottinghamshire *Cortlingstock* may also be connected. It does not seem probable that *cyrtla or *cyrtle represents the Frankish-Latin *curtilla* or *curtile*, as the meaning of these words was covered by the OE. *weorðig*. Cf. Laws of Ine, c. 40. If *cyrtla or *cyrtle be a substantive, the mention of its gate in the boundaries would be parallel to that of the *hagan get* of line 4.

11 (= I. 20). **on suran apuldre,** 'sour apple-tree or crab.' This was, probably, in the neighbourhood of Higher Berry Camp.

Apple-trees are frequently mentioned in OE. charters, both with and without qualification. The 'sour apple-tree' occurs in *CS*. i. 229[11]; ii. 270[26]; 436[42]; 438[29]. The 'sweet apple-tree' is mentioned in *CS*. iii. 232[86] (*to þare swete apuldre*). The 'hoar-apple-tree' is referred to in *CS*. ii. 41[5], 295[31]; iii. 52[9], 63[26]; 303[35]; 'broad apple-tree' in iii. 352[20]; 'twisted apple-tree' in ii. 79[4]; 'long apple-tree' in iii. 586[8]; 'rough apple-tree' in ii. 585[8]; 'large apple-tree' in iii. 655[36]. There was an apple-tree in 969 at the junction of the boundaries of Woburn and Wavendon, co. Bucks, and of Apsley, co. Bedford (*CS*. iii. 517[29]).

---

[1] Cf. Elworthy (*West Somerset Word-Book*, E. D. S. 1886, p. xvii), who also cites the pronunciations *Foxydown, Dartymoor*. A similar tendency is recorded for the dialect of the Hundred of Berkeley, co. Gloucester, in the 17th cent. by J. Smyth; cf. *The Berkeley MSS.*, ed. by Sir J. Maclean, Gloucester, 1885, iii. 23.

CHARTER II. 53

The OE. name of the apple-tree is recorded in the Devonshire local names *Appledore* at Clannaborough, near Crediton, and *Appledore* near Bideford. *South Appledore*, a tithing of Burlescombe, but in Halberton Hundred, co. Devon, is an interesting corruption of (*æt*) *sūran apuldre*. It was still called *Sourapledere* in 1316, according to the *Nomina Villarum*, p. 387 a. A manor of *Surapla*, co. Devon, is mentioned in the Exon Domesday, p. 368.

The OE. word occurs in two forms: *apuldre*, weak feminine (*Ælfric's Grammar*, ed. Zupitza, p. 20, *ðeos apuldre;* CS. ii. 79⁶, *on þa . . . apoldran, of þere apoldran;* cf. also CS. i. 229¹¹; ii. 270²⁸, 436⁴²; iii. 303³⁵; 352²⁰, &c.); and *apuldur, -dor, -der*, strong fem. (Wright-Wülcker, 31³¹ *apuldur;* CS. ii. 542³ *of ðære apuldre;* cf. also ii. 585³; iii. 52⁹, 63²⁶, 164²¹, 232²⁶, 240⁷, &c). The former corresponds to the OHG. *affoltra*, which is also a weak fem., and the latter to the ONorse *apaldr*, a strong masculine. No doubt the OE. *apuldor* was originally masculine, like the Scandinavian form, but its gender has been influenced by the weak *apuldre*. We have noted but one instance in which the old gender has been preserved, viz. CS. iii. 586⁸, *on þone longan apuldre* (for *-der*), *of þam apuldre*.

grenan weg. Probably the road from the Okehampton road to Black Down Plantation near Posbury, which passes by Higher Berry Camp.

12 (= I. 21). **wulfpyt.** 'Wolf-pits' are mentioned about 765 at Stanmer, co. Sussex (CS. i. 280²⁰); in 829, 939, and 956 at Droxford, Hants (*Ib.* i. 548²⁰; ii. 460⁴¹; iii. 134²¹); in 955 at Chalk, co. Wilts (*Ib.* iii. 84¹⁵); in 955-9 at Alveston, co. Gloucester (*Ib.* iii. 113⁸¹); in 1033 at Polhampton, Hants (CD. iv. 49⁷); in 1062 at Passefield, co. Essex? (*Ib.* iv. 157¹¹); and in 1004 at Littlebury, co. Essex (*Lib. Elien.*, p. 175). Probably an artificial excavation or pitfall for catching wolves, although it may merely mean a depression in the ground haunted by wolves, a wolf's lair.

Woolpit, near Stowmarket, Suffolk, derives its name from 'wolf-pit,' as it is recorded in Domesday as *Wlfpetta* (vol. ii. p. 362 b). A *wulf-seað* or wolf-pit occurs at Broadwas, co. Worcester, about A.D. 779 (CS. i. 326²⁰), and in 978-92 at Bredicot (CD. iii. 264⁶). The *wulf-hagan* of 959 at 'Ermundeslea' or Appleton, co. Berks (CS. iii. 258²⁶), and of 972 at 'Longandun,' co. Worcester (*Ib.* iii. 587³⁰) were probably enclosures or 'haws' to protect the flocks from wolves. The first example describes the *wulf-hagan* as 'old.' Other compounds into which the name of the wolf enters are: *wulfbeorh*, CS. ii. 81¹⁶, 512³⁰; iii. 48¹⁴; *wulfa broc*, CS. iii. 16⁸³, 137³²; *wulvesburghe*, CS. iii. 43¹⁹; *wulfcumb*, CS. ii. 232¹⁵ (cf. *wulfcumbes heafod*, Charter I. l. 36); *wulfandun*, CS. i. 176²⁹; *wulfflodan*, CS. ii. 482³¹; *wolfgate*, CS. ii. 471³⁶; *wulfhlype*, CD. iv. 157³¹; *wulfhricg*, CS. iii. 113³; *wulfhylle*, CD. iii. 279²⁹; *wulfleag*, CS. i. 342⁵; ii. 295³⁸; *wulfa leag*, CS. ii. 490¹⁶; *wulfmere*, CS. i. 388¹; *wulfa mere*, CS. iii. 556²⁵,

558 [35]; *CD.* iii. 292 [16]; *wulforan, CS.* iii. 10 [13]; ii. 301 [17]; *wolfpol, CS.* ii. 512 [30]; *wulfslæd, CS.* iii. 212 [21]; *CD.* iii. 456 [6]; *wulfwælles, CS.* ii. 34 [24]. Some of these may be from the personal names *Wulf, Wulfa*.

oþ þa laca tolicgaþ. The junction of the brook at Eastford with the Fordbrook near Tillerton, or the junction of the brooks from Langridge, Cadaford Moor, and West Down, which form the brook at Eastford. The Crediton boundary follows the united streams until they flow into the Fordbrook. The word *lacu* here means 'stream,' not 'lake.' Cf. *CS.* iii. 624 [19], boundaries of Copplestone, near Crediton: *adune on Secgbroc oð seo lacu scyt west þanon ut on hæðfeld.* Cf. also *CS.* ii. 541 [26]. This meaning has survived until the present day in the south-west of England. In the modern dialects of Devonshire, Cornwall, and Somersetshire, the word *lake* is not applied to a pond or sheet of standing water, but is always used of running streams. Numerous instances of its use in this sense may be found in the Ordnance maps of Devon.

14 (= I. 23). sceaftrihte, 'in a straight line.' Cf. Charter IV. 1. 42, 44, &c. Also *CS.* iii. 336 [22] *þanon west sceftrihte* (also a Devonshire charter). The word is not recorded in the dictionaries.

alr, 'alder.' *Aller* is a very common local name in Devonshire, but we have been unable to identify this one.

on hlypan. Two forms of this word are met with: *hlyp*, strong fem., and *hlype*, weak fem. (?). It occurs both alone and preceded by names of persons (*Freobarnes, Wullafes, presta,* &c., *hlyp*), and is not uncommon in compounds of which the first element is the name of an animal or bird (*swealewan-, hinde-, wulf-hlype*). It is also found as the first part of compounds where it is followed by a noun denoting some common boundary mark, like *cumb, burna, geat.* It is not impossible that we have here more than one word. The meaning 'leap,' which is sometimes given to it, certainly does not suit in all cases. In the case of *hindehlype* one might think of something like a 'deer-leap,' a ditch over which the deer could get one way, but not back, and *hlypgeat* might mean a gate in such a line of enclosure. Unfortunately the prepositions *into, æt,* which we find used with *hindehlype,* point rather to an enclosed space than to a mere line. Cf. also *CS.* iii. 443 [18], *þ synd .iii. hida þe fram cuþum mannum hindehlep is gehaten.*

The following are instances: I. *Hlyp,* strong fem., *into presta hlype . . . to Freobearnes hlype . . . to ðære ældan hlype . . . of ðare hlype . . . into Æðerices hlype . . . into wulfhlype (CD.* iv. 157); *þe . . . hindehlep is gehaten (CS.* iii. 443 [18]); *on hindehlyp . . . of hindehlype (CD.* iv. 19 [24]); *clifhlep, -hlyp* (Wright-Wülcker, 39 [1], 469 [1]).—II. *Hlype,* weak fem. (?), *to preostan lypan (CS.* ii. 310 [25]); *to swacan hlypan (CD.* iv. 27 [20]); *to Wullafes hlipan (CS.* iii. 33 [8]); *to (æt,* &c.) *hindehlypan (Ib.* i.

CHARTER II.

342 [3]; ii. 541 [2]); *on swealewan hlypan* (*CD.* iv. 27 [19]).—III. Compounds: *hlypget* (*CS.* i. 502 [10]; ii. 354 [24], 474 [29], 575 [22]; iii. 44 [20], 212 [32], 351 [4], 586 [26]; *CD.* iii. 180 [26], &c.); *Ælfwines hlipgeat* (*Ib.* iii. 320 [26]); *hlypcumb* (*Ib.* iii. 204 [19]); on *hlypeburnan* (*CS.* iii. 288 [26]). Cf. also *hleapmere* (*Ib.* i. 82 [37]).

The word probably exists in these modern local names: *Lipe* Hill, West Buckland, Somerset; *Lype* Hill, near Luxborough, Somerset; *Lepe*, about two miles east of Exbury, Hants; *Leapyate*, Upper Wraxhall, Wilts; *Lypyate*, near Holcombe, Somerset; and Clerken*leap* near Powick and Kempsey, co. Worcester; Bird*lip* and Post*lip*, co. Gloucester; Islip (*Gihtes-hlype), co. Oxford; and Hindlip, co. Worcester. Cf. (?) Devil's Leap, Doddinham, co. Worcester.

suþ ofer, 'southwards over it' (i.e. the Alr). Cf. Alfred's *Orosius*, ed. Sweet, 244 [2], *he eode to þære burge wealle, 7 fleah ut ofer, þæt he eall tobærst.*

byrccumbes heafod. This seems to have been known as 'Brygcombes heauyd' in the fifteenth century (No. III. 15).

15 (= I. 24). hananford. There is a *Honyford* (farm or hamlet) about a mile west of Cheriton Bishop. This might possibly record the *hananford*, but it is not on the parish boundary. If *hananford* was on the line of the modern boundaries, it was probably on the brook between Hooke and Caddiford. Honyford is probably derived from *hunig*, like *Honeybourne*. There is a *Hannaford*, west of Kenn, and another in Swimbridge, co. Devon. Cf. *hananwelle*, *hananwurðe* (*CS.* ii. 232 [9]).

16 (= I. 26). Eowan. The River Yeo. The modern boundary of Crediton touches the boundary of Hittesleigh just above the crossing of the Yeo by the road from Cheriton Bishop to Hittesleigh, near West Pitton. From here the Hittesleigh boundary ascends the Yeo for nearly a mile. It then makes a bend westward, returning to the Yeo near Fursham. From this point the Yeo forms the boundary between Cheriton Bishop and Drewsteignton.

17 (= I. 26). eorþgeberst, 'a landslip, chasm in the ground.' It seems to have been still known as *yeorþberst* in the fifteenth century (No. III. 18). This compound is not recorded in Bosworth-Toller, where only the uncompounded *geberst* is cited from Cockayne's *Leechdoms*; the word does, however, occur elsewhere in the charters: *CS.* ii. 557 [26], *up to þam eorþgeberste; Ib.* ii. 579 [15], *on thar eorðbriste; Ib.* iii. 531 [31], *in þæt eorþebyrst, of þon eorðgebyrste.*

17 (= I. 27). on grenan dune. This name is probably preserved in *Grendon*, a hamlet in the extreme west of the parish of Cheriton Bishop, near Whiddon Down, and close to the road from Okehampton to Exeter. Grendon is close to the head of the Yeo, the present boundary between the parishes of Cheriton Bishop and Drewsteignton.

18 (= I. 27). hereþaþ. Probably the road from Okehampton to Exeter;

see preceding note. The name is preserved in *Harepath*, a hamlet immediately south of the road, in the parish of Drewsteignton.

Puttan stapul. From the personal name *Putta*. This was probably in the vicinity of Puddicombe, which lies between the *herepað* and Drewsteignton, if this name be derived from *Puttan cumb. Cf. *Puttan . . . ealh* (*CS*. i. 315 [10]), *Puttan crundell* (*Ib*. i. 316 [14]), and *Puttan pytt* (*Ib*. iii. 52 [29]).

19. **stanford on Eowan.** This second mention of this ford does not occur in No. I, which goes directly from Beornwyn's tree to Bucgan ford. If it be not a mistake in No. II, another *stanford on eowan* must be meant, as otherwise the land encircled by the boundaries since the previous mention of *stanford* must have been entirely cut off from the other land conveyed by the charter.

19 (= I. 28). **Beornwynne treow.** From the fem. personal name *Beornwyn*. Cf. *Beornwyne stan* (*CS*. iii. 33 [1]), and *Beornwynne dene* (*Ib*. iii. 586 [29]). With the form *Beornwunne* in No. I may be compared *Sigewunne dic* (*Ib*. ii. 232 [10]). The linking of personal names with trees in the boundaries in OE. charters is very common.

20 (= I. 28). **Bucgan ford.** There is a *Bugford Bridge* on the (western) River Yeo, west of Morchard Bishops, but this, of course, cannot be the *Bucgan ford* of our charters. There is a *Budbrook* (farm or hamlet) in the parish of Drewsteignton, close to the Woodbrook brook. Budbrook was, no doubt, the name of an affluent of the latter, taking its rise near the farm or hamlet. *Budbrook* may possibly be derived from an older *Bucgan-broc* by an inverse process to that by which our *bug*, 'cimex,' has been supposed to have arisen from OE. *budda*.

Bucgan-ford contains the rare OE. fem. personal name *Bucge* (or masc. *Bucga*?). A poem of Aldhelm's is entitled *De basilica aedificata a Bugge filia regis Angliae*. She was, as we learn from line 2, a daughter of King Centwine (of Wessex). *Bucge* occurs in 736–737 (*CS*. i. 225 [19]) and in 772 (*Ib*. i. 297 [12]; 298 [15]). The first of these is noticeable for having led Kemble to make the astounding suggestion that this 'was a familiar, though not very graceful name,' meaning *cimex*, 'perhaps upon the principle of that insect being also a "familiar beast and friend (!) to man"' (*Proceedings of the Archaeolog. Institute at Winchester*, 1845, p. 96. See *English Historical Review*, iv. 354, note 2). A masc. *Buca* occurs in 727 (*CS*. i. 213 [8]), but, unless it be a mistake for *Bucga*, this name cannot be connected with the one now under consideration. The only full-name recorded is *Buggild*, in *Buggilde stræt*, now *Buckle Street*, part of the Icknield Way, near Evesham (*CS*. i. 184 [21]; *CD*. vi. 220), elsewhere called *Bucgan*, *Buggan stræt* (*CS*. iii. 479, 480; *CD*. iii. 396 [15]). As these charters are late copies, it is probable that the name was *Burghild*, not *Buggild*. The (Latinized)

Bugga, according to Stark, *Die Kosenamen der Germanen*, Vienna, 1868, p. 14, represents the full-name *Eadburga*, in the epistles of S. Boniface (Winefriŏ). But it could, of course, be a hypocoristic form of any name (masc. or fem.) commencing with *Burg* or of any fem. name ending with that word. It occurs frequently in compounds mentioned in boundaries. A Somersetshire *Buchan* (=*Bucgan*?) *ford* occurs in *CS*. ii. 74²³. There is a Bughead Cross lying to the west of Moreton Hampstead, co. Devon.

Brunwoldes treow. This was still known, apparently, in the fifteenth century as 'Brymwoldys tree' (No. III. 20). The OE. *brūn* in compound local names is preserved in many cases as *Brim*.

21 (= I. 29). **Won broc.** This is probably the stream running by Woodbrooke into the Teign at Clifford Barton. The northern boundary of the parish of Drewsteignton proceeds from near Grendon along the Okehampton road to the point where that road crosses this stream; the boundary then goes down the stream to the Teign. The boundaries given in the charter between Grendon and the *Won broc* do not, apparently, agree with the modern boundary. Woodbroke might possibly be a corruption of *Wōnbroc*, through the form *Woobrook. The *won broc* of *CS*. iii. 227²² is one of several names contained in the charter there printed that agree in name but not in position with some of the features of the Crediton boundaries.

(Cf. I. 11). **andlanges**, formed from *andlang* with adverbial ending -*es*, occurs elsewhere in the charters: *CS*. i. 179⁷; ii. 41⁵, 60²⁸, 305¹⁰, 494¹²; iii. 290³¹, 476¹⁸, 496³³, 497⁹, 528⁵ (*olluncges*), 532⁴; *CD*. iii. 172²⁹, 320²⁸ (*onlonghes*); vi. 168²³, 217⁵. For later forms, see *NED*. s. v. *alongst*.

21 (= I. 30). **Teng.** The River Teign. Although thus spelt in both versions of the boundaries, it is probably mis-written for *Tegn*¹. The latter form is recorded in the form *Tegntun*, King's (?) Teignton, in the Parker MS. of the Chronicle, A.D. 1001, and in the manor-names *Teigna* in the Exon Domesday, pp. 126, 274. It is also confirmed by the modern name of the river.

22 (= I. 30). **Papford.** This is probably recorded, in a very corrupt form, in *Parford*, a hamlet in Drewsteignton. The ford was, in this case, probably where the road from Easton crosses the Teign. Cf. *Patforda*, Exon D. B. pp. 421, 428.

Francan cumb. If the preceding identification be correct, this must have been the name of a combe north of Parford. There is a *Frankford* (East and West) in the parish of Whitestone, some distance to the NE. of Parford. Cf. *Frankaborough* in Broadwood Widger, co. Devon.

The personal name *Fronka* is recorded in the Durham *Liber Vitae* (*O. E. T.* p. 155⁵³). Frankley, co. Worcester (*Franchelie*, D. B. i. 177, c. 2), Frankton, co.

¹ Metathesis of *g* and *n* is not uncommon, cf. Sievers, § 185, and *PBB*. ix. 216.

Warwick (*Franchetone*, ib. i. 239, 240), and Frankton, co. Salop (*Franchetone*, *Ib.* i. 255), may be from *Franca* (*Franc).

22 (= I. 31). **Drosncumb.** Probably Drascombe, in the parish of Drewsteignton. The fifteenth-century boundaries have the form 'Droscomb.'

The OE. *drōsn* has no recorded meaning except that of 'dregs, sediment,' and the remark holds good of the cognate OHG. *truosana*, NHG. *Drusen*. If it had been possible to connect *drōsn* with OE. *drēosan* 'to fall,' it might have been assumed that it meant 'slope,' like Gothic *driusō*, or 'landslip,' but the phonology of the word absolutely forbids the connexion.

23 (= I. 31). **Deormere.** Probably the small lake called 'Bradmere Pool' on the old one-inch Ordnance map, and 'Bradford Pool' on the new one. The line of boundary from Parford, above indicated, is slightly to the east of the Drewsteignton parish boundary. As *Deormere* is written *Deremere* in the fifteenth-century version of the boundaries, it is probable that the name still existed.

23 (= I. 32). **on langan stan.** This can scarcely be Longstone in the adjoining parish of Throwleigh, which is nearly two miles distant from Bradmere or Bradford Pool.

24 (= I. 32). **Hurran cumb.** Probably Hollycombe, in the parish of Spreyton, called Hollacomb in the old one-inch Ordnance map. Kelly's Devonshire Directory mentions a Horracombe at Spreyton, which does not appear on the maps, and is, therefore, probably identical with Hollycombe. Hollycombe is near the Drewsteignton boundary, which does not, apparently, agree with the line indicated in the charter. There is a *Horrabridge* in Buckland Monachorum, and another in Whitchurch, co. Devon.

24 (= I. 33). **riscford.** Probably Hollycombe Ford on the river Troney, at the junction of the Spreyton and Drewsteignton boundaries. There is a Rushford Barton, Mill, and Bridge in the parish of Chagford close to Parford, but they cannot very well derive their name from the *riscford* of the charter.

25 (= I. 33). **Nymed.** The course of the boundaries from *Hurran cumb* and *riscford* is very doubtful. If they include the parish of Spreyton and follow its western boundary, they should proceed across country from Hollycombe to the (western) River Yeo and down that river to Coxmoor. In this case the *nymed* may be, as it seems undoubtedly to be, in line 31, the River Yeo itself. If, however, Spreyton is excluded, and the boundaries follow the western boundary of the parish of Hittesleigh, then the *nymed* may be the River Troney. There are grounds, as will be seen below, for identifying each river with this name. With either alternative, we have to assume that *on nymed* means 'to the river, and along the river,' which is certainly an unusual meaning. As Spreyton is not included in the Hundred of Crediton, whilst Hittesleigh is, the probabilities

CHARTER II. 59

incline in favour of the exclusion of Spreyton. The name of this *nymed* seems to have been unknown in the fifteenth century, for No. III. 26, writes *nimed* instead of *nimet*, the form then borne by the other places called by this name.

The name of the *Nymed* is preserved in the various 'Nymets' dotted about the country by the sides of the (western) river Yeo and the river Troney. On the six-inch Ordnance map we find *Nymet* Wood in Hittesleigh, abutting upon the Troney, *Nymet* Cross in the same parish, Broad *Nymet*, *Nymet* Barton, *Nymet* Wood, *Nymet* Chapel at Bow or *Nymet* Tracy. The hamlet or farm by Nymet Wood, Hittesleigh, called 'Easterbrook' on the new Ordnance map, is called *Nymph* on the old one-inch. This seems, therefore, to be a corruption of *Nymet* (cf. the Gloucestershire *Nymphs*field from *Nymdes*-feld). This form occurs in *Nymph* and West *Nymph* at South Tawton, Nickels *Nymph* at North Tawton, and *Nymphays* at Zeal Monachorum. All these are to the west of the (western) Yeo, but in its vicinity. There is also a *Nymph* at Spreyton. These are all near enough to the Troney or the Yeo to derive their name from those rivers. *Nymet* Rowland is further afield, but as it lies close to the junction of the river Taw and of the river formed by the Yeo and the Dalch, it is not impossible for it to derive its name from the Yeo. King's *Nympton*, *Nympton* St. George, and Bishop's *Nympton* are some distance to the north of Nymet Rowland. They are by the river Mole, which flows into the Taw some considerable distance below Nymet Rowland. We can hardly assume that the Mole was also known as Nymed. It would be easier to account for this diffusion of the name in a limited district on the theory that Nymed was the name of a forest; it can hardly have been a common noun. But we see from line 31 of our boundaries that the Nymed was a stream. The same Nymed seems to be clearly a stream in the boundaries ' æt Nymed' (Down St. Mary?) in *CS*. iii. 624[21]: *ðanon adune andlang streames oð riscbroc scyt on nymed; þanon east on riscbroc*, as *scyt* in the boundaries generally means 'flows.'

A *Nimet* is mentioned in a Glastonbury charter of A. D. 744 (*CS*. i. 242[25]), and a *Nymede* (the same as above?) occurs at Lottesham, Somerset (*Ib*. ii. 14[17]). A Somersetshire *Nymed* is mentioned in the Bath manumissions (Thorpe, *Diplomatarium*, p. 644[19]). The *Nymdesfeld* of A. D. 872 (*CS*. ii. 151[26]) is the present Nymphsfield, co. Gloucester.

As regards the form of the word, the spelling *nymed* is probably the correct one. It is not only the spelling of our No. II, which preserves the distinction between older *y* and *i* better than No. I, but it is also thus written in the tenth-century ' æt Nymed' charter cited above. The other charters, with the exception of the Bath manumissions, containing this word are all late copies. Yet two out of three of them retain the *y*, which we may therefore conclude to be original.

This being the case, the word cannot be equated with the Old Low Franconian *nimid*, 'sacred grove,' in the *Indiculus Paganiarum*, although it may be cognate with it. Fick, *Vergleich. Wörterb. der indogerm. Sprachen*, 4th ed. i. 97, connects this Franconian *nimid* with Zend *nema*, *nemata*, *nimata*, 'grass, meadow.' As the name occurs in a Celtic district, it may be of Celtic origin. It may be from the Celtic *nemeton* (Welsh *nemet, nevet*, Breton *nemet*, 'silva, quae uocatur Nemet'; C. W. Glück, *Die bei C. I. Caesar vorkommenden keltischen Namen*, p. 17). The word seems to have meant 'sacred grove,' and, secondarily, 'temple,' undergoing the same development as *hǫrgr* has done in ONorse, as evidenced by the retention of the original meaning of grove by OE. *hearh* and OHG. *haruc*.

25 (= I. 33). healre dune. This can scarcely be Hillerton, in the parish of Bow, spelt 'Helliton' on the old one-inch Ordnance map. It is close to the boundary of Spreyton. The fifteenth-century boundaries write 'Alre down' (No. III. 26).

The first word seems to occur only in the great Pershore charter in *to healre mere* (*CS.* iii. 587 ³³). As *mere* is masc., *healre* cannot be, as might at first sight appear, a strong dat. fem. adjective, and it is, moreover, the weak form that is required in this position. Nor can it well be a form of *healh*, as it is considered to be in the glossary to Earle's *Land Charters*.

25 (= I. 34). wærnan fæsten, 'the wren's fastness'? It may, however, be from *Werna, a hypocoristic personal name (cf. *Uern-frith, -bercht, -bald, -gyth, -ðryð* in the Durham *Liber Vitae*). The wren seems to be meant in *Wrænnan leah* (*CS.* iii. 45 ¹). The following may be compared: *on wernan broc, ðonne on wrennan wylle*, co. Wilts (*Ib.* ii. 65 ²⁶); *wernan wylle*, co. Berks (*Ib.* ii. 516 ¹); *on wærnan hylle*, co. Berks (*Ib.* iii. 228 ³⁶); and *wernan ford ... wernan strem*, co. Somerset (*Ib.* iii. 609 ⁷). These names have been derived from the *Warni* (OE. dat. pl. *Wernum, Wærnum*, Widsið, 25, 29), the neighbours of the Angles in Germany, by Seelmann, *Jahrbuch des Vereins für niederdeutsche Sprachforschung*, Jahrgang 1886, p. 23. The use of the gen. sing. forbids this derivation.

26 (= I. 34). ciddan ford. This cannot be *Chidden*brook near Crediton, as the latter is too far away from the parish boundaries. There is a *Kiddicott* on the six-inch Ordnance map in the parish of Bow, lying east of Nymet Wood by the river Troney, and close to the western boundary of Colebrooke. There are here two fords, one of them being on the parish boundary. If the latter was the *Cyddan ford*[1] of this charter, it is clear that the boundaries excluded Spreyton and Bow.

There is a Chiddencombe farm south of Bicknoller, co. Somerset.

---

[1] Kiddicott represents, no doubt, an OE. *Cyddan-cot, from the personal name *Cydda* (*CS.* i. 371 ¹⁴, 388 ³¹). If *Cyddan ford* is connected with Kiddicott, we should have to adopt the spelling *Cyddan* of No. I.

CHARTER II. 61

26 (= I. 35). **Cæfcan græfan.** Can *Cæfca* be a hypocoristic name with the suffix *ica*? The adj. *cāf* suggests itself as a likely one for a name-stem, but there is no proof of its use. The *Caua* of the Durham *Liber Vitae* can scarcely be related. There is a *Chaffcombe* (farm or hamlet), in the parish of Down St. Mary, and Chaffcombe Cross, on the road from Copplestone to Clannaborough, marks the boundaries of these two parishes. This could only be connected with *cæfcan* by the assumption that that word is mis-written for *ceafcan*. The Exon Domesday, p. 462, mentions a manor of *Chefecoma* and a *Caffecoma* at p. 127. Both these forms represent a guttural and not an assibilated initial. Chaffcombe is a considerable distance from Kiddicott, so that the identifications of these places with *Ciddan-ford* and *Cæfcan græfan* are incompatible.

The word *grāfa, -e* (weak masc. or fem.?) appears to mean 'bush, bramble, brushwood, thicket, grove.' We have noted the following instances of its occurrence: Wright-Wülcker 406³³ and 526³⁷ *frondosis dumis = þæm gehilmdum græfum*; 517³⁶ *per dumos = þurh græfan*; 225²⁴ *dumas = spinas uel græfe* (have we here a strong fem. *grāf*?); *CS.* ii. 364⁸ (original charter, A.D. 931) *on ða blacan græfan* (either acc. sing. fem. or acc. plur.); *CS.* iii. 655¹² (Codex Winton.) *on hincstes grefan, of hincstes grafan*¹ ... *on þonne mearcgrefan.* The same word is found once in the Ormulum (l. 9210):—

> 7 whærse iss all unnsmeþe gett þurrh bannkess 7 þurrh grafess,
> 7 sharrp 7 ruhh 7 gatelæs þurrh þorrness 7 þurrh breress,
> þær shulenn beon ridinngess nu, 7 effne 7 smeþe weȝȝess.

The context shows that close impenetrable thickets are here meant. The same word occurs frequently throughout the ME. period in the form *greve*, meaning 'grove, wood': cf. Chaucer's *Knight's Tale*, l. 637:—

> And with his stremes dryeth in the greves
> The silver dropes, hanging on the leves.

Palsgrave, 1530, gives '*greave* or busshe, *boscaige*,' and this form survived until Elizabethan times. As a suffix it still exists in Sheffield local names².

The word is probably related to the OE. *grāf* masc. neut., which occurs in the charters³, and which survives as NE. *grove*, the *v* of which, however, rather points to an OE. feminine *grāf*⁴, or to a weak *grāfa, -e*, than to a masc., or neut. *grāf*, which should have become *grofe* in Modern English. Compare, however, the

---

¹ Kemble (*CD.* iii. 134²⁷) prints this as *grǣfan.*
² S. O. Addy, *Sheffield Glossary*, E. D. S., p. 95.
³ It is found in *CS.* ii. 199³, 241³⁶, 245⁷¹, 540³⁵; iii. 486¹¹, 532¹⁰, 588⁸⁴, 589¹²; *CD.* iii. 261⁶; Earle, *Land Charters*, pp. 239⁴, 248¹², etc.
⁴ Does the Latinized *grava* 'lucus' point to the use of *grāf* as a feminine? Cf. *PBB.* xiii. 315.

form *grafan* cited above. Moreover the *v* might be due to the influence of the form *greve*.

Orm's *græfess*, standing, as it does, at the end of a line, where the metre only permits words of the form — ⌣, show that the *æ* must represent a long root vowel in OE.; and his spelling with *æ*, as well as that of the OE. recorded instances, prove that the correct OE. form was *grǣf-*, not *grĕf-*, which latter spelling we have only met with in the late twelfth-century Codex Wintoniensis. An OE. *ǣ* corresponds both to a Primitive Germanic *ǣ* and *ai*, and if, as is highly probable, the word is connected with *grāf*, it must in this instance be the latter. But in neither case can the word be connected with *grafan* 'to dig, to grave, to carve,' or *græf* 'a grave, trench, hole,' which belong to an entirely different ablaut series. The explanation of *grǣfa* in Bosworth-Toller, as 'pit, cave, hole,' and of Orm's *græfess* in Holt's edition as 'ditches,' is obviously based on the assumption of such a connexion and is therefore untenable. The *grǣfe* 'speluncam' quoted in the former work (s. v. *grǣfa*) from Matth. (Lindisfarne) xxi. 13, is the dative of *grǣf* 'a grave, &c.,' in spite of the accent over the *æ*, whilst the *græfan* (*twælf foðr grafan*) in the Peterborough Chronicle, an. 852, standing as it does between *sixtiga foðra wuda* and *sex foðr gearda*, evidently means 'brushwood' (and not 'coal,' or, as Earle suggests, 'gravel') and affords another instance of our *grǣfa* or *grǣfe*.

27 (= I. 36). **stanbeorg.** The fifteenth-century boundaries (No. III. 29) call this 'Stansbrygg' and 'Stanbrugge,' but this is probably merely a substitution of 'bridge' for the obsolete *beorg* of the old boundaries. The latter would be more likely to assume the usual West of England form 'burrow' or 'borough.'

28 (= I. 36, 37). **cærswille,** 'cress-well.' As this is written 'Carswyll' in the fifteenth-century version (No. III. 29), it is possible that the name still existed. There is a Kerswell (farm?) in the parish of Crediton Fitzpaine, according to the old one-inch Ordnance map. The name occurs elsewhere in Devon in Abbots *Kerswell* or *Carswell*, *Kingskerswell*, *Kerswell* Rocks, Chudleigh, and *Kerswell* in Broadhembury and in South Brent. Outside Devon it occurs in the form *Cresswell*. There is a hamlet of *Carswell* in Buckland parish, co. Berks.

28 (= I. 37). **dyðford.** There is a *Diddy* Mill in Sandford, and a *Tid*lake in the parish of Thelbridge, but neither of these is in the position required for *Dyðford*. Cf. *Didworthy* in South Brent, *Didland* in East Down, and *Diddywell* in Northam, co. Devon. The word *dyð* occurs in *dybmere*, co. Berks (*CS*. iii. 234 [18], 279 [29]). Cf. *dyddan þorn*, *ðyddan þorn*, co. Hants (*Ib*. ii. 245 [23], [24]).

29 (= I. 37). **dices get.** The 'Dychys yeate' of the fifteenth-century version suggests that this name still existed at that time. Ditcheat, co. Somerset, is from *dices geat* (*CS*. ii. 13 [16]); this is, no doubt, the *Dicesget* of the Exon Domesday, pp. 157, 483. There is a *Ditchett* in the parish of Rose Ash, north of Crediton.

CHARTER II.

30 (= I. 38). **Egesan treow**. This was probably in the vicinity of the *Eisan* (= *Egesan*) *dun* mentioned in the boundaries of Nymed (Down St. Mary?) in *CS*. iii. 624[17]. This was on the *herepað* west of Copplestone, which evidently means the road from Copplestone to Bow, the present boundary between Clannaborough and Down St. Mary. Does the latter derive its name from 'Egesa's down'?

'Egesan treow' might mean 'tree of terror,' but this seems improbable, especially as there is also an 'Egesan down' in its vicinity. It is better to derive it from the personal name *Egisa* (*CS*. i. 68[21]), a shortened form of some name in *Egis-*, like *Egis-berht, Eges-noð, Agesmund*. An *Egsa ford* occurs in *CS*. ii. 167[19], and an *Egsan mor* in iii. 590[10].

30 (not in I). **riscbroc, scipbroc.** These brooks, or other brooks of the same names in the immediate neighbourhood, are mentioned in the boundaries of Nymed (Down St. Mary?) in *CS*. iii. 624. But whilst in our boundaries the *riscbroc* falls into the *scipbroc*, and the *scipbroc* into the *nymed*, in the Nymed boundaries the *riscbroc* flows into the *nymed*, and the *scipbroc* into the *riscbroc*. In the latter the *scipbroc* is named at Copplestone: it seems to be the *riscbroc* of our charter, for the boundary between Down St. Mary and Crediton goes by Copplestone down a brook by the railway side, running into the Ash Brook and the Knathorn Brook. These united brooks, under the name of Knighty Brook, flow into the (western) River Yeo near Lapford. The boundaries of Down St. Mary, on the one side, and of Crediton, Sandford, and Morchard Bishop, on the other, follow these brooks up to the junction with the Yeo.

The Exon Domesday, pp. 364, 461, mentions *Eschipabroca, Eschipebroca*.

31 (= I. 39). **nymed.** This is clearly the (western) River Yeo. See note to line 25.

32 (= I. 39). **Doflisc.** The River Dalch, which joins the Yeo near Lapford. It is called 'Doflysch' in the fifteenth-century version (No. III. 32). This is the same river-name as that preserved in *Dawlish* (probably the *doflisc* of *CD*. iv. 275[3], and of *OS. Fcs*. II. Exeter, plate 12), and in *Dowlish*, co. Somerset. There was another name *deflisc*, which is recorded in the *Dewlish* and *Divelish* rivers, co. Dorset (*deuelisc, CS*. ii. 143[12, 15]; *deflisch, Ib*. ii. 144[24]; *deulisc, Ib*. ii. 510[16]; *deuelisch, defelich, Ib*. iii. 494[26]). Some of the late forms here cited might seem at first sight to favour Mr. Davidson's comic derivation of the name from our adj. *devilish* (*Transactions of the Devonshire Association*, 1878, p. 352, note 6).

wiþigslæd, 'willow slade.' As this is written 'Wydeslade' in the fifteenth-century version, it is probable that the name still existed in that form. This may possibly be the *wiðig slæd* of the Æscford and Beohyl boundaries (*CS*. iii. 227[30]), which contain several names that occur in the Crediton boundaries. It is difficult, however, to identify the two sets of boundaries.

The compound *wiðig-slæd* is of frequent occurrence (*CS.* i. 229[1]; ii. 171[22], 436[33], 441[5], 504[25]; iii. 143[12], 297[27]). These are all in Dorset, Somerset, and Wiltshire.

As we cannot identify *wiðigslæd*, we are unable to say at what point the boundary leaves the River Dalch. The present boundary of Morchard Bishop ascends the Dalch from its junction with the Yeo to Cann's Mill near Horridge Wood and Lower Curriton.

34 (= I. 41). **Beonnan ford.** This is, no doubt, Binneford on the Binneford Water[1], in the parish of Stockleigh English. This is somewhat south of the point where the Kennerleigh boundary (which is probably the line followed by these boundaries) strikes the river. There is another Binneford in the parish of Hittesleigh.

We have here the personal name *Beonna*, which occurs frequently amongst the names of witnesses in the OE. charters. A local Beonna may be found in *Benna*, the name of the father of St. Sativola or Sidefull of Exeter, one of the names whereof Freeman (*Exeter*, p. 15) says 'it is hard to make anything.' Stark, *Die Kosenamen*, p. 25, quotes continental instances where *Benno* is used as a short form of *Berngerus* and *Bernhardus*, and therefore concludes that *Beonna* represents *Beorna*. The few instances of the latter name may be explained as late formations from the stem *Beorn*. There was no name-stem *Beon-*. *Beonna* is not infrequent in compounded local names in the charters.

35 (= I. 42). **þone ealdan herepaþ.** The road from Woolfardisworthy to Stockleigh English and Cheriton Fitzpaine? The Sandford boundary runs roughly parallel to this road, but a little to the south of it.

þa easteran cridian. This seems to be the stream now known as Holly Water Stream, which flows into the Creedy. It partly bounds the parish of Sandford on the north-east.

III.

This version of the boundaries is written on paper in a late fifteenth-century hand. In some cases the names seem to be given in their fifteenth-century form, but not consistently, for the scribe copies such inflected forms as *Tettanburna*, *Crydyan*, *Lyllan broke*, &c. In these cases the scribe, if he had any local knowledge, must have known the forms of the names in use in his day. Similarly he writes *landsceare*, although he probably knew this word in his own dialect. The boundaries are copied or translated from No. I, not from No. II, for they omit, like No. I, the passage from *þanon* to *oþ nymed* in No. II. 30, 31.

---

[1] That the Binneford Water was formerly known as the Creedy, seems to be proved by the name Creedy Mill Farm near Binneford.

IV.

This is the original charter, which is here printed for the first time. It is an addition to the very brief list of charters of Æðelstan that have come down to us in their original form. The turgid proem is the same as that of Æðelstan's Chichester charter (*CS.* ii. 348), with which it agrees very closely down to *episcopo* in line 26 [1]. This proves that the Chichester text, which is derived from a very late copy, is a copy of, or is based upon, a genuine charter.

Bishop Eadulf of Crediton procured a charter from this king in 933 conferring certain immunities upon the lands of the bishopric (*CS.* ii. 390). The original of this is preserved in the Cotton collection.

In 997 King Æðelred granted to Ælfwold, bishop of Crediton, two hides at Sandford, the boundaries of which agree in many points with those given in the present charter. Æðelred's charter is not printed by Kemble or Thorpe, and is not mentioned by Wanley. A *facsimile* of it is given in the Ordnance Survey *Facsimiles of Anglo-Saxon Charters*, part II, No. 35.

The phraseology of the present charter is so inflated that frequently the sense can only be made out with difficulty. We have ventured to add a few notes to assist in its more rapid comprehension.

2. **Iduma**, abl. sing. This word occurs frequently in Æðelstan's charters, and in a dubious charter of King Æðelred, A.D. 990 (*CD.* vi. 122 [20], *per eiusdem pantocratoris iduniam*, for *idumam*), which elsewhere recalls the wording of Æðelstan's charters. *Iduma* means 'hand,' and is derived, in some unexplained way, from the Hebrew *yad*, dual *yadayim*. It occurs in the *Lorica* glossary ascribed to Gildas (Cockayne, *Leechdoms*, i. lxx ; Sweet, *O.E.T.*, p. 172): '*binas idumas*, twa honda.' In a version of this glossary with Irish glosses (Whitley Stokes, *Irish Glosses*, Dublin, 1860, p. 133) *idumas* is glossed by the Latin '*i[d est] manus.*' Stokes remarks, p. 144, that '*idumas* seems formed from the Hebrew *yādhayim*. The abl. sing. occurs in the Book of Hymns, *Altus*, line 70, "*Suffulta dei iduma omnipotentis ualida*," where the scholiast says, "*i. manu*, iduma *ebraice*, cirus *graece*, manus *latine*."' In the glossary entitled *Hisperica Famina* we read: *Arboream capto iduma pellam, quae cerneas cluit tutamine pernas*. Here *iduma* is glossed by *manus*. See *Incerti auctoris Hisperica famina denuo edidit et explanauit J. M. Stowasser*, in *XIII. Jahresbericht ubtr das K. K. Franz-Joseph Gymnasium in Wien*, 1886–7. The authorship of this work is discussed by H. Zimmer, *Nennius Vindicatus*, 1893, p. 291 *sqq.*[2]

---

[1] Compare also lines 54–69 with the corresponding portion of the Chichester charter.
[2] We are indebted to our friend Mr. Henry Bradley for supplying us with the clue to this explanation.

3. **iusta**, abl. sing. with *lance*.
4. **infra**, 'within (the balance).'
5. **motata** = *mutata*. Cf. *commotatione* for *commutatione*, line 39. Similarly the Corpus Glossary has *motatio* (D 366) for *mutatio*, and *permotatio* for *permutatio* (E 466). So also *CS.* ii. 211[20], *sine motatione et disceptatione*.
6. **inaccessibili**, 'unapproachable, inattainable.'
rimatur, 'examines.' The subject is *iduma*.
que, *sc. iduma.*
7. **patria naturalis sinceritatis**. The Garden of Eden.
8. **cyrographum**. Used in the sense of 'sentence.' Cf. *CS.* ii. 440[24], iii. 446[2].
9. **temporibus ... uoluentibus nouissimis**, ablative of duration of time.
10. **precepto**. The Chichester charter has here incorrectly *praecepta*.
pantacratoris. The παντοκράτωρ of 2 Cor. vi. 18, etc., and of the Septuagint. Cf. Corpus Glossary, ed. Hessels, P 50: '*Pantocraton*, omnipotens.' The OE. scribes, not understanding *crator*, sometimes connected it with the Latin *creator*, and spelt it accordingly. The scribe of this charter first wrote the word as *pantocreatoris*, and in line 24 the charter speaks of *eiusdem omnipatrantis dexteram*, which can only refer to *pantocratoris* in line 10. The words *Theo pantocratori* occur in a charter of Beorhtwulf, king of the Mercians, *ante* A.D. 840 (*CS.* ii. 2[6]), and in another charter of the same king's in A.D. 845 (*Ib.* ii. 32[27]). It also occurs in the dubious charter of Æðelred's referred to in the note on *iduma*, line 2 above.
11. **cuiusque**, *sc. massa humane conditionis.*
12. **timpora**, 'temples,' τὰ καίρια. This is a not uncommon spelling of *tempora*.
eam, *sc. massam humane conditionis.*
14. **atria**. So correctly in the Chichester charter. Birch needlessly suggests the emendation *altera*.
16. **altero**. Read *altera* (*sc. pars*), as in the Chichester charter.
21. **ego Æthelstanus**. The same stile is used by Æðelstan between 930 and 937 (*CS.* ii. 349[20], 357[15], 360[11], 363[14], 383[27], 385[21], 392[13], 394[11], 403[6], 407[31], 423[16], 465[28]). It also occurs with variations in other charters of this king (*CS.* ii. 378[18], 390[13], 406[2], 426[12]; iii. 684[14]).
21. The same phrases are used, *mutatis mutandis*, to express the date in other charters of this monarch. See *CS.* ii. 349[21], 379[30], 384[36], 387[39]. With slight variations they are met with in other charters of his (*CS.* ii. 359[5], 361[3], 362[14], 364[22], 393[4], 395[10], 401[22], 403[37], 406[25], 423[27], 425[11], 427[13]; iii. 685[1]). They also occur in a charter in the *Liber de Hyda* purporting to be a grant of Edward the Elder and dated 921 (*CS.* ii. 311[23]). But the wording of this

CHARTER IV.

charter is that of the time of Æðelstan, and the witnesses prove that it must be dated 931.

28. **census.** Read *censu*.

32. **aliqui ex familia**, etc. This exemption from forfeiture for offences committed by any of the *familia* is unusual. A charter of Edward the Elder to Friðestan, bishop of Winchester, A.D. 909 (*CS.* ii. 292 [8]), records that an estate had been taken from Winchester church *pro stupro cuiusdam militis, cui accommodatum fuerat, ut censum singulis annis persolueret indictum*, and that Bishop Denewulf procured the restoration of the estate by giving a former king a *pateram centum auri siglis appendentem*. This is described as 120 mancuses in Edgar's charter (*CD.* iii. 145 [12]), which continues the history of this estate. Lands given to Winchester cathedral in 737 (*CS.* i. 228) are recorded, in a dubious charter of Æðelstan (*Ib.* ii. 436 [18]), to have been forfeited by those *qui eorum possessores fuerunt, quia aperto crimine furti usque ad mortem obnoxii inuenti sunt*. It will be noted that the king states in the present charter that the land conveyed by it formerly belonged to the bishop, *sed tamen mihi census* [read *censu*] *iniquorum actuum prius reddebatur* (line 28). In 1008 Æðelred restored to Abingdon monastery an estate that had been unjustly obtained from them by a knight of his, the abbot having claimed it upon its forfeiture by the knight's widow and her second husband (*CD.* vi. 160).

35. **ergasterio** = *monasterio*. Cf. Corpus Glossary, E 299: '*ergasterium, monasterium.*' Ducange quotes a MS. glossary to the like effect.

38. **alium**, *sc. agellum*.

39. **commotatione** = *commutatione*. See note to *motata*, line 5.

cartula ... hereditaria. This stipulation is important. It is intended to secure that the lands received in exchange shall be protected by a charter restricting the right of alienation like the present one. In other words, the land received in exchange must be *bócland*.

40. **tellus ... clarescit.** This phrase occurs in some of Æðelstan's charters between the years 930 and 934 (*CS.* ii. 349 [30], 378 [26], 384 [7], 386 [8], 392 [25], 403 [17], 466 [8], and, with slight changes, 362 [10], 363 [54], 378, 383, 394 [23]). Cf. also the dubious charter of Æðelred (*CD.* vi. 123 [8]) mentioned in note to line 2.

41. The land herein described is contained within the boundaries of No. I. It had been forfeited to the king as stated in line 28. We have identified some of the local names mentioned, but these are not sufficient to enable us to lay down the boundaries accurately. It is evident, however, that the land comprises the western half of the parish of Sandford.

fintes leage. Cf. *fintes hrigc* (*CD.* iii. 202 [10]). As this quotation is from a fifteenth century copy, *fintes* may be a mistake for *finces* (cp. *finces stapul*,

CS. iii. 176 [18], 655 [35]). This suggestion cannot apply to the present charter, as there is no graphic confusion of *t* and *c* in writings of this period.

herepað. The road from Crediton to Creedy Bridge, the boundary between Crediton and Sandford.

holan cumbes heafod. This combe is recorded in the name of the hamlet of *Hollacomb*, which is called *Hollowcomb* in the old one-inch Ordnance map. *Holancumbes landscare* is mentioned in *CS.* iii. 227 [27], a charter containing other names occurring in the Crediton and Sandford boundaries, but the position does not seem to agree with that of Hollacomb.

42. **sceaftryht,** 'in a straight line.' See No. II, note to line 14.

42. **Cuddan cnoll.** The personal name *Cudda* occurs in the Durham *Liber Vitae*, and is, no doubt, a short form of a name in *Cūð-* with hypocoristic consonant doubling. There are a *Knowle* Barton and *Knowle* Lake to the west of the present boundary between Crediton and Sandford, but they seem to lie too far west to be identified with *Cuddan cnoll*.

43. **þorniscea weg.** No other instance of *þornisc* is known. It is clearly not an adjective, as in this position the weak flexion would be used, and no such adjective is known. The adjectives derived from *þorn* are *þornih/*, *þornig*, and *þyrnen*. If it be a substantive, it may be a derivative of *þorn* and mean 'collection of thorns,' 'thicket,' 'ground covered with thorns.' But substantives from adjectives in *-isc* are rare, and the collective *þyrnet* exists. If it be such a substantive, the use of the gen. sing. is irregular. The use of this case suggests that *þornisc* is either the name of some animal, bird, &c., or a man's name (for the suffix, cp. *Velhisci*, gen., A.D. 679, *CS.* i. 71 [27]). We can, however, find no instance of the use of *þorn* in the formation of personal names, and the name would, therefore, be an irregular one.

44. **scip broc.** This is possibly the *scipbroc* of No. II, which partly forms the western boundary of Sandford parish.

Lilles ford. Cf. *Lillan broc*, II. 8. The personal name *Lil* is preserved in *Lilles beam* (*CS.* iii. 632 [25]) and *Lilles ham* (*Ib.* ii. 81 [3]). Cf. *Lil-sǣtan*, Lilleshall, co. Salop (*Ib.* iii. 355 [29]).

45. **cealdan hlinc.** The *hlinc* is probably recorded in *Linscomb* (from *Linchcomb?*), on the southern slope of the hill forming the parish boundary, which is slightly to the north of Linscombe.

45. **wyrtrum.** The *wyrtruman* of the 997 boundaries. The only recorded meaning of this word is 'root' or 'tree-root.' This is evidently the primary meaning of the word, which is a compound of *wyrt* and *trum*. It occurs most frequently in the weak form *wyrt-(t)ruma*. In local names it had, probably, some secondary meaning, although we are unable to say what it was. That

CHARTER IV.   69

it means more than 'tree-root' is evident from the frequent occurrence of *wyrtrum* in the boundaries of the present charter. This deduction holds good even if the word in each of the five cases do not refer to the same *wyrtrum*. In lines 45, 46 the boundary leaves the *wyrtrum* and returns to it (*on wyrtrum þonne git norð*). Kemble explains *wyrttruma* as the 'roots or foot of a hill, forest, shelf of land, &c.' In the case of a hill, *wyrttruma* would, if Kemble's suggestion be correct, mean merely 'foot' or 'edge.' In a charter of 984, the boundaries touch the *wyrttruman* of a grove, thence proceeding by a ditch (*of Dynningegrafes wyrttruman eall swa se dic sceot*; *CD*. iii. 208 [5]). This is probably the origin of Kemble's application of the word to a forest. The *wyrtruman* of a wood are mentioned in *CS*. iii. 142 [2]. The reference to a hill is probably founded upon *CS*. iii. 39 [8]: *ðurh Wippan hoh, þæt swa be ðæm gretan wyrtruman*. But here the *wyrtruman* are not, apparently, part of the *hoh*. The phrase in a charter of 961 (*CS*. iii. 301 [4]) *of þam seaþe swa wyrtruma sceat oð ramleah weg*, 'as the *wyrtruma* runs as far as Ramleah way,' proves that the *wyrtruma* was something much longer than a tree-root. Moreover, the stub of an elder-tree (*ellen-styb*) is mentioned immediately before the *seaþ*. The contention that *wyrtruma* was something possessing considerable length is supported by the following passages, in which the boundary proceeds 'along' a *wyrtruma*: A.D. 944, *of þam byrgelse forð norð be wyrttruman oð ðæs heges ende* (*CS*. ii. 541 [15]); A.D. 956, *on wiðigleas wyrtruman . . . on Eatan beares wyrtruman . . . norð be wyrttruman on ða east langan dic wale . . . andlang hagan suþ on feld on wyrttruman oþ wederan grafes suð ende* (*Ib*. iii. 106); A.D. 979, *on ðone feld, ðæt andlang wyrttruman on Hildes hlæw* (*CD*. iii. 170 [7]); A.D. 968, *of langan riple* [=riþie?] *up be wirtrume on wlfgedyte* [=dyce?], *of wlfgedyte be wirtrume, . . . forðe be wirtrime on Heahstanes quabben forð be wirtrime andlang riple* (*CS*. iii. 499 [17]); A.D. 994, *of wulfhylle to wuda, swa be ðan eald wyrttruman* (*CD*. iii. 279 [31]); A.D. 931, *be wyrttruman oþ þa rode* [=clearing?] *neoþewearde . . . of þam west slo be wyrttruman* (*CS*. ii. 354 [21], [25]); A.D. 996, *of ðan hamme a be wurtruman* (*CD*. vi. 137 [22]). It will be noticed that *wyrtruma* is several times mentioned in close connexion with a hedge or enclosure (*hege, haga*). Can the word have meant an enclosed clearing in a wood? Leo's explanation of the word (*Ags. Glossar*. p. 499) as *die Wurzelfeste* (*was beim Abfressen des Grases, Abhauen der Bäume übrig bleibt*) finds no support in the passages cited by him. It may be mentioned in this connexion that the place where a tree had stood (*treowsteall*) is mentioned in *CS*. ii. 557 [14], 558 [2]. The word *wyrt-wala*, which undoubtedly means 'root' (=Germ. *wurzel*), has apparently the same meaning as *wyrtrum* or *wyrtruma* in local names[1].

[1] In *CS*. iii. 492 [16] it is in close connexion with a 'haw': *forð þonne be uurtwalan þær se*

70   NOTES.

Earle's explanation of the meaning of *wyrtwala* (*Land Charters*, p. 462) seems to us unlikely.

46. **Brocheardes hámm.** This is, perhaps, recorded in the name *Broxham* Copse, near Pidsley, in Sandford parish. The personal name *Brōc-heard* occurs in *Broc-hardes ford* (*CS*. iii. 588 ⁸), and in *Brocardes-cote*, co. Leicester (Domesday Book, i. 232 a, col. 1). Names in *Brōc* are rare. *Brōc-wulf* is preserved in *Broxtowe*, co. Nottingham (*Brocholvestou*, *Brochelestou*, and *Brolvestou* in Domesday) and possibly in *Brocklesby*, co. Lincoln (*Brochesbi*, D. B.). The short form *Brōc* is probably preserved in *Brooksby*, co. Leicester (*Brochesbi*, D. B. i. 236 b, col. 1, 237 a, col. 1) and in *Brocheshale*, co. Dorset (D. B. i. 82 b, col. 2). Förstemann, *Altdeutsches Namenbuch*, i. 286, has only the name *Bruoh-braht* (=O.E. *Brōc-beorht). The first-stem pet-form occurs in 990 *on Broccæs hlæw* (*CD*. iii. 252 ²⁵), for this cannot well be from *brocc* 'a badger.' The word *hlǣw* in the charters is almost invariably joined with a personal name, no doubt recording the person buried therein.

haga. This is probably the *haga* referred to in the Sandford boundaries of 997, which proceed direct from the *wyrtruman* to the *haga* and thence by the brook to *ðelbricg*.

bromleah. Probably *Brimley*, to the west of Pidsley, near the parish boundary.

Pideres leah. Pidsley (East and West), in Sandford. Cf. *piddes meres weg* (*CS*. iii. 586 ²¹), *Pyddes geat* (*Ib*. ii. 363 ²⁷).

48. **hlosleah.** *Hlos* is one of the numerous unexplained words that enter into the composition of OE. local names. It is evidently a substantive, as it is, with one exception, uninflected in composition. We have noted the following instances of the word: *hlos-stede* (*CS*. iii. 449 ²⁶), co. Dorset; *hlos-hám* (*Ib*. iii. 474 ³¹), co. Essex (?); *hlos-hrycg* (*Ib*. iii. 84 ¹³), co. Wilts; *hlos-dionu* (*Ib*. ii. 403 ²³), co. Kent; *hlos-wudu* (*Ib*. ii. 301 ²¹), co. Surrey; *hlos-moc* (*Ib*. i. 229 ⁸, ¹⁰; ii. 436 ⁹), co. Wilts; *hlossan-ham* (*Ib*. i. 207 ⁹), co. Kent¹. The *hlīos-sole* cf. *CS*. i. 565 ¹⁷ may be connected, if it is wrongly copied for *hlos-sol*.

49. **fileð leah.** Cf. *Filleigh*, in Lapford parish, to the west of Sandford. *Fileð* is another unexplained word that occurs several times in local names. A *fileð-leah* occurs in the charter printed in *CS*. iii. 227 ²⁶, which has several names agreeing with those in the present charter, but we are unable to identify the *fileð-leah* there mentioned with that in our text. The compound occurs also in *CS*. i. 314 ³⁸; iii. 494 ²¹, 589 ⁴, and, as *filid-leah*, in *CD*. iii. 208 ³. A *Fileð-ham* is

haga ut cymð, be þam wyrtwalan to pædes paþe. In *CS*. iii. 44 ²⁸ a *wyrtwala* is mentioned next to an oak wood.

¹ This is from a post-Conquest copy, and is probably corrupt.

mentioned in *CS*. iii. 44[30], a *filed-hamm* at iii. 95[2], and a *fylet-* or *fælet-hamm* in ii. 171[37]. In *CS*. iii. 290[31] a *fileð-cumb* occurs, and the sub. occurs uncompounded in *CS*. ii. 519[11] *on fileþa*. Cf. (?) *on fildena wega* (*CS*. ii. 167[14]). Domesday, i. 248 b, col. 1, mentions a *Felede* in co. Stafford (now Fauld?). It is dubious whether the *Filleicham*, i. 17 a, col. 1, now Filsham, in Bexhill, Sussex, is derived from *filið*. Felixstowe, co. Suffolk, apparently represents a *Filið-stow*, as it is called *Filthstowe* in 1316 (*Nomina Villarum*, 319 a). A John de *Fylethe*, of Kent, is mentioned in the Close Rolls in 1318 and 1325 (*Calendar*, pp. 406, 612), but this does not prove that the word was then current, since this Fylethe might be a local name, and not an appellation in common use.

þelbrycg. 'Plank-bridge.' This is not the parish of Thelbridge near Sandford, but a bridge in Sandford parish recorded in the name *Thelbridge Ford*, where the road from Sandford to South Molton crosses, at Waddely Hill, the small brook running into the Binneford Water opposite Dowrish Mill. It is the *ðelbricg* mentioned in the Sandford charter of 997 (*Ordnance Survey Facsimiles*, Part III, No. 35). .

The word *þelbrycg*, which is identical with the German *Delbrück*, occurs several times in the charters (*CS*. i. 82[31]; iii. 15[7], 356[7]; *CD*. iii. 236[30], [31]). Elmbridge, near Gloucester, has been etymologized from *Elbridge*, which arose from a thirteenth century interpretation of *Thelbridge* as *Th' Elbridge* (Stevenson, *Calendar of Gloucester Corporation Records*, 1893, p. 109).

Æsculfes weorðig. 'Æsculf's homestead or farm.' Cf. the laws of Ini, c. 40 (Schmid, p. 38): *ceorles weorðig sceal beon wintres and sumeres betyned*. Here it appears to mean 'croft.' Ælfric's *Gram*., ed. Zupitza, has *'fundus*, wurðig' (28[12]), and *'praedium*, worðig' (318[18]). The word had also the meaning 'street' (*Vesp. Psalter*, 17, 43 *worðigna = platearum*, 54, 12 *of worðignum = de plateis*, 143, 14 *in worðignum = in plateis*; cf. also Matth. (Lindisfarne) vi. 5 = *worðum platearum*, and 12[10] *worðum = plateis*; *Leechdoms*, ii. 44 *on worþium = '*by the road side,' &c., &c.). In *Beda*, ed. Miller, p. 194[18] it is used for 'village' (*from Cetrehl weorþige = a uico Cataractone*). It is preserved in local names in the former meaning. In Devonshire it occurs frequently in the names of farms and small hamlets.

53. henne stigel. This name is preserved in *Henstill* (Middle, Cobley's, Adam's, and Reed's Henstill) and in West *Henstill*, in the parish of Sandford. It is the *henne-stigel* mentioned in the Sandford boundaries of A. D. 997 (*Ordnance Survey Facs.*, Part III, No. 35), where it is north of Ruxford (*Hroces-ford*), and, therefore, in the immediate vicinity of the present *Henstill's*. The 997 boundaries agree hereabouts exactly with those of the present charter, proceeding, however, in the opposite direction.

72   NOTES.

The name is puzzling, as it means literally 'hen's stile.' It may be compared with *Henna-rið* or *Henne-rið* (*CS.* iii. 165 [19], 326 [19], 391 [26], 392 [11]; *CD.* vi. 116 [8]), now Hendred, co. Berks. The *Wifeles stigel* in *CS.* ii. 246 [28] derived its name, no doubt, from the man's name *Wifel* and not from *wifel* 'weevil.'

Hroces ford. Ruxford Barton, in West Sandford. It is spelt in the same way in the Sandford boundaries of 997. Cf. *hroces-wylle* (*CS.* ii. 81 [16], [20]), *et hroces seaðum* (*Ib.* ii. 29 [8]). Probably from a personal name **Hrōc*. This name-stem is not uncommon in continental Germanic names (*see* Förstemann, col. 712), but it does not appear to have been much used in England, although possibly preserved in the surname *Rooke*. Hrōc is interesting as the name of the Alemannic king who played so important a part in the creation of Constantine as emperor at York (Aurelius Victor, c. 41, where the text has *Erocus* in mistake for *Crocus*).

54. **weardsetl.** The *weard-setl* of the 997 boundaries, lying south of Ruxford. One is tempted to identify this with Beacon Hill or Beacon Cross, which lies NW. of Ruxford Barton, but the boundaries appear to proceed in the opposite direction.

Weard-setl means the 'seat or place where watch was kept,' and thus it may denote a watch-tower or beacon or merely some elevated place where watch was kept in time of war. The word occurs several times in boundaries (*CS.* i. 257 [18]; ii. 114 [17], 458 [19], [20], 532 [11]; iii. 66 [14], 610 [33]; *CD.* iii. 227 [26]; vi. 243 [20]). It was also used to denote the watch itself, *e.g.* Ælfric's *Homilies*, i. 452 [13]. In Wright-Wülcker, 342 [26], &c., it glosses *excubias*. Cf. *weard-hangra* (*CS.* ii. 246 [1]) and *weard-steall*.

Si uero, &c. The same anathema occurs in the Chichester charter (*CS.* ii. 350), and, with slight variations, in *CS.* ii. 358, 362, 364, 379, 384, 387, and 403. Compare also *CS.* ii. 340, 390, 392, 395, 406, and 408. These are all charters of Æðelstan. The same phraseology occurs in the charter wrongly ascribed to Edward the Elder (*CS.* ii. 311), mentioned in the note to line 21 above.

57. **breuiculam.** In addition to the references given in the preceding note, Æðelstan calls his charter *breuiculam* in *CS.* ii. 341. The charter there printed was probably composed by the same rhetorician as the present one.

61. **filius perditionis.** Ioh. xvii. 12.

62. **huius namque.** This same attestation clause is used, with the omission of the words *uirgineo* ... *destillante*, and with slight variations, in other charters of this king (*CS.* ii. 350, 359, 362, 364, 379, 384, 387, 393, 395, 403, 406, 408, 423, 427).

63. **inspirate atque inuente uoluntatis.** This phrase has been singularly perverted by the copyists of Æðelstan's charters. The correct reading is obviously *inspiratae atque inuentae uoluntatis* as given here and in two original charters

CHARTER IV.

(*CS*. ii. 364, 403), and in several charters preserved only in later copies (*CS*. ii. 379, 393, 408, 427). Several of the printed texts read *inspirante atque uiuente* (*CS*. ii. 350, 387, 406 ; *CD*. ii. 190). In the first case Mr. Birch unfortunately suggests *iuuante* for *uiuente*. In *CS*. ii. 406 the scribe has justified the misreading by omitting the preposition *a* before *deo*. The copyists of the charters in *CS*. ii. 423 and 425 have the strange reading *innuente*, although the preposition is retained. It is probable that some of these errors are due to the editors, for a mediaeval scribe would not be puzzled by the use of *e* for *ae*.

64. **Cyppan hamm.** Chippenham, co. Wilts. This form proves that the long-prevalent derivation of this name from *cȳping* 'market,' is unfounded. It is called *Cippan-hamm* in the Parker Chronicle, A. D. 878, and *Cyppan-ham* in some of the other chronicles. In King Alfred's will (*CS*. ii. 178 [15]) it is *æt Cippan hamme*. The *to Cyppan-hamme* of *CS*. i. 342 [2] was in the parish of Bishop's Cleeve, near Cheltenham, co. Gloucester. The second part of the name is clearly not *hām*, but *hamm*, which is still applied to meadows in the West of England. From the gemination it is probable that *Cippa* is a personal name. A *Cyppinge leuita* is recorded in the Hyde *Liber Vitae*, ed. Birch, 1892, p. 29 [26]. Cf. *Cipes broc* (*CS*. iii. 344 [19]).

65. **uirgineo... destillante.** This inflated sentence merely means 'with ink on white parchment,' *forcipe* being evidently used in the sense of *calamo*. Cf. *CS*. ii. 341 [34], Æðelstan to Bishop Friþestan : *hanc ... breuiculam atrae fuscationis pallore depictam ac lacrimosa uirginei forcipis destillatione fedatam ... corroboraui*.

70. **Æthelstanus.** The king subscribes in the same or a very similar phrase in *CS*. ii. 350, 379, 385, 388, 395, 400.

73. **Wulfhelmus.** The witnesses are, in the main, the same as those of the Chichester charter (*CS*. ii. 348), which is dated twenty-four days earlier. The latter omits Bishop Friþestan, and omits the *duces* Æscbriht, Styrcær, Guþrum, Þurferð, and Fræna, having an equal number of other *duces* in their places, to wit Ælred, Ælfred, Urum, Regenwold, and the blundered name Scrices. There are also differences in the names of the *ministri*. The *Busa* of the Chichester charter arises from a common misreading of OE. ʒ as *s*, and is therefore the *Buga* of our charter. The name *Syfred* clearly represents the *Sigered* of the present charter, arising from a misreading of the latter as *Sisered*, which a later scribe has read as *Sifered*.

85. **Eadweard episcopus.** This bishop signs in 930 (*CS*. ii. 350 [31]) and 931 (*Ib*. 359 [22], 365 [15]). He was, according to Bishop Stubbs, *Registrum Sacrum*, p. 14, a suffragan of York. He is not named amongst the suffragans of York in 929 (*CS*. ii. 344). The present charter is witnessed principally by southern and western bishops.

87. **Ælfwald dux.** Ælfwald signs pretty regularly from 925 to 938 and in 944 (*CS.* ii. 550 [20]). He also signs a charter ascribed to Edward the Elder and dated 921 (*Ib.* ii. 312 [9]), but this is, as the *formulae* and witnesses prove, a charter of Æðelstan, and should be dated 931. Ælfwald is called *princeps* in 925 (*Ib.* ii. 317 [22]). There is a grant of land in Kent to a *minister* of this name (*Ib.* ii. 403). This is probably the Ealdorman, as the charter is witnessed by him and no Ælfwald is named amongst the *ministri*.

88. **Æsobriht dux.** Signs regularly from 931 to 934.

89. **Ælfstan dux.** Signs regularly from 930 to 934. He also signs the charter wrongly dated 921, described in note to line 87. The charter dated 943 (*CS.* ii. 528 [13]) witnessed by him is obviously wrong. Although professing to date from the sixth year of Æðelstan (i. e. 930–1), the stile of this charter is that of Eadred and his successors, not of Æðelstan, and it is witnessed by three archbishops, two of whom are unrecognizable. Ælfstan was probably the brother of Ealdorman Æþelwold, as the latter makes a bequest to the son of his brother Ælfstan in his will (*CS.* ii. 583 [26]), which must be dated in 946 or 947 [1]. As the bequest is to Ælfstan's son and not to Ælfstan, it seems that Ælfstan died before the date of this will; the Ælfstan *dux* who witnesses the present charter ceases to sign in 934. This Ealdorman Æþelwold is to be distinguished from his nephew (?) Æþelwold, Ealdorman of East Anglia, the son of Æþelstan 'Half-King' (see below, page 83). The first-named Æþelwold was in possession of Ashdown, co. Berks, which was granted by Cenwealh of Wessex to his kinsman Cuðred in 648 (Chron. A), and was probably an estate inalienable to others than members of the royal house of Wessex. It seems from this Æðelwold's will that he was brother to Æðelstan 'Half-King' (see below, page 83). If our identifications of the men named in Æðelwold's will are correct, it is clear that Ælfstan, the witness of the present charter, was also a brother of Æðelstan 'Half-King.'

90. **Uhtred dux.** There is a grant of land in Derbyshire to a *fidelis* Uhtred in 926 (*CS.* ii. 333 [29]). This is perhaps Uhtred, brother of Eadred, son of Ealdwulf, of Bamburgh [2], who made peace, together with several other 'kings,' with Æðelstan at Emmot in this year (Chron. B). With the exception of Uhtred, *regulus* of the Hwiccii (*CS.* i. 266–290), most of the bearers of this name were members of the great Northumbrian family. Uhtred signs as *dux* from 934 to

---

[1] Kemble and Birch date the will '946–955,' the duration of the reign of Eadred, to whom it is addressed. But as two of the estates therein bequeathed to Ealdorman Eadric were confirmed or granted to the latter by Eadred in 947 (*CS.* ii. 593, 602), it is evident that the will was executed between 946, the date of Eadred's accession, and 947, the date of the above confirmations.

[2] *Historia de Sancto Cuthberto*, ed. Hinde, p. 147.

CHARTER IV.　　　　　75

946 and in 949 [1]. In the latter year he received a grant of lands in Staffordshire (*CS.* iii. 40). Two *duces* of this name sign in 931, 932, and 934, and one as late as 958. An 'Uhtred Child' received a grant of land in Derbyshire in 955 (*Ib.* iii. 73).

91. **Styrcær dux.** This represents the ON. *Styr-kār* [2]. No other signatures of this Styrcær occur. A later bearer of the name occurs between 972 and 992 (*CS.* iii. 369 [18, 36], 370 [2], 371 [11]). For the orthography, cf. *Eadgær*, line 81.

92. **Guþrum dux.** The ON. *Goðormr* [3], from *guþ* + *þormr* [4]. He subscribes from 928 to 937, the date of the battle of Brunanburh. Æþelstan's charters are witnessed by several Northmen. Steenstrup, *Normannerne*, iii. 70, has collected their signatures, but he is wrong in stating (p. 69) that they only occur between 928 and 935. It will be seen from our notes that some of the signatures are subsequent to the latter date.

93. **Þurferð dux.** By the action of phonetic laws of later date than this charter, ON. has reduced the sub. -*friðr* of several compound names to *rfðr* [5], so so that this ON. name occurs as *þorrfðr*. Þurferð signs in 931 (*CS.* ii. 365 [12]), and 934 (*Ib.* 402 [9], 407 [28]; iii. 685 [41], a very late MS., wherein his name has been corrupted by the copyists into *þurberd*). The name occurs in Domesday as *Turverd, Turvert*.

94. **Fræna dux.** Like Styrcær, Fræna is an addition to the list of Norsemen who witness Æþelstan's charters. The name represents the ON. *Frāne, Frāni*, from the adj. *frānn*, 'bright, gleaming.' *Fræna* occurs in Chron. A, in 871, as the name of a Danish *eorl*. The same form is used in the Chronicles in 993 of a leader who was, according to Florence of Worcester, of Danish origin. This is, no doubt, the *Fræna minister* who signs from 980 to 1004 (*CD.* iii. 177 [8], 280 [25], 284 [14], 289 [36], 292 [14], 308 [29], 315 [35], 334 [28]). He is called *Frana* in 1001 (*Ib.* iii. 317 [27]). Another (?) *Frena minister* witnesses in 970 and 971 (*CS.* iii. 559 [27], 567 [30]). He is possibly the *Frena* of *CS.* iii. 368 [3], 369 [17, 22], 370 [14, 18, 29, 41], 371 [22], 372 [12]. As these *Frena* forms are from post-Conquest copies, they, no doubt, represent the form *Fræna*. In Domesday the name is spelt *Frane*.

95. **Grim dux.** This witness occurs in 930 (*CS.* ii. 350 [35]). A *Grim* [*eorl*] witnesses in 946 (*Ib.* 578 [4]), and in 949 (*Ib.* iii. 39 [39]), where his position suggests that he was a Northumbrian. He was, no doubt, a Norseman, as *Grim* was little used in OE. personal names.

[1] He also signs the charter of 921 = 931 described in the note to line 87.
[2] P. A. Munch, *Om Betydningen af vore nationale Navne*, in his *Samlede Afhandlinger*, Christiania, 1876, iv. 125, 175.
[3] The name also occurs, with accent-variation, as *Guttormr* (Noreen, in Paul's *Grundriss*, i. 456; *Altnord. Grammatik*, ed. 2, § 51, 1 a, § 186).
[4] Munch, iv. 88; Noreen, *Altnord. Gr.*, § 51, 1 n.　　　[5] *Ib.* p. 71; *Ib.* § 245, 4.

NOTES.

ENDORSEMENT.

116. A corrupt text of this endorsement, which is now printed for the first time from the contemporary MS., is preserved in a thirteenth century roll in the British Museum (Cott. Roll, ii. 11). It was printed in 1878 from this roll by Mr. J. B. Davidson in the *Transactions of the Devonshire Association*, vol. x, p. 250, and it has been reprinted by Earle, *Land Charters*, p. 422.

As the endorsement is witnessed by Cnut, it cannot have been written before the end of 1016, whilst, of the other witnesses, Archbishop Lifing died in 1020 and Ealdorman Æðelwerd was outlawed in the same year. The fact, pointed out by Davidson, that the names of the witnesses are all found in a charter of 1018 (*CD*. iv. 3), renders it probable that this record was drawn up in that year.

This endorsement is a mortgage for securing thirty mancuses of gold, which Beorhtnoð had lent to the bishop. As the bishop states that this money was 'for the redemption of his land' (*to minre landhreddinge*), there need be little doubt that he required the money for payment of his portion of the Danegeld imposed by Cnut in 1018 for the purpose of paying off his fleet[1]. The word *landhredding* is used because, if the bishop had not paid the sum due from him for the Crediton lands, the lands would have been forfeited to the king. The wording of the deed is not quite clear. The bishop grants to Beorhtnoð a yard of land as security for the money, which land Beorhtnoð is to hold for life, bequeathing the sum for which the land was charged to whomsoever he wished. Probably the meaning is that Beorhtnoð was to take the profits of the land until his debt had been satisfied, and that he might bequeath the sum still remaining due at his death to whomsoever he wished.

A close parallel to the transaction recorded in this deed may be found in a charter of Eadric, abbot of Ealdanham (Gloucester), in 1022, which probably relates to the Danegeld of 1018. In this he witnesses that he had demised two abbey estates to a man for life, adding *et hoc feci pro eiusdem placita pecunia mihi pro xv. libris, quibus redemi omnia alia praedia monasterii ab illa magna heregeldi exactione, quae per totam Angliam fuit* (*Hist. Mon. S. Petri Glouc.*, i. 8; *CD*. vi. 180). The use of *redemi* strongly supports the meaning that we have given to *landhredding*. A somewhat similar transaction is recorded in *CD*. iii. 285. The Danes, whilst ravaging Kent, *promittebant se ad aecclesiam Sancti Saluatoris, quae in Dorouernensi ciuitate sita est, ituros, et eam suis incendiis funditus delere, nisi pecunia, quae eis ab archiepiscopo Sirico promissa fuerat, ad plenum daretur.*

---

[1] Earle, *Land Charters*, p. 422, translates *minre landhreddinge* by 'management of my estates' apparently identifying the *redding* of his MS. with *rǣding*. But the correct reading of our charter (*hredding*) can only mean 'saving, redemption.' Moreover, Earle's explanation altogether misses the point of the mortgage.

CHARTER IV. 77

Archbishop Sigeric sent to Bishop Æscwig begging him that *sibi pecuniam, quae deerat, pro sui amoris diligentia donaret, et antedictum rus quo in suo potestatis arbitrio, pro hac accipere non renueret.* Æscwig sent the money, and the land was demised to him *ut habeat et possideat quamdiu se esse praesentialiter cognoscat; et post se haeredi, cui uoluerit, concedat.* The next charter (*CD.* iv. 286) records that Æscwig—to whom, presumably, the money had been paid—restored the land, which he describes as the land *quam . . . Sigericus . . . dedit mihi in uadimonium pro pecunia, quam a me mutuo accepit.* Cf. also *CD.* iii. 249 [32]. In a charter of 1014 (*CD.* vi. 168) land is recorded to have been conveyed in perpetuity by the Bishop of Sherborne *ob malorum infestationes direptionesque Danorum.* Domesday, ii. 360 b, records that the Abbot of St. Edmunds held certain land *in uadimonio pro xi. marcis auri, concessu Engelrici, quando redimebant Anglici terras suas.* But this redemption was from the Normans (Freeman, *Norman Conquest,* iv. 25, note).

Translation :—I, Bishop Eadnoð, make known in these writs that I borrowed thirty mancuses of gold by lead-weight from Beorhnoð for the redemption of my land, and I delivered to him as security a yard[1] of land by the Creedy on these conditions, that he should have it for his life, and that after his life he should bequeath the money that stands on the land [i. e. the thirty mancuses wherewith the land is charged] to whomsoever he please. These are the land-boundaries of the yard by the Creedy : first into Shobrook ford, thence east along the 'herpað' to the little gore [of land] on the east, south thence by the dead lake into the Creedy, up against the stream to the single acre, thence east along the 'herpað' to Shobrook ford again. These are to witness : King Cnut, [&c.] . . . Abbot Aðelwold, and all the monastery at Exeter, and the monastery at Crediton. And the bishop made this known to the *witan* of the borough at Exeter, and at Totness, and at Lidford, and at Barnstable.

117. **Eadnoð bisceop.** Eadnoð, bishop of Crediton, subscribes from 1012 to 1019 (*CD.* iv. 6 [7]); Stubbs, *Registrum Sacrum.*

118. **leadgewiht.** Mr. Davidson suggested that this was a mistake for *leodgewiht,* and that this meant the 'national or common law, as opposed to customary, weight.' This suggestion is adopted by Earle. The alteration is plausible when dealing with such a corrupt text as Mr. Davidson had before him. But as our text is contemporary, we are not justified in departing from the MS., which has clearly *lead. Lead-gewiht* therefore means 'lead-weight,' and is, apparently, the term applied to some heavier scale of weights, a sort of avoirdupois weight, as compared with the pre-Conquest Troy weight, the 'silver weight' referred to in Cockayne's *Leechdoms,* iii. 92, *and se sester sceal wegan twa pund be sylfyr-gewyht.* About 964 Bishop Æðelwold of Winchester bought some land for the extension

[1] That is a 'yardland' or virgate, a quarter of a hide.

of New Minster, Winchester, and *ad unumquemque pedem mancam auri publico pondere pensitauit* (W. Malm., *Gesta Pontificum*, p. 173). In the *Historia Rameseiensis*, p. 130, a bishop paid a sum in gold plate by public weight, *promissam fului massam metalli publico pondere pensitauit*. In 1032 land is recorded as being sold for eighty marks (mancuses?) of white silver *be hustinges gewihte* (*CD.* iv. 37 ²³). In the following instance, A.D. 1015, the mancuses are paid by unspecified weight, whilst the pounds are paid by silver-weight¹: *þæs landes . . . þe ic gebohte . . . mid twam hund mancusan goldes be gewihte* (Earle, *L. C.*, 224). The seventy-two marks (mancuses?) of white silver by weight (*CD.* iv. 305 ⁸), and the ora-weight of gold (*æn nore wichte goldes*) of *CD.* iv. 308 ² probably mean by silver-weight and gold-weight respectively, if there was a separate gold-weight. It is clear from these passages that there was more than one weight in use. The *publicum pondus* ² may be the *hustinges gewiht*. The price of certain land in Æthelred's time is said to be nine pounds of purest gold *iuxta magnum pondus Normannorum* (*CD.* iii. 368 ²⁰, *Hist. Eliensis*, p. 193). This is an early mention of the use of the Norman pound in England, but it is not altogether free from the suspicion of being an addition to the charter made after the Norman Conquest. Cf. the *ducentas libras auri et argenti ex appensione Danorum* of *CD.* iii. 249 ³⁶, in a somewhat dubious charter of 996.

120. **þone sceat. . . þe on þam lande stent,** 'the money wherewith the land is charged.' A similar use of *standan* in this sense occurs in the will of Ulf and Madselm, his wife, about 1066 : *þat land . . . þæron stent þam bisceope eahta marca goldes* (*CD.* iv. 288 ⁸, Thorpe, *Dipl.* p. 595). In this case the money was to be repaid upon the testators' return from Jerusalem ; if they did not return, the bishop was to have the land, and to expend for the benefit of their souls the excess of the value of the land over the sum for which it was mortgaged (*swa mycel swa þat land is betere þene þæt gold sy*). *Sceat* has possibly the same meaning as in the present deed in *CD.* iii. 352 ⁷, but in *CD.* vi. 178 ⁹ it means simply rent.

122. **gyrde,** ' yardland.' Mr. Davidson, p. 252, identifies this with Lower Creedy Farm, in the parish of Newton St. Cyres, but there is much hypothesis in this identification. Mr. Davidson thought that the *elpenian acer*, which in his version represented the *ænlypan æcer* of line 124, was a mistake for *æc*, and this suggestion is reproduced by Earle, but the reading in the original charter shows that it is groundless. Mr. Davidson nevertheless identified the 'single oak,' and

---

¹ In King Eadred's will (*CS.* iii. 75 ¹⁹) *mancus* seems to be used as a denomination of weight. He directs that 'twentig hund [2400?] mancusa goldes' shall be taken and minted into mancuses.

² The *publicum pondus* is mentioned in a charter of Æðelred, A.D. 1002 (*CD.* vi. 141 ¹⁴): *quam [tellurem] ipse a me cum una talentis exigebat ponderosa trutinationis publice probatis liberatione*.

marks it on his plan, placing it about half way between the Creedy and the
'herpað,' although the *ænlypa æcer* should evidently be close by the Creedy.

sceocabroc. The river Shobrook, which runs into the Creedy below Crediton. It was called *Shogbrook* in the 17th cent. (Pole, *Description of Devon*, 1791, p. 222). A Devonshire *Sceocabroc* is mentioned in *CS.* ii. 434 [28], 435 [2].

124. **þa deadan lace.** A 'dede lace' is mentioned in a very corrupt copy of a charter of 966 (*CS.* iii. 452 [12]). It means, no doubt, a sluggish stream, or perhaps standing water on each side of the stream.

128. **Æðelwerd ealdorman.** This is, no doubt, the Ealdorman Æðelweard who was exiled by Cnut in 1020 (Chron. C; D, E, and F). He witnesses as *dux* in 1018 (*CD.* iv. 3 [18]). He appears to have succeeded Æðelmær as Ealdorman of the western counties about 1016. There are several men of this name at this period, and it is difficult to distinguish them. But as Æðelweard the son of Ealdorman Æðelwine was slain at Assandun in 1016, and Æðelweard the son of Ealdorman Æðelmær was slain by Cnut's order in 1017, it is probable that the present Æðelweard was the son-in-law of Æðelmær who is mentioned in 1005 in *CD.* iii. 340 [20]. This would account for his holding the important ealdormanship that had been held by Æðelweard, the father of Æðelmær, who was of the West-Saxon royal house. See page 118 below, note to line 68. An *Æþelweard miles* or *minister* signs between 1004 and 1015 (*CD.* iii. 330 [20] erroneously called *comes* [1]; 345 [29], 357 [37]; vi. 169 [12], 171 [33], 177 [12]), but this may be the *Æþelweard minister* who signs from 967 to 998 [2].

Aðelwold abbud. Æðelwold, abbot of Exeter, subscribes in 1018–19 (*CD.* iv. 4 [36], 6 [15]), and an abbot Æðelwold subscribes between 1018 and 1024 (*CD.* iv. 3 [16], 9 [18], 31 [19]).

131. **to Hlidaforda and to Beardastapole.** Lidford and Barnstaple. Lidford is, no doubt, the *to hlidan* of *CS.* iii. 672 [5], where Barnstaple appears as *Bearstaple*. But the whole list is very corrupt. Barnstaple is given as *Barnestaple* in Domesday. It is evident from the present charter that the old form of the name was *Beardan-stapol*, and it is to Barnstable that the OE. coins minted at *Bard*, *Beard*, *Beardan*, &c. [3] belong, although they are, even in the British Museum *Catalogue of Anglo-Saxon Coins*, ascribed to Bardney (*Beardan-īg*), co. Lincoln, which is unknown except as the site of a monastery. Barnstable was a borough in 1018, as we see from the mention of its *burh-witan* in the present charter.

[1] The more correct *minister* is used in the better text of this charter given from the Charter Roll of 6 Edward II, No. 21, m. 10, in the *Register of St. Frideswide*, Oxford Historical Society, 1894, vol. i, p. 6.

[2] The 967–998 signatures may be those of the 'king's high reeve' slain in 1001.

[3] On a coin of Cnut described by Hildebrand, *Anglos. mynt*, 1881, p. 203, no. 11, the minting place reads *Beardas*, which may well stand for *Beardastapol*, but not for *Beardanig*.

In the later copy (Earle, *L. C.* 422) the endorsement is followed by the words: *And þisses iwrites idoua is on cridiamtone . mid hure elder boken*, the meaning of which is evidently, 'And the counterpart, or duplicate, of this document is at Crediton, amongst their old books,' i.e. muniments. Light is thrown upon the puzzling word *idoua* by a similar expression which occurs at the close of a charter in *CS*. iii. 547[12]: *And þysses gewrites geclofan nam se ealdorman Ælfhere to swytelunga*. Here we have evidently the same word: *idoua* is miswritten for *icloua*, OE. *geclofa* (a scribe could easily misread *cl* as *d*); it is connected with the verb *clēofan* 'to cleave, cut off,' and means 'the part cut off.' The term was, no doubt, used in the first instance of short documents, such as wills and the like, the two or three copies of which were actually written on the same skin, and then cut apart. Thence it naturally came to be applied to the counterpart or duplicate copy of a document generally, even when originally written on separate pieces of parchment.

Another term for the counterpart of a document appears to have been *gēn* (*geān-*)*bōc*, 'counter-deed': cf. *CD*. vi. 177[24] *geanboc to beonetleage*, and *CD*. iii. 208[25], 256[1]. But the formula most frequently employed was that which we find, for instance, in *CD*. iv. 170[26] : *Ðissa gewrita syndan twa, an is on Ealdan mynstræ, and oðær hæfð Æðelmær*; cf. also *CD*. iv. 307[19], vi. 196[14]. In other cases three copies are mentioned, e.g. *CS*. iii. 172[26], 218[19], 220[12]; *CD*. iii. 316[1]; iv. 11[8], 76[10], 87[16], 117[26], 118[21], 260[19], 269[17], 291[26]; vi. 191[8], 198[27], 201[22]; Earle, *L.C.*, p. 236[9]; Thorpe, *Diplom.*, p. 575[9]. In *CS*. iii. 329[17] the formula varies slightly. Occasionally as many as four copies are spoken of, cf. *CD*. vi. 207[25]. In *CS*. iii. 417[6] the expression *cyrografum*, the ordinary mediaeval Latin term for an indented deed[1], is used, *þara ðinga þe on þissan þrim cyrog*[*r*]*afum þe on ðissum þrym mynstrum to swytelungum gesette syndon*.

V.

This charter is printed in Kemble, No. 465, vol. ii. p. 342, from a copy in Cole MS. xviii. fo. 4 (Brit. Mus., Add. MS. 5819), and, from the same source, in Birch, vol. iii. p. 196. This copy was made by William Cole on May 22, 1773, from the original charter in the possession of Dr. Mason, Rector of Orwell, co. Cambridge. The copy, which is a very accurate one, was evidently taken from the charter here printed by us, as Cole's original had the hole in line 2 before *Eadwig* that occurs in this charter. It is, therefore, clear that this charter was in Dr. Mason's possession in 1773.

[1] The use of *chirographum* in this sense seems to have originated in England (Bresslau, *Handbuch der Urkundenlehre*, i. 503), the word having a different technical meaning amongst the Romans (Brunner, *Zur Rechtsgeschichte der römischen u. germanischen Urkunde*, p. 44).

CHARTER V.

As no boundaries are given, it is difficult to identify the locality of the grant. Kemble and Birch state that it is Ely. Ely is thus spelt in *CD*. iii. 362 [26], but it is *Elig* in the superior text in Earle, *L. C.*, p. 226. It cannot be the subject of the present grant, since the whole of the Isle of Ely was then in the possession of St. Æðelþryð's monastery. A somewhat later endorsement states that the grant relates to Eðandun, but this is merely the place where the grant was made. The form of the name is curious. It may be intended for *Æthelig*, as the space between the *t* and *h* is very little greater than between the other letters. In this case it may be a name embodying *ig* 'an island,' but, although not altogether unknown, the use of the nominative is exceedingly rare in such a position. On the other hand if the name be *æt Helig*, it is clear that the name cannot be a compound of *ig*, since the dative *ige* would be required. It is possible that *Helig* is a river-name, used like the River Wiley, which occurs as *æt Wilig* (*CS*. ii. 244 [11], 583 [17]; *CD*. iii. 158 [7]). We are unable, however, to find a river-name corresponding to *Helig*: it can scarcely be the Hel, co. Cornwall. In the Cornish DB. there are several names that may be compared with Helig, but we should expect Helig to be nearer the archbishop's see. It is not Monks' Eleigh, co. Suffolk, as this place, *Illanleáh* (*CS*. iii. 215 [23], 602 [76]), did not come into the possession of the monks of Canterbury until about fifty years after the date of this charter. There is a Hilegh in Selsey (*CS*. i. 115 [3]), but this charter is preserved in a very late copy. Helig cannot, we think, be *Isle* Abbots near Athelney, which occurs as *Ile Abbatis* in 1316 (*Nomina Villarum*, p. 378 a), and as *Hile Abbatis* in 1284 (*Inquisit. post Mortem*, i. 84 a). This place is probably the *Iglea* of Chron. A, *anno* 878.

11. **Eðan dun.** This was a royal possession, and, as such, was bequeathed by King Alfred (*CS*. ii. 178 [24]). It was the site of Alfred's great victory of 878, and is probably to be identified with Edington, co. Wilts, as Edington, Somerset, seems to lie outside the line of campaign. It is noteworthy that there is a ' white horse' on the hill under the earthworks known as Bratton Castle, close by Edington, just as there is under Uffington Castle, by the reputed site of Alfred's other great victory of Æscesdun. In 968 King Edgar granted land at 'Edyndon,' co. Wilts, to Rumsey Abbey, according to the fifteenth century chartulary of this house (*CS*. iii. 495).

15. **ite maledicti**, &c. Matt. xxv. 14.

31. **Aþulf.** According to Stubbs, *Registrum Sacrum*, p. 16, Athulf, bishop of Hereford, was consecrated between 951 and 973, and subscribes between 973 and 1012. The present charter shows that he was bishop in 957. He subscribes in 956 (*CS*. iii. 108 [27], 121 [36], 128 [5]), in 957 (*Ib*. iii. 203 [16]), in 958 (*Ib*. iii. 244 [24]), in 960 (*Ib*. iii. 275 [14]), in 961 (*Ib*. iii. 289 [20]), and in 963 (*Ib*. iii. 335 [10]), &c.

33. **Daniel.** Stubbs, *Reg. Sac.*, p. 15, conjecturally assigns the bishop Daniel

who signs between 955 and 959 to Rochester or Selsey. There is no mention of a bishop Daniel in the list of bishops of these sees in the Hyde *Liber Vitae*. Daniel is, no doubt, the bishop of Cornwall mentioned in our No. VII. See below, page 104. The charter witnessed by Daniel assigned by Kemble to 947 (*CD.* v. 305⁹), is dated 957 (*CS*. iii. 182, note 2). The names of the ealdormen and bishops who witness it prove that it cannot be earlier than 956. The copyist has in this case copied the King's name wrongly, which is not an unusual mistake in the chartularies.

34. **Æðelstan dux.** There are two ealdormen of this name at this period, of whom (I) signs from 923 to 958 and (II) from 940[1] to 974. This distinction is here made because two *duces* of this name subscribe from 940 to 958. It is presumably the elder one who ceases to sign, and he is, apparently, the one who takes precedence[2]. This elder one was, no doubt, Æðelstan, the ealdorman of East Anglia, who was called 'Half-King' by reason of his great power (*Vita S. Oswaldi*, p. 428; *Hist. Rameseiensis*, p. 11). Mr. E. W. Robertson (*Historical Essays*, 1872, p. 180), followed by Green, *Conquest of England*, p. 260, states that Æðelstan was a member of the royal race of Wessex, whilst Mr. Hunt (*Dict. of Nat. Biography*, xviii. 35) says that he was 'certainly a member of the royal house of Wessex.' The *Vita S. Oswaldi* says that his son was *progenitus ex regali prosapia*, and the Ramsey history, p. 11, describes him as *ab atavis regibus praeclara ingenuae successionis linea transfusus*. The great offices held by him and his brothers certainly favour the view that they were scions of the royal house of Wessex, and their names are favourite names of the house of Wessex[3]. King Edgar's charter to Ramsey (*CS*. iii. 636⁶) speaks of Æðelwine, Æðelstan's son, as *michi* ... *propinquitatis consanguinitate connexus*, which may refer to kinship on the maternal side. This charter cannot, however, be trusted implicitly, as it has been much tampered with, if it be not, indeed, a forgery entirely[4]. Robertson, Green, and Hunt allege that Æðelstan was the son of Æðelred, who, as Robertson argues, cannot be the

---

[1] He signs once only in this year (*CS*. ii. 483³³), once in 941, and twice in 942. Afterwards the two signatures appear frequently.

[2] Unfortunately the evidence of the charters is not clear upon this point. Some of the signatures have been displaced by the copyists of the chartularies, whilst it is possible that the editors or printers are responsible for other dislocations.

[3] We cannot lay such stress upon this argument as Robertson, Green, and Hunt do, because *Æðel* and *Ælf* and *Ead* are some of the most common OE. name-stems.

[4] The statement ascribed to Æðelwine, Æðelstan's son, that the latter exchanged land at Hatfield for his patrimony in Devon, at the instance of King Edgar (*Liber Eliensis*, p. 115), is very different from Robertson's assertion that he 'exchanged his patrimonial forty hides, in his native province of Devon,' which is quoted by Green. Even if his patrimony was restricted to this one county, a view that is contradicted by *CS*. ii. 264, this is not a proof that Æðelstan was a member of the royal house of Wessex, or that he was born in Devonshire.

CHARTER V. 83

ealdorman of Mercia, King Ælfred's son-in-law, since he left by Æðelflæd only a daughter named Ælfwyn (Chron. B, C, D, an. 919). Robertson, quoted by Green, contends that Æðelstan can hardly be a son of Æðelred I, who died in 871. Mr. Hunt thinks he was probably a grandson of Æðelred I. The sole authority for making Æðelstan a son of an Æðelred is the charter given in *CS.* ii. 263. This is the record of the confirmation, in 904, of the title of a *dux* Æðelfrið to land at Wrington, Somerset, made by Edward the Elder, Elredus or Athelret (i. e. Æðelred) of Mercia and his wife Æðelflæd, and by the Mercian *witan*. It is preserved in very late and very corrupt Glastonbury MSS., and it has a clause added that *Æthelstan dux, filius Etheredi*, granted the estate to Glastonbury when he became a monk there, and that King Æðelstan had given this *hereditas* to him[1]. As the MSS. are so corrupt, it is quite possible that there is a confusion between Æðelred and Æðelfrið, and that the latter was Æðelstan's father[2]. That the *dux* Æðelstan who bestowed this estate upon Glastonbury was Æðelstan 'Half-King' is proved by the record of his becoming a monk in that abbey (*Vita S. Oswaldi*, p. 428; *Hist. Rames.*, p. 12). Robertson, Green, and Hunt assert that Æðelstan retired in 956, Hunt justifying the statement by the fact that his son Æðelwold signs as Ealdorman in that year. But it is evident that he did not resign in 956, as two *duces* Æðelstan sign in 956, 957, and 958 in addition to Æðelwold *dux*[3]. The Ramsey historian, p. 12, makes Æðelstan 'Half-King' live until the reign of Edgar (959). By this he means that he subscribes until then, as he refers to the charters preserved in the abbey as his authority for this statement. He must, however, have had the same difficulty as we have in identifying the signatories. Freeman, *Norman Conquest*, i. 634, says that Æðelstan 'Half-King' signs for the

[1] This charter is a puzzling document. From its wording it has the appearance of being genuine, although the King is called *Edred* in line 28 (through a confusion of Æðelred and Eadward?). It is obviously a Mercian charter, although it relates to Wrington, which is in Wessex. It corresponds almost word for word with the original charter to Æðelfrið in *CS.* ii. 258.

[2] Æðelfrið was a Mercian *dux*. He witnesses a charter of Æðelflæd's bearing the impossible date of 878 (*CS.* ii. 308⁶), which is witnessed by Bishop Æðelhun, who was consecrated bishop of Worcester in 915 (Florence of Worcester, *in anno*). An *Æðelferð dux* witnesses a charter of Æðelred, the Ealdorman of Mercia, in 883 (*CS.* ii. 174¹⁰), and another of the same potentate's in 884 (*Ib.* 175²⁹), where he is called *Ealdorman*. He is, no doubt, the *dux* who subscribes a charter of King Edward's in 901 (*Ib.* ii. 244²⁹). These subscriptions in all probability belong to the Æðelfrið in question, since he was, according to the Glastonbury charter, a Mercian *dux* having lands in Wessex. Cf. *CS.* ii. 258. It is possible that the *Etheredi* of the Glastonbury charter represents *Ethelfredi* = Æðelfrið.

[3] This Æðelwold must not be confused with the *dux* of the same name who signs from 931 to 946, and whose will occurs in *CS.* ii. 583. It should be dated 946 or 947. See above, page 74, note 1. This earlier Æðelwold seems to have been a brother of Æðelstan 'Half-King.' See above, note to line 89, p. 74. If this be so, the latter had brothers named Æðelwold, Ælfstan, Ælfsige, and Eadric, who are mentioned in the will.

M 2

last time in 967, but this signature clearly belongs to Æðelstan No. II, who signs throughout 968, 969, 970, and in 973 and 974. It is, no doubt, this second Æðelstan who is spoken of in the *Liber Eliensis*, p. 183, as the husband of Æðelflæd, sister of Ælflæd, the wife of the famous Byrhtnoð. Freeman and Hunt are clearly wrong in identifying Æðelflæd's husband with Æðelstan 'Half-King,' since the Ramsey history, which is a pretty good authority for the family of the founder of the abbey, says that the wife of Æðelstan 'Half-King' was named Ælfwen, and that she was the foster-mother of Edgar [1] (p. 11). Robertson thinks Ælfwen was the sister of Bishop Eadnoth (of Dorchester). Ælfwen is said in the Ramsey History, p. 11, to have had *inclyta genealogia*. It is hardly possible that she was the daughter of Æðelred and Æðelflæd of Mercia. Æðelwine, her son, had an *eam* or maternal uncle Æþelsige (*CS.* iii. 368 [4]). It was by the side of Æðelstan 'Half-King' that Dunstan was riding, in the train of King Edmund, when he saw the evil spirit presaging the king's death (*Vita S. Dunstani, auctore B*, ed. Stubbs, pp. 44, 471).

35. **Eadmund dux.** Signs from 937 to 963.

36. **Ælfhere dux.** The well-known Ealdorman of Mercia, the enemy of the monks, who died in 983 (Chron.). His signatures extend from 956 to 983. The former is probably the date of his creation as Ealdorman, as the *Ælfhere, ex parentela regis, minister*, who subscribes in 956, is, no doubt, the ealdorman [2]. An account of him is given in Freeman, *Norman Conquest*, i. 633, and in the *Dict. of Nat. Biography*. His brother Ælfheah (*CS.* iii. 86 [3]), who was created an Ealdorman at about the same time, is referred to in 958 as King Eadwig's *mǣg* and *propinquus* (*CS.* iii. 127 [1], 231 [28], 232 [10]). Ælfheah in his will (*CS.* iii. 432) calls Ælfþryð, the wife of King Edgar, his *gefædere* (for *gefædere*), which usually means 'godmother.' This cannot well be the meaning here. Kemble renders it 'cousin.' Thus Ælfhere and Ælfheah were related to Edgar and to his wife. The latter was the daughter of the West-Saxon Ealdorman Ordgar, and widow of Ealdorman Æðelwold (*Vita S. Oswaldi*, p. 428). Green, *Conquest of England*, p. 306, note 2, has made a curious mistake in citing the charter printed in *CS.* iii. 123, to prove that Ælfere was King Eadwig's '"kinsman," descended "a carissimis praedecessoribus."' The charter really states that Ælfhere was *a suis carissimis praedecessoribus claro insignitus nomine Ælfhere*— a characteristic way of saying that he was named Ælfhere.

37. **Æþelsige dux.** A *dux* of this name witnesses in 937 and 938 (*CS.* ii.

[1] See also the Ramsey chartulary, iii. 165, 166.
[2] The Ealdorman is described by Florence of Worcester, *anno* 983, as *propinquus* of King Edgar. Freeman thinks this means kinship by the mother's side. An earlier *dux* of this name witnesses between 931 and 941.

CHARTER V. 85

430³¹; 434¹¹). The present witness is, no doubt, the third son of Æþelstan 'Half-King,' who signs between 950 and 958. An almost contemporary account of him is given in the *Vita S. Oswaldi*, p. 429, the MS. of which calls him by mistake *Athelwinus*.

38. **Æþelwold dux.** The eldest son of Æðelstan 'Half-King.' He subscribes from 956 to 962, and an Exeter charter with the wrong date of 950 (*CS*. iii. 337⁷), for which Mr. Saunders suggested 961. He also witnesses a dubious Worcester charter dated 964 (*Ib.* 381²⁶). An account of Æðelwold is given in the *Vita S. Oswaldi*, p. 428, by Freeman, *Norman Conquest*, i. 634, and in the *Dict. of Nat. Biography*, xviii. 35. He was succeeded as Ealdorman by his brother, the well-known Æþelwine, who occurs in 962 four times as a witness¹. His widow Ælfþryð married King Edgar in 965 (Chron. D, F), or in 964 or earlier if the date of the charter in *CS*. iii. 393 is correct. In the strange story preserved in Malmesbury and Gaimar King Edgar is said to have slain Æðelwold for deceiving him as to the beauty of Ælfþryð, whom the king himself thought of marrying.

39. **Byrhtnoð dux.** This is, no doubt, the hero of Maldon. He signs from 956 to 990². Freeman (*Norman Conquest*, i. 635) thinks that he is the *minister* of 967 (*CS*. iii. 479¹⁶), an error for 972-3. He is clearly the *dux* who signs from 956. Mr. Hunt suggests that he succeeded his father-in-law Ælfgar as Ealdorman of East Anglia probably about 953. But, if the charters at *CS*. iii. 149, 153, are trustworthy, we have evidence that he was raised from *minister* to Ealdorman in 956, and Ælfgar appears to have died in 951. Nothing is known of his family³, except that his father was named Byrhthelm (*Song of Maldon*, line 92). It is possible that he was related to Byrhtsige, son of Æðeling Beornoð (Chron. A) or Beorhtnoð (Chron. B, C, D), who fell in 905 fighting with the Æðeling Æðelwald against King Edward. Of the Æðeling Beorhtnoð⁴ nothing is, unfortunately, known, but he must from his title have

¹ He witnesses a dubious charter in *CS*. iii. 693³⁶ (see page 90 below) dated 951, for which Birch suggests 959, apparently because it bears the name of King Eadgar. But it must be subsequent to November 29, 963, the date of the consecration of Bishop Æðelwold, who witnesses it.
² The charter of Æðelstan witnessed by him (*CS*. ii. 452²⁴) is in form a charter of Æðelred's. It is a dubious document, as it is witnessed by Ealdorman Ælfere, who died in 983, and Archbishop Æðelgar, who succeeded Dunstan in 988. Byrhtnoð's subscription in 948 (*CS*. iii. 24⁵) is appended to one of the Ingulf forgeries.
³ Birch (*CS*. iii. 604) makes Ælfþryð his mother, evidently on the strength of the bequest at 602²⁰ by his widow to *Ælfþræðe minæs hlauordæs medder*. But this is clearly Ælfþryð, the mother of King Æðelred, who died between 999 (*CD*. iii. 314¹¹; *Chron. Mon. Abing.*, i. 376) and 1002 (*CD*. iii. 323³⁴).
⁴ A Beorhtnoð *minister* witnesses West-Saxon charters in 868 (*CS*. ii. 133⁶, 136⁴), in 874 (*Ib.* ii. 157¹⁶), 871-877 (ii. 163¹⁵), and a Byrhtnod *dux* witnesses in 882 (172¹⁹). Amongst the

been of royal descent, and was probably a near relative of both Edward and Æðelwald. Brihtnoð of Maldon married Ælflæd[1], the youngest daughter of Ælfgar, who mentions her (not by name) in his will (*CS.* iii. 215), in which Brihtnoð is clearly regarded as her husband. The will is preserved in a corrupt copy, and it is undated. It is evidently subsequent to the death of King Edmund in 946. If the corrupt sentence in line 4 is intended to refer to Bishop Theodred and Ealdorman Eadric as still living, the will cannot be later than 951, the date of the last subscription of Theodred. Ealdorman Eadric, apparently the brother of Æðelstan 'Half-King' (*CS.* ii. 583[23]), subscribes only from 942 to 948, and once in 949 (*CS.* iii. 27[25]). The will may, therefore, be dated about 950. This Ælfgar was evidently an East Anglian, and he was an Ealdorman. This is proved by the Worcester Chronicle (B), which records that King Edmund's wife at the time of his death, in 946, was Æðelflæd æt Domerhame, daughter of the Ealdorman Ælfgar[2]. He is, no doubt, the Ælfgar *dux* who witnesses twice in 945-6 (*CS.* ii. 569[27], 583[6]), frequently in 947 and 948, twice in 949, and once in 951 (*CS.* iii. 53[22]). Thus he was probably made Ealdorman by Edmund when he married his daughter[3]. The Ælfgar *dux, consul,* who signs in 956, 958, 960, and 961, is King Edgar's kinsman, who died in 962 (see note 2), as he is called *propinquus* by Eadwig, Edgar's brother, in 958 (*CS.* ii. 239[7]). That Æðelflæd, the sister-in-law of Byrhtnoð, was Æðelflæd æt Domerhame is proved by her will, wherein she bequeaths land at Damerham (*CS.* iii. 600). She is also the *una matrona* to whom King Edgar grants land

witnesses to the last charter is Æðelwald *dux.* There is a *dux* or *aldorman* (175[26]) who witnesses Mercian charters between 855 and 888, whose name appears nine times as *Biornoð* or *Beornoð* (90[21], 91[31], 110[31], 126[32], 127[20], 153[17], 161[22], 175[28], 195[11]), and thrice as *Beorhtnoð* (95[28], 157[16], 160[26]). These are all, with the exception of the charter at p. 157, from post-Conquest copies, five of the Mercian ones being from Heming's chartulary. It is probable that the name of the Mercian *dux* was *Beorn-noð,* as at 89[14], and that the scribes have identified it with *Beorhtnoð.* This Mercian *dux* Beornoð mostly appears as a witness to charters of Burhred of Mercia, so that, if he be the Æðeling, he may have been a member of the Mercian royal house. Beorhtnoð of Maldon had possessions in Oxfordshire, a part of Mercia (*CS.* iii. 149, 152; *CD.* iii. 341), but these were all acquired by him. The name-stem *Beorht* occurs in the names of the Mercian king Beorhtwulf and of Beorhtulf, Ealdorman of Essex, who died in 897, whilst there was a Beornred and a Beornwulf amongst the Mercian kings.

[1] Freeman (*N. C.* i. 634) and Mr. Hunt call her Æðelflæd, and hence produce confusion. The cause of this seems to be the mistake of the *Liber Eliensis,* p. 183, where she is called *Ædelfleda* and *Ælfleda Domina.* But the evidence of her will, of which the original or a contemporary copy is preserved (*CS.* iii. 602), is conclusive proof that her name was Ælflæd.

[2] This is not Ælfgar, King Edgar's kinsman (*mæg*), whose death in Devonshire and burial at Wilton is recorded in the Winchester Chronicle (A) in 962. Æðelflæd's father was, apparently, buried at Stoke by Nayland, co. Suffolk. Damerham was granted to her by Edmund (*CS.* ii. 580).

[3] The signature of 930 (*CS.* ii. 348[10]) obviously belongs to 950 or thereabouts.

CHARTER V.

at Chelsworth, co. Suffolk, in 962 (*CS.* iii. 311), as she bequeathed this estate to Ælflæd and Brihtnoð (*CS.* iii. 601)[1]. The will of Ælflæd records that Rettendon [co. Essex] was her 'morning-gift' (*CS.* iii. 603[11]), so it is evident that Brihtnoð had possessions in Essex at the time of his marriage (*circa* 950). In Ælflæd's will, which was drawn up after Brihtnoð's death (991), a kinsman of his named Æðelmær is mentioned. This is not the Ealdorman, who is mentioned separately, and probably not the man of Bishop Oswald (*CD.* iii. 255[5]), as the latter is called *familiaris artifex* (257[27]). The kinsman whom Ælflæd mentions seems to be Æðelmær, son of Ealdorman Æðelweard, the chronicler (see below, page 118, note to line 68), as he bestowed estates upon his foundation of Eynsham abbey that formerly belonged to Ealdorman Brihtnoð (*CD.* iii. 341). One of them seems to have been bequeathed to him by Brihtnoð[2]. Robertson (*Hist. Essays*, p. 184) assumes that Æðelweard's ealdormanship was divided between Æðelmær and Ordulf, son of Ordgar, shortly after Æðelweard's death in or after 998. Both appear in the charters one after the other as *ministri*[3] from 997 (*CD.* iii. 315[84]) to 1006, and Æðelmær in that year is described as the king's *discðen* (*CD.* iii. 351[12]). Yet it is assumed that the Ealdorman Æðelmær who submitted to Swein in 1013, with the western thegns, was Æðelmær the son of Ealdorman Æðelweard. Æðelmær is called 'the Fat'[4] in the Chron.

[1] Æðelflæd's marriage with King Edmund seems to have occurred shortly before his death. According to Æðelwerd, Ælfgifu, Edmund's first wife, died in the same year that Anlaf was expelled from Northumberland, i.e. 944. The wording of the Chronicle in 946 is noteworthy: *Æþelflæd at Domerhame . . . wæs þa his cwen.* In her will (*circa* 975?) she makes bequests for the souls of Kings Edmund and Edgar. She does not refer to her position as a king's widow, and the *Liber Eliensis*, p. 183, which makes her the wife of Ealdorman Æðelstan (see above, page 84, note to line 34), knows nothing of her royal marriage. Her will contains no mention of Æðelstan. Mr. Hunt, by some mistake, calls Æðelflæd the sister of Brihtnoð, and makes her, like Freeman (see above, page 84, note to line 34), the wife of Æðelstan 'Half-King.' From Edgar's cold reference to her, it would seem that his father's marriage with her was not to his liking. Is this the reason why she makes no reference in her will to Edmund as her husband? These considerations make Birch's blunder (*CS.* iii. 604) of calling her the mother of both Eadwig and Edgar by King Edward (*sic*) the more incomprehensible. They were, of course, the sons of (St.) Ælfgifu, the first wife of Edmund.

[2] We read that Æðelmær *Micclantun similiter ad monasterium dedit, quam ille Birhtnoðus dux praedictus ultimo commisit dono.* The pronoun *ei* appears to have been overlooked by the copyist, unless *ille* is a mistake for *illi*.

[3] The *Æðelmær dux* and *Ordulf dux* of 986 (*CD.* vi. 136[6] from 12th cent. MS.) are probably mistakes for *minister*. Both Æðelmær and Ordulf are described as *comes* in *CD.* iii. 330, but the better text of this St. Frideswide charter given on the Charter Rolls, 6 Edward II, calls them *ministri*. See *Register of St. Frideswide's*, 1894, vol. i. p. 6.

[4] The words of the Chronicle *Æþelweard Æþelmæres sunu greatan* have caused many historians to call him 'Æðelmær the Great,' but there is no reason for such a misleading epithet. His actions do not entitle him to any such title. The OE. chronicler meant to call him 'the Gross,' and refers undoubtedly to his physical appearance. An *Æthelnoð Æþelferðes sunu*

in 1017, which records the murder of his son Æðelweard. But he is not described as Ealdorman. The charter of 987, in which he is described as *filius Æðelwerdi, satrapa regis Æðelredi* (*CD:* iii. 224 [31]) is clearly spurious. An Æðelwine, son of Ealdorman Æðelmær [1], is mentioned in 995 (*CD.* iii. 291 [16]), whom Robertson says must be distinguished from Æðelmær, the son of Æðelweard. This may be the Æðelmær who died in 982, but he is more likely the Ealdorman mentioned in Ælflæd's will. We have, however, no signatures of his, unless some of those linked with Ordulf's belong to him. There is, it may be noted, a second Æðelmær who witnesses a few charters between 998 and 1005 (*CD.* iii. 308 [31], 330 [18], 334 [26], 345 [29]). Out of all this nothing emerges clearly except the great probability that Brihtnoð's kinsman Æðelmær was the son of the chronicler Æðelweard, an undoubted scion of the royal house of Wessex. The Eynsham charter (*CD.* iii. 341 [37]) also tells us that Bishop Byrthelm of Winchester, Edgar's kinsman (*CS.* iii. 303 [12]), was a *propinquus* of Æðelweard. It is noteworthy that he bore the same name as Brihtnoð's father. Brihtnoð's sister's son Wulfmær fell at Maldon (*Song of Maldon*, line 113). Another relative of Brihtnoð's who distinguished himself in the battle was the Mercian Ælfwine, son of Ælfric, and grandson of Ealdorman Ealhelm (lines 209 to 224). This is, no doubt, the Ealdorman Ealhelm who subscribes from 940 to 951 [2]. It may be noted that the Battle of Maldon, which was fought in 991 according to the Chronicle, occurred on August 11, for the *Obitus Byrhtnoði Comitis* is given upon this day (III. Id. Aug.) in an eleventh century calendar (Cott. Tib. D. xxvii). This calendar was printed by Hampson, *Medii Aevi Calendarium*, London, 1841, i. 435, who first drew attention to this fact (preface, p. vi). The calendar has been since reprinted by Birch, *Transactions of the Royal Society of Literature*, Series II, xi. 495 (1878). Charter No. IX, below, page 122, is, apparently, the will of the son of another of the Maldon heroes.

VI.

The text of this charter is printed in the *Monasticon*, i. 291, in *CD.* ii. 363 and iii. 39, in Thorpe, *Diplomatarium*, p. 219, and in *CS.* iii. 548. These texts

---

greatan occurs as a surety in 972–992 (*CS.* iii. 371 [17]), and he was, apparently, an ordinary countryman.

[1] If the charters at *CD.* iii. 192, 195, are to be trusted, an estate granted to the *dux* Æðelmær in 983 was granted in the same year to an Æðelwine *minister*.

[2] The charter of Æðelstan dated 931 witnessed by him (*CS.* ii. 353 [33]) must be dated 941, as it is witnessed by Bishop Ælfric (of Hereford), consecrated 941, and by Oda (of Ramsbury), who was translated to Canterbury in 942. Ealhelm also signs a charter of [958–9] wrongly ascribed to King Eadred, who died in 955 (*CS.* iii. 224 [5]).

CHARTER VI.

are derived from Cott. MSS. Titus A viii, fo. 4 *b* (now numbered 5 *d*) and Faustina, A iii, fo. 17. The first of these is a late thirteenth century MS. containing Sulcard's history of Westminster Abbey, and copies of deeds relating to the abbey. The other is of about the same age, and is of a similar nature. Thorpe also quotes 'Westm. Nig[ra] Quat[ernio],' a register preserved in the abbey. The text given in *C.S.* iii. 514, from Alford, *Fides Regia Anglicana*, 1663, iii. 354, merely consists of portions of the present charter with the same witnesses.

Our text is derived from what purports to be the original charter, and is in many respects superior to the texts hitherto printed. The charter is written in a curiously compressed handwriting in OE. letters, but it is unlike any OE. hand. It may be described as an imitation of OE. handwriting with exaggerated features. Under these circumstances it is difficult to fix the date of the hand, but it seems, from the shape of some of the *compendia* and from other details, to have been written shortly before or after the year 1100[1]. The words are very much contracted, the abbreviations being very much more numerous than they are in genuine OE. charters, in which abbreviations are used very sparingly. The hand is almost, but not quite, identical with that of the forged charter of Dunstan to Westminster (*C.S.* iii. 262), of which a *facsimile* is given in the *Ordnance Survey Facsimiles*, Part II, Westminster, plate 5[2].

This charter was still in possession of the abbey in Humphrey Wanley's time (*Catalogus*, 1704, p. 303), who describes this and Dunstan's charter as *chartae supposititiae*, and as being *sigillis munitae*[3]. Hickes, *Dissertatio Epistolaris*, 1703, p. 66, was indebted to the Dean of Westminster for copies of this and Dunstan's charter, but he, no doubt, examined the originals. That the Bodleian charter was at Westminster in his time is proved by his description (p. 71) of the gap in line 211 of our text, caused by the cutting out of the parchments over the seal: *locus membranae e quo per retinaculum [sigillum] pendebat, etiamnum cernitur.* Hickes, p. 82, also describes the arrangement of dots about the crosses in lines 146, 147. The charter was in the possession of Robert Austen, F.S.A., in 1791, when a letter of Astle's, deciding against its authenticity, was read before the

---

[1] As the *Cisseniensis* of line 162 is intended for Chichester (*Cissan-ceaster*), the date of the fabrication of this charter cannot be earlier than 1070, when the South-Saxon bishopric was transferred from Selsey to Chichester. Indeed, the date must be a generation or so later than this, for the forger would not make the mistake of speaking of a bishop of Chichester in 969, at a time when the transference of the see thither in 1070 was still fresh in men's minds. From the note to line 29, it seems that the date of the charter must be later than 1082.

[2] Both charters purport to be written by Abbot Ældred.

[3] Wanley probably means that Edgar's charter was originally *sigillo munita*, as we have the evidence of Hickes to prove that the seal was then missing.

Society of Antiquaries (*Archaeologia*, x. 232). Astle describes the traces of gilding on the · A · ⠪ · of line 1, the arrangements of dots about the crosses in lines 146, 147, and he remarks that, at the bottom of the charter, 'is the word SIGNV ... then some of the parchment is cut off for several inches, and afterwards appears part of the word CRUCIS.' This clearly refers to line 211, Astle having read the *gis* of [*Re*]*gis* as *cis*.

As Hickes, *Dissertatio*, pp. 66, 82, has proved that this charter is a forgery, and it has been condemned by Wanley and Kemble, it is not necessary for us to insist upon its numerous incongruities. It contains many Frankish Latin words, such as *baronibus*, line 39; *indominicatis terris*, line 36; *curtes*, line 86; *freda uel bannos, paratas*, line 90; *fiscus*, lines 93, 138, &c. The *uicecomitibus* of line 2 is alone sufficient to condemn the charter as a forgery of Norman times.

Fortunately, we have been able to trace the process of the manufacture of this famous forgery. There is a copy of a charter of King Edgar's in existence, granting to the abbey the estate at Westminster, which had been granted to the abbey by King Offa (*CS*. iii. 260)[1]. This is dated wrongly 951, but as no witnesses' names are preserved, we are unable to correct the date. As Dunstan, who became archbishop of Canterbury in 960, is described in it as archbishop, the date cannot be 959, as suggested by Birch. The date is probably 971[2]. At some time intermediate, apparently, between the date of Edgar's charter and the fabrication of the Bodleian charter, an expanded version of Edgar's charter was produced (*CS*. iii. 692). The additions are pointed out in the note to lines 111–112 below. One of the added clauses also occurs in Æðelred's charter to St. Albans (*CD*. iii. 249), but as this is derived from Matthew of Paris's *Liber Additamentorum* (Cott. Nero D i.), we are unable to decide whether this charter was used by the Westminster forger, or was copied from the Westminster charter, or was derived from a common original[3]. This expanded form of Edgar's charter is clearly the kernel of the forgery. Instead of the Westminster estate the names of numerous other abbey estates, concerning which there were, presumably, no charters in existence, were inserted. The forger had, in addition to these, copies of the spurious charter of Dagobert I to the abbey of St. Denis, near Paris, dated 631–2, and of

---

[1] A facsimile of this copy, which is in an early eleventh-century hand, is given in the *O. S. Fcs.*, part ii. Westm. pl. iv. Kemble has starred this charter, which reads like a genuine charter.

[2] The witnesses to the expanded charter probably belong to this one. They fall between 963 and 975. See below, p. 97, note 1.

[3] Prof. Earle, *Land Charters*, p. 395, says that the OE. charters in the *Liber Additamentorum* are 'transparent fabrications.' We are by no means sure of this, and No. XI of the present collection proves beyond doubt that at least one of the charters contained in it was copied from a genuine original.

CHARTER VI. 91

some other muniments of St. Denis[1]. From this diploma of Dagobert's he copied, with slight alterations, the first fourteen lines of our text, prefixing an invocation that frequently occurs in OE. charters. For lines 15 to 42, the narrative portion, we have been unable to find a source. They are probably the composition of the forger[2], as the other forgeries of this school have somewhat similar narrative-portions. He next (lines 42 to 69) concocted a papal letter, which is based upon and largely copied from the spurious (?) letter of Pope Nicholas I to King Charles the Bald of France, in favour of St. Denis[3]. Lines 70 to 95 he copied from Dagobert's grant, occasionally changing the order of the paragraphs. Lines 95 to 103 appear to be the composition of the forger. Lines 103 to 121 are derived from the expanded version of Edgar's charter. Lines 121 and 122 and part of line 123 are taken from Dagobert's diploma; lines 123 to 135 are from Chlodowig the Second's confirmation to St. Denis. For the remainder of the body of the charter (to line 145) the forger returned to Dagobert's grant.

The familiarity herein displayed with the voluminous muniments of the great French abbey favours the view that the forger was a French monk, and a former inmate of St. Denis. Some of the passages ascribed to the St. Denis documents may have been derived from the Frankish formulary of Marculf, but this work could have supplied only a small portion of the Frankish phraseology, and the agreement with the St. Denis charters is so close as to preclude any other explanation than that of direct copying from the muniments of that abbey. The Norman abbots of Westminster after the Conquest were Geoffrey, who had been abbot of Jumièges, Vitalis, who had been abbot of Bernay, a cell of Fécamp, and Gilbert Crispin, who came from Le Bec Hellouin. Of the next abbot's origin nothing is known. The forgery was concocted during the times of these abbots, but there is nothing to connect any one of them with the forgery. There

---

[1] These charters are:—(*a*) a genuine charter of Chlodowig II, A.D. 653 (*Monumenta Germaniae Historica: Diplomatum Imperii Tomus I*, ed. Karl Pertz, Hanover, 1872, p. 19); (*b*) a spurious charter of Dagobert I [A.D. 631, 632], (*Ib.* p. 143); (*c*) a spurious grant by the same king of the right of sanctuary, A.D. 632 (*Ib.* p. 143); (*d*) another spurious charter of the same king [A.D. 637?] (*Ib.* p. 161); (*e*) a genuine charter of Chilperic II, A.D. 716 (*Ib.* p. 72); (*f*) a letter of Pope Nicholas I, A.D. 863 (see note to line 42). Of these most use has been made of *b*, of which *d* appears to be another form; both are probably expanded from *e*. It is possible that in some cases *d* and *e* were used, but the weight of probability is greatly in favour of *b*. This will be seen from our notes, wherein the parallel passages in *d* and *e* are noted.

[2] This narrative was perhaps suggested by that in the charter of Ludwig the Pious A.D. 832, confirming the reforms in the abbey of St. Denis (printed in *Archives de l'Empire* ... *Inventaires*, vol. i, No. 124. *Par Jules Tardif*. Paris, 1866).

[3] It is possible that the forger merely copied the spurious letter of Pope Alexander II in favour of Coventry monastery (see note to line 42), but it is equally possible that Alexander's letter is copied from this Westminster forgery.

were, however, Norman or French monks in the abbey. This is proved by the name of the earliest historian of the abbey, Sulcard, whose name is rather French than Norman. But Sulcard must be acquitted of the forgery (see note to line 29), unless we assume that he compiled this charter after the completion of his history[1].

The compiler of this charter not only borrowed large portions of the St. Denis muniments, but he also makes the English king refer to St. Peter as his *peculiaris patronus* or *specialis patronus*, just as the Frankish kings speak of St. Denis. The monks of Westminster also followed the monks of the great French abbey in claiming for their abbey a miraculous dedication. The abbey of St. Denis was alleged to have been dedicated by Our Saviour; the Westminster monks, showing unusual moderation, were satisfied with the ascription of the dedication of their abbey to St. Peter. But they were probably confined to this choice by the fact of the abbey bearing St. Peter's name. The tale of the dedication by St. Peter, which is mentioned in this charter (lines 31, 113), is given by Sulcard. The monks of Westminster, moreover, imitated the example of their brethren at St. Denis in fabricating charters, for, in addition to the present one, they forged about the same time the great charter of Dunstan (*CS.* iii. 262), two charters of Edward the Confessor (*CD.* iv. 173, 181), one of which recites a forged papal letter, and a charter of William the Conqueror, dated 1067 ('Cartae Antiquae,' Pub. Rec. Office, CC. No. 2). It cannot be said, however, that they attained anything like the success of their continental exemplars, for their forgeries, besides being much less numerous than those of St. Denis, are much less skilful productions. The present charter, notwithstanding its magnificent appearance, is a clumsy forgery, outraging nearly every canon for establishing the authenticity of OE. charters. It is, nevertheless, an interesting document, for these monkish forgeries are by no means unworthy of serious study.

2–4. **rex . . . futuris.** Slightly altered from Dagobert I (Pertz, 143 [b]):
Omnibus episcopis, abbatibus, ducibus, comitibus, centenariis, ceterisque agentibus nostris, praesentibus scilicet et futuris[2]. Cf. Marculf, i. 2.

4–14. **dignum . . . igitur.** Also from Dagobert I (144 [1]), with slight changes:
Oportet clementiae principali inter ceteras petitiones illud, quod pro salute animae ascribitur et pro diuino nomine postulatur, placabili auditu suscipere et procul dubio

---

[1] The text of the charter is given in the MSS. of his history, which are of later date. The history given in the charter does not agree with that given by Sulcard, so that the charter appears to be a later insertion in his text.

[2] In our quotations from the St. Denis muniments, we have, for the ease of the reader, normalized the Vulgar-Latin grammar and orthography of the Merovingian documents. We have compared our normalized texts with the late St. Denis copies, which do not reproduce the Vulgar-Latin characteristics.

ad effectum perducere; quatinus de caducis rebus praesentis saeculi aeterna uita conquiratur, iuxta praeceptum Domini dicentis: Facite uobis amicos de mammona iniquitatis. *Ergo de mammona iniquitatis, iuxta ipsius dictum, nos oportet mercari aeterna et caelestia, et dum aecclesiis Christi impertimur congrua beneficia, retributorem Dominum ex hoc habere mereamur in aeterna tabernacula. Igitur*, &c. The same proem occurs in the genuine diploma of Chilperic II (*e*), in favour of St. Denis (Pertz, *Diplomata*, p. 72), which, however, reads *sacerdotum* instead of *aecclesiis Christi* before *impertimur*.

10. **date elemosinam . . . uobis.** Luc. xi. 41.

20. **omnia monasteria . . . circumirent ac reedificarent.** Cf. *CS.* iii. 547, derived from the Westminster *Niger Quaternio*. This '*telligraphus*' has a decidedly Frankish tinge.

25. **ecclesiam . . . specialis patroni.** Founded upon the *basilica peculiaris patroni* of Chilperic II and Dagobert I. The phrase occurs frequently in the St. Denis charters.

29. **Sæberhto.** Sæberht, King of Essex, the nephew of Æðelberht of Kent (Bæda, *H.E.* ii. c. 3). Bæda states that London was the *metropolis* of the East Saxons, although he records that Æðelberht, the overlord, built the church of St. Paul in it in 604. Sulcard, whose history of Westminster is dedicated to Abbot Vitalis, 1076–1082, alleges that the abbey was founded by *quidam ciuium urbis non infimus* (Cott. MS. Faustina, A iii, fo. 12). The other MS. of his work (Cott. Tib. A viii, fo. 2 d) has *nomine Sebbertus* inserted after *quidam* in a later hand. The name is, no doubt, derived from this charter, which is the oldest authority for assigning the foundation to Sæberht. This ascription is clearly later than the compilation of Sulcard's history, and its presence here affords a strong presumption that the charter was fabricated after the conclusion of his history. It is, in all probability, an invention of the fabricator of the charter, based upon the passage in Bæda cited above.

31. **ab ipso sancto Petro . . . dedicata.** The account of the consecration of the abbey by St. Peter occurs in Sulcard's history. It is printed in the *Monasticon*, vol. i. p. 288. See also line 113.

32. **Kenulfo.** Nothing is otherwise known of any benefactions of King Cenwulf of Mercia to Westminster. His name was probably inserted because he was known as a benefactor of monasteries. Possibly the proximity of the abbey estates in Gloucestershire to Winchcombe Abbey, Cenwulf's foundation, may have had something to do with his selection for mention as a benefactor of Westminster.

37. **concilio.** This council at Westminster appears to be a figment of the forger's, possibly suggested by the mention in the St. Denis muniments of councils

being held for the confirmation of the abbey privileges. For instance, a council of bishops is mentioned in the charters of Chlodowig II (Pertz, p. 20) and of Dagobert I (*Ib.* p. 144).

42. **Iohannes.** John XIII (965-972). See Jaffé-Wattenbach, *Registrum Pontificum Romanorum*, No. 3712, where it is said that this bull *non est a suspicione remota.* It is evidently copied from the letter of Pope Nicholas I to Charles the Bald of France, A.D. 863, in favour of St. Denis (Tardif, No. 125; Migne, *Patrologiae Cursus*, vol. cxix. p. 819; Jaffé-Wattenbach, No. 2718). The forger has omitted the proem of this letter and, consequently, the *igitur* before *quia* in line 44. With the exception of the necessary changes, and the insertion of *cuiusque ordinis uel dignitatis sit* in line 55, the wording of the Westminster letter agrees closely with that of St. Denis down to *permaneat* (line 56). The latter then proceeds: *quatinus abbas et fratres eiusdem loci uenerabiles pro statu regni uestri . . . Deo grates et uota soluere delectet.* The forger has made the fourth, fifth, sixth, and seventh words into the commencement of a fresh paragraph. The passage from *ut ipse locus* (line 52) to *dampnamus* (line 67) occurs in the letter of Pope Alexander II to Edward the Confessor, in favour of Coventry monastery, dated 1043[1], with the exception of *praepotentis hominis* (line 55), *uenerabiles* (line 57), *ex auctoritate* to *amplius* (line 59), *neque* to *elegerit* (lines 60, 61), *priuilegia* to *indulta* (lines 63, 64), and *rata inuiolataque* (line 66). The Coventry letter substitutes *uexatione* for *repet[it]ione* (line 54), *cuiuscumque dioecesani* for *Lundonicae urbis* (54), and *regalis* for the more correct *ratus*[2] (56). The passages from *igitur* to *eligendi* (lines 57, 58), and from *habeant* to *prohibemus* (lines 59, 60), which are given word for word in the Coventry letter, also occur in one of Edward the Confessor's Westminster charters (*CD.* iv. 184) in the bull of Pope Nicholas as follows: *habeantque potestatem, secundum regulam Sancti Benedicti, per successiones eligere ex se idoneos abbates.* This bull then proceeds with *neque introducatur per uiolentiam extranea persona, nisi quem concors congregatio sibi praeesse elegerit*[3]. This agrees closely with line 60 of our text. This charter of Edward the Confessor has several phrases in common with the present charter, and it is obviously of the same workmanship. We cannot be far wrong

---

[1] Printed in the *Monasticon*, vol. iii. p. 191, Migne, vol. 146, p. 1299. It is recited in Edward's charter of 1043 (*CD.* iv. 255), which has other passages in common with the Westminster charter (see note to line 114). The date of this pope's letter cannot be altered to 1063, as Jaffé-Wattenbach, No. 4543, suggest, since Earl Leofric, who died in 1057, is spoken of as dead.

[2] The copy of the Coventry letter in the Charter Roll, 19 Edward II, mem. 3, reads *ratus*.

[3] *Regula S. Benedicti*, iv. § 1: *In abbatis ordinatione illa semper consideretur ratio, ut hic constituatur, quem sibi omnis concors congregratio . . . elegerit.* Cf. the Newminster Statutes, c. 13 (*CS.* iii. 461). Cf. the Lateran Council of 601: *nisi de eadem congregatione, quem si propria uoluntate concors fratrum societas elegerit* (Labbe and Cossart, x. 487).

CHARTER VI.

in concluding that lines 57 to 61 are expansions from the Rule of St. Benedict. The next passage, which also occurs in the Coventry letter with the exception of the reference to St. Dunstan, is partly repeated in Pope Leo's bull in the other Westminster charter of Edward the Confessor (*C.D.* iv. 175 [27]). The clauses *obseruatores . . . mereantur, causa . . . perueniat* (lines 67 to 69) are taken from the St. Denis letter of Pope Nicholas, their order being reversed. The wonderfully close agreement between these Westminster and Coventry letters and the St. Denis letter cannot be explained away on the hypothesis that it arises from the use of stereotyped phrases in the papal chancery, for, even if the St. Denis letter were free from suspicion, it is clear that the phraseology of these English papal letters is not that of the ages of the popes to whom they are assigned. We may, therefore, conclude that the three Westminster and the Coventry bulls are spurious, and that they have been fabricated on the lines and in the language of the St. Denis letter.

54. repetione. Read *repetitione*, 'claim' (Marculf, i. 32, ii. 9).

70. cognoscat ergo magnitudo seu utilitas uestra. From Dagobert I (Pertz, 144 [14], 162 [8]) or Chilperic II (*Ib.* 72 [29]). The phrase is common in Merovingian charters. Cf. Marculf, i. 15.

decernimus, &c. From Dagobert I (*Ib.* 144 [17], 162 [6]): *per hoc praeceptum, quod specialius decernimus et in perpetuum uolumus esse mansurum, iubemus atque constituimus.* Cf. Marculf, i. 15.

71. pro reuerentia, &c. From Dagobert I (Pertz, 144 [16], 162 [8]) following *utilitas uestra* (line 70): *quod ita nos pro reuerentia ipsorum sanctorum, uel pro quiete monachorum ibidem Deo famulantium.* Part of the phrase in the Westminster charter from *pro quiete* to *obseruetur* is used in the charter of Edward the Confessor (*C.D.* iv. 186 [9]).

72. honor, &c. From the grant of sanctuary by Dagobert I to St. Denis (Pertz, 143 [19]): *pertractauimus . . . qualiter honor et laus ecclesiae beatorum martyrum . . . haberetur et obseruaretur ; id est, ut quisquis fugitiuorum pro quolibet scelere ad praefatam basilicam beatorum martyrum fugiens Tricenam pontem aduenerit, ... siue de palacio nostro egrediens.*

76. quocunque delicto, &c. From the grant mentioned in the preceding note (Pertz, 143 [21]): *magis dignum est homines rationabiles, quocunque delicto facinoris siue contra nos, uel succedentes reges Francorum, uel contra quemlibet alium fidelem sanctae Dei ecclesiae, aliquod crimen commiserint, relaxentur et liberentur.*

79–81. ut neque nos . . . immanentes in ipsa. From Dagobert I (Pertz, 144 [19]), following *constituimus* (see second note to line 70): *ut neque nos, neque successores nostri, neque quilibet episcopus uel archiepiscopus, nec quicumque de iudiciaria potestate accinctus, in ipsam sanctam basilicam uel immanentes in ipsam.* Parts of this passage occur in the genuine charter of Chilperic (Pertz, 72 ³⁵), and in the second charter of Dagobert (162 ⁷). These clauses are used in the charter of Edward the Confessor (*CD.* iv. 186 ¹¹).

81, 82. **uel in homines ... uoluerint.** From Dagobert I (Pertz, 144 ¹²) granting immunity to the abbey *uel homines qui se cum substantia eorum uel rebus ad ipsam sanctam basilicam tradere et deuouere uoluerunt* (*sic*). The passage occurs also in the other charter of Dagobert (Pertz, 161 ⁴⁶). It is differently worded in Chilperic (*Ib.* 72 ²⁶). It is also used in the charter of Edward the Confessor cited in the preceding note.

82–95. **nisi ... confirmamus.** These passages agree, with a few trivial exceptions and with the exception of the necessary changes from St. Denis to St. Peter, with Dagobert I (Pertz, 144 ²¹⁻³⁴). The words from *nisi* to *uideantur* (line 86) occur only in the charter here quoted, but the clauses from *in curtes* (*maneria uel* are Westminster additions) to *concedimus* are used in the other charter of this king (*Ib.* 162 ⁸) and partly in the charter of Chilperic II (*Ib.* 72 ³⁴). The clauses from *nisi* (line 82) to *uideantur* (line 86) are used in the charter of Edward the Confessor mentioned in the two preceding notes. For the latter part of the clauses embraced in the present note, see Marculf, i. 4.

93. **exauctare.** Both charters of Dagobert have *exactare*, while that of Chilperic II has *esperare*. *Expectare* appears to be the more usual word.

97. **Hamme.** Ham, co. Essex (DB. ii. 15).

Winintune. In Essex (*CD.* iv. 220 ¹⁶). Wennington, called *Wemtuna* in DB. ii. 15, where it is said that it was always held by St. Peter's, Westminster. According to the writ of Edward the Confessor (*CD.* iv. 220), Wennington was given to Westminster by Atswere Swerte (ON. *Ogurr* the Swart) and his wife Alsi.

Mordune. Morden, co. Surrey (DB. i. 32, col. 2).

98. **Fentune.** The *Phantuna*, co. Essex, of DB. ii. 14. It is called *Fantuna* at 17 b, and was in the Hundred of Barstable, and is now absorbed in either Bemfleet or Bulphan. The charter of Henry I (in Cott. Tib. A viii. fol. 49) confirms *Fentune* and *Pantune* in Essex to the abbey. The manor of Fanton is mentioned in the ministers' accounts, 33 Henry VIII (*Monasticon*, i. 329).

Aldenham. Aldenham, co. Hertford (DB. 135 a, col. 1). It was granted to Westminster Abbey by Offa in 785 (*CS.* i. 339), and was confirmed by Edward the Confessor (*CD.* iv. 190).

Bleccenham. It is stated in the *Monasticon*, i. 266, that Sulcard says that Offa gave to Westminster five plough-lands at Blekenham, in the parish of Hendon. This is derived from Dart's *Westmonasterium*, 1742, p. 8, who states that Offa gave to the abbey 'Blekingham or Bleccingam, in the parish of Heandune, in the county of Middlesex.' His marginal reference 'Sulcardus' is probably intended as the authority for the statement that Offa granted Staines to the abbey. Sulcard does not say where the *uilla Blekenham* was situate (Cott. Faust. A iii. fo. 14; Tit. A viii, fo. 2 d). Dart, p. 11, says of Hendon 'in which, or at least to which appertaining, were the former gifts of Blakenham, Cowenlow, and Loyersley.' The latter is the *Lopereslege* of our next note, and Dart is right as to its situation. Widmore, *Hist. of St. Peter's, Westminster*, London, 1751, and *An enquiry into the time of the foundation of Westminster Abbey*, London, 1743, does not identify the site of Bleccenham. From the boundaries given in King Edgar's expanded charter (see page 90 above)[1] it is clear that 'Blecceanham' (*CS.* iii. 693) lay between Hampstead (Middlesex), the Watling Street, and the River Brent. The name was in existence some time after the Norman Conquest, for a Thomas de Blechenham is mentioned in a fine relating to Hendon in 10 Henry III, and another of the same name in 8 Edward II in a fine relating to Hendon, and in another one relating to Finchley (Hardy and Page, *Middlesex Fines*, pp. 17, 88, 89).

98. **Lopereslege.** It is evident from *CS.* iii. 604 that Dunstan bought this estate from the king, as here stated. This name has entirely vanished. It is called *Lohðeres leage* at the above reference, which relates to events between 972 and 978, and *Loceres-leage*[2] in a charter of 957 (*Ib.* iii. 188). Neither of these MSS. is contemporary. The name seems to be *Hlōð(h)eres lēage*. It lay, according to the boundaries in the aforesaid deeds, between Hendon and Brockley Hill, and about Edgeware, co. Middlesex. It is noteworthy that Brockley Hill, the site of the Roman *Sulloniacis*, is referred to as *þam ealdan tunstealle* in *CS.* iii. 605[12] and as *þam tunstallan* in iii. 188[26]. Lopereslege is not mentioned in Domesday; it is probably included in Hendon or Hampstead, both of which belonged to Westminster Abbey.

99. **una cum praedicto loco.** It is noteworthy that all the lands here said to be of the ancient endowment of the abbey are, with the exception of Morden, in the counties of Essex, Middlesex, and Hertford. If this is trustworthy, it favours the supposition that Westminster was an ancient East Saxon foundation, the lands lying within the kingdom of Essex, in which Middlesex and Hertfordshire, or at all events part of the latter, were included.

101. **sigillo suo et anulo episcopali.** Referring to the words of Dunstan's charter (*CS.* iii. 265[25]), which is dated six weeks earlier than the present one.

---

[1] With the impossible date 951, for which Mr. Birch proposes to substitute 959 (i.e. the date of Edgar's accession). But the signature of *dux* Æðelwine makes the earliest date 962, whilst Bishop Æðelwold, another witness, was not consecrated until 963. The date is probably 971.

[2] A *lokeres leage* is mentioned in the boundaries of Fovant, Wilts, in *CD.* iii. 279[18].

103. **Holewelle.** Holwell, co. Bedford (DB. i. 211 a, col. 1).
Dęcewrthe. Datchworth, co. Hertford (DB. i. 135, col. 2; *CD.* iv. 190).
104. **Wattúne.** Watton-at-Stone, co. Hertford (DB. i. 135, col. 2; *CD.* iv. 190).

Cillingtúne. The site of this has not been identified. Dart, p. 10, calls it 'Cillinton, or Shillengton, or Chellington.' It is not Shillington, co. Bedford, which occurs as *Sethlindone* in Domesday, i. 210 b, col. 2, and as *Schutlingdone*, *Schitlingdone* in the Ramsey History, p. 143, *Schitlingedune* in the charter of William the Conqueror (*Ib.* p. 202), &c. Thorpe, *Diplomatarium*, says that Cillingtune is 'Chillington, Middlesex,' but he has evidently derived this from Kemble's hypothetical '*Chillington*, co. Middlesex.' In the twelfth century copy of the charter of Edward the Confessor amongst the *Cartae Antiquae* (*CC.* No. 1) in the Public Record Office, three hides in *Sillingtune* and four in *Cillingtune* are confirmed to the abbey (cf. the text given in *CD.* iv. 177 [27], from a later copy, where the former is called *Collingtune*). In the charter of William the Conqueror (*CC.* No. 2), he is said to restore to the abbey the *uilla* of *Cillictune*, which Boselin de Diva had taken by force. The juxta-position of *Sillingtune* and *Cillingtune* in Edward's charter is curiously like that of *Cilletone* (West Chiltington) and *Sillintone* (Sullington), co. Sussex, in DB. i. 24 b, col. 1, but these were held in Edward's time by Azor and Wulfweard. Moreover, Parham is close to Chiltington and Sullington, and *Pereham* precedes *Sillingtune* and *Cillingtune* in Edward's charter. At the time of Domesday, Parham was held by the abbot of Westminster (i. 17 a, col. 1), so that it is probable that he had lands in Chiltington and Sullington [1]. Earl Roger, the Domesday tenant of Chiltington and Sullington, also held Parham (i. 24 b, col. 1), no doubt a separate manor from the abbot's, so that it is very probable that *Cillingtune* and *Sillingtune* are the Sussex Chiltington and Sullington. Perhaps the abbey had lost or exchanged these lands by the time of the survey.

105. **Stána.** Staines, co. Middlesex.

Tudintún. Teddington, co. Middlesex, as given by Kemble. It is not mentioned in Domesday, but it appears as *Tudinton* in 1197-8, and as *Todinton* in 1279-80, and as *Tudynton* in 1297-8 (Hardy and Page, *Calendar of London and Middlesex Fines*, vol. i., 1892, pp. 1, 55, 71).

106. **Halgeford.** Lower Halliford, a hamlet of Shepperton, and Upper Halliford, a hamlet of Sunbury, co. Middlesex. The *Nomina Villarum*, A.D. 1316, has two places called *Halgheford* in Shepperton (p. 327 a). As Shepperton

---

[1] According to the Dunstan charter (*CS.* iii. 265) three hides in Sillinctune were given to the abbey by Ælfwine, *prefectus regis de Kent*, and Dunstan bought the reversion of the land in Perham from one Wulfnoð. Sillinctune cannot possibly be Islington, as Birch suggests, since the Domesday name of the latter is *Iseldone* and *Isendone*.

CHARTER VI.   99

and Sunbury both belonged to Westminster Abbey at the time of Domesday (i. 128 a, col. 1), it is probable that the *Halgeford* of the charter includes both Lower and Upper Halliford.

Feltham. Feltham, co. Middlesex.

Ecelesford. Ashford, on the stream called the Echel or Exe, co. Middlesex. It is called *Exeforde* in Domesday, i. 127 a, col. 2, where it is noted that its soke formerly lay in Staines. In the *Nomina Villarum*, p. 327 a, it is joined with Littleton; both of them belonged to Westminster Abbey. It is called *Echelesford, Ecchilesford*, &c., in the thirteenth, fourteenth, and fifteenth centuries, and *Eglesford* in 1444–5 (Hardy and Page, *Calendar of London and Middlesex Fines*, vol. i. pp. 60, 102, 158, 193, 238, &c.).

106–109. **priscis ... iussit.** This is copied from the first charter of Edgar to Westminster (*CS*. iii. 260): *Haec particula terrae priscis temporibus ad eandem [perhibetur ecclesiam pertinere], sicut legitur in antiquo telligrapho libertatis, quam rex Offa illi*[1] *monasterio [dudum contulit, quando] aecclesiis per uniuersas regiones Anglorum recuperatiua priuilegia, Wulfredo archiaepiscopo hortan[te, scribere ius]sit.* This charter relates, however, only to the abbey land at Westminster.

109. **Wlfredo archiepiscopo.** Archbishop Wulfred was a considerable benefactor of monasteries, but he was not consecrated archbishop until 805, whereas Offa died in 796.

111, 112. **Hanc ... concessi.** This is based upon the clause following *iussit* (see note to lines 106–109) in Edgar's first charter: *Hanc ea[n]dem libertatem prefate aecclesiae Sancti Petri Dunstano commendaui archiaepiscopo*. It is, however, taken from the expanded copy of Edgar's charter. This inserts, between *Petri* and *Dunstano* of the above quotation, the words: *principis apostolorum, cui locus praedictus, dedicatus ac consecratus mirabiliter ab antiquis temporibus, Dei prouidentia, ab ipso clauigero, fuit confirmatus,* and reads *concessi* instead of *commendaui* in the passage quoted above from the genuine charter. This is the origin of the *concessi* of line 112 of the present charter, the concoctor whereof has added *qui templum fuerat dudum Apollinis.* This is the earliest mention of this imaginary Temple of Apollo, which is not referred to by Sulcard.

114. **quatinus ... seruitute.** From the intermediate charter (*CS*. iii. 692 [27]).

114–121. **et ne quis ... cenobii.** From the intermediate Edgar charter (*CS*. iii. 692 [27]), which, however, reads *abbas, qui ipso praefuerit coenobio* after *ordinauerit,* instead of *fratres eiusdem cenobii* of this charter (line 121). The same phrases occur, with the above reading *abbas,* etc., in a charter of Æðelred's to St. Albans (*CD*. iii. 249 [19]), which is preserved only in Paris's *Liber Addi-*

[1] So the MS. Birch has *illa.* Cf. *OS. Facs.* ii, Westm. pl. iv.

O 2

tamentorum. If this charter be spurious, as Kemble and Earle hold, it is a singularly clever imitation of the phraseology of Æðelred's charters. The only serious objection to its authenticity is the unusual exemption from the *trinoda necessitas.* It is possible that these clauses were taken by the Westminster forger from this charter of Æðelred's. They are used in Edward the Confessor's spurious Coventry charter (*C.D.* iv. 254 [27]), which was either founded upon the Westminster charter or was forged by the same hand.

121-123. **omnes successores ... iudicis.** From Dagobert's grant of the right of sanctuary to St. Denis (Pertz, 143 [24]).

123. **quoniam ex munificentia.** From Chlodowig II to St. Denis (Pertz, 20 [17]): *dum ex munificentia parentum nostrorum, ut diximus, ipse sanctus locus uidetur esse ditatus, nullus episcoporum, nec praesentes, nec qui futuri fuerint successores, aut eorum ordinatores, uel qualibet persona, possit quoquo ordine de loco ipso aliquid auferre, aut aliqua*[*m*] *potestate*[*m*] *in ipso monasterio uindicare, uel aliquid quasi per conmutationis titulum, absque uoluntate ipsius congregationis uel nostrum permissum* (sic), *minuere, aut calices uel cruces, seu indumenta altaris, uel sacros codices, argentum aurumue, uel qualemcumque speciem de quod* (sic) *ibidem conlatum fuit aut erit, auferre aut minuere, uel ad ciuitate*[*m*] *deferre non debeat nec praesumat. Sed liceat ipsi sanctae congregationi, quoniam per rectam delegationem conlatum est, perpetim possidere et pro stabilitate regni nostri iugiter exorare; quia nos, pro Dei amore uel pro reuerencia ipsorum sanctorum martyrum et adipiscenda uita aeterna, hunc* (sic) *beneficium ad locum ipsum sanctum cum consilio pontificum et inlustrium uirorum, nostrorum procerum, gratissimo animo et integra uoluntate uisi fuimus praestitisse; eo scilicet ordine, ut sicut tempore domni et genitoris nostri ibidem psallencius per turmas fuit institutus, uel sicut ad monasterium Sancti Mauricii Agaunis die noctuque tenetur, ita in loco ipso celebretur.* Cf. Marculf, i. 1, 2.

126. **commutationis titulum.** Marculf, i. 2, 31, 33, 34.

127. **nostrum permissum.** The forger, who generally normalizes the Merovingian grammar, has not altered this to *nostro permissu.*

130. **delegationem.** A Frankish term frequently used by Marculf and in the other formularies.

134. **uisi fuimus prestitisse.** Marculf, i. 15: *promptissima deuotione cum omni integritate uisi fuimus concessisse.*

136-140. **si autem ... indultum.** From Dagobert I (Pertz, 144 [34]), the only changes being *se ipso* for *semetipso* (line 137), .*v.* for *triginta ex auro purissimo* (line 137), *persoluat* for *componat*, and, of course, *Petri* for *Dionisii.* There are considerable changes in the clauses in the other charter of this king (*Ib.* 162 [17]). The clauses from *et ut dictum est* to *indultum* (lines 138

CHARTER VI.

to 140) occur in the charter of Chilperic II (*Ib.* 72⁴⁸). All three add after *indultum* the words *ita ut eis melius delectet pro stabilitate regni nostri uel pro quiete et quibuslibet leudis nostri Domini misericordiam attentius deprecari.*

140-145. **et ut haec ... sigillare.** From Dagobert I (Pertz, 144⁴¹), where it follows after *deprecari* as quoted at the end of the preceding note. The only change is that of *anulo* into *sigillo* (line 144). The passage also occurs in the other charter of this king (*Ib.* 162²³). It is evidently expanded from the genuine charter of Chilperic (*Ib.* 73¹).

148. **acsi peccator.** Even these words are borrowed from St. Denis, for Landeric, Bishop of Paris, attests the confirmation of Chlodovig II as *ac si peccator episcopus* (Pertz, 20⁴⁰). In the same way he attests Dagobert's grant of the right of sanctuary to St. Denis (*Ib.* 143³⁶), and the attestation is used frequently by the Bishops of Paris in the St. Denis muniments printed by Father Jacques Doublet (*Histoire de l'Abbaye de S. Denys*, Paris, 1625, 4to). Dunstan is made to use the same phrase in his Westminster charter (*CS.* iii. 265), where his attestation speaks of *hanc libertatis scedulam*, and he says that *agalmate sanctae crucis ... consignaui*, like the present charter. The florid attestations ascribed to Dunstan in these and other forgeries contrast strongly with the brevity of his genuine attestations.

153. The witnesses are in many cases impossible. The charter is dated 969, yet it is witnessed by Archbishop Oswald, who was bishop of Worcester until 972, and the first signature of Bishop Æscwig of Dorchester, another witness, is in 979, his predecessor Eadnoð signing until 975. Bishop Ælfheah of Lichfield was not consecrated until 973, whilst Æðelsige of Sherborn was not consecrated until five years later. 'Wulgarus Wiltuniensis' is probably intended for Wulfgar of Ramsbury, consecrated in 981. The 'Æþelgarus Cisseniensis' must be Æðelgar of Selsey, who was consecrated in 980; the see was not transferred to Chichester until 1070. Sigar (Sigegar) of Wells was consecrated in 975, and Ælfric of Crediton in 977. Nothing is known of a Sigegar of Elmham, but Bishop Eadwulf of Elmham signs between 956 and 964 and Bishop Theodred in 975. Ælfric was probably the bishop at the date of this charter. Kemble (*CD.* ii. 363) thinks that the charter was 'probably meant to bear the date 971 or 972,' but even this date is impossible, as will be seen from the above notes.

Of the witnesses, the following abbots appear as witnesses to Edgar's charters of this and following years: Ælfric (*CS.* iii. 513, 518, 520, 525), Cyneweard (*Ib.* 518, 520, 525, 541), Osgar (*Ib.* 518, 520, 525, 541), Æþelgar (*Ib.* 518, 520, 525), Sideman (*Ib.* 520), Foldbriht (*Ib.* 541), and Godwine (*Ib.* 541).

Of the *duces*, the following occur: Ælfere (*Ib.* 518, 520, 522, 525, 541),

Oslac (*Ib.* 520, 541), Byrhtnoð (*Ib.* 518, 520, 525, 541), and Ælfeg=Ælfheah (*Ib.* 518, 520, 522, 525, 541), whilst Eanulf occurs as a 'minister' or 'miles' (*Ib.* 520, 541, etc.). *Marchere*, no doubt, represents OE. *Morcere* (=ON. *Mǫrukari*). A 'Morcar dux' witnesses a York charter in 958 (*CS.* iii. 250 [21]), and a 'Morcar' witnesses in 949 (*Ib.* iii. 38 [14]).

180. **singrapha**. This word is probably borrowed from a genuine OE. charter. See below, page 117, note to line 46. The writer is never mentioned in genuine OE. charters. See Heinrich Brunner, *Zur Rechtsgeschichte der römischen und germanischen Urkunde*, Berlin, 1880, i. 161, 232 ; Julius Aronius, *Diplomatische Studien über die älteren angelsächsischen Urkunden*, Königsberg, 1883, p. 12 ; *English Historical Review*, vi. 739.

VII.

This letter, which has hitherto been entirely unknown, is written in characters of the end of the tenth or beginning of the eleventh centuries. Owing to the OE. custom of copying charters without distinguishing the copies as such, it is frequently impossible to determine whether a document is an original or a copy. This difficulty exists in regard to this letter. It would add considerably to its interest if we could feel sure that it is the original letter of Dunstan. In our opinion, however, the probabilities are against this view. The original was sent to the king, and hence would be preserved or destroyed with the OE. state records. It is clear that the person who benefited by the letter was the bishop of Cornwall (St. Germans), and a copy would, no doubt, be kept at St. Germans for the protection of the right of the bishop and his successors. This copy would doubtlessly be transferred to Crediton when the see of Cornwall was united to Crediton, between 1027 and 1036 [1]. By adopting this hypothesis, we can account for its presence in this collection amongst the other Crediton documents [2].

The letter is a report [3] of the archbishop upon the right to certain episcopal

[1] Malmesbury, *Gesta Pontiff.*, p. 200, states that the see of Cornwall was united to that of Crediton upon the death of Bishop Brihtwold of Cornwall, by Lyfing, bishop of Crediton, after Cnut's return from Rome. Cnut's journey to Rome occurred in 1027, and the transfer must therefore have been made between that year and 1036, the date of Cnut's death.

[2] The insertion on an erasure of the important sentence in line 19 favours the view that this is a copy, as the scribe seems to have jumped from the *þa gelamp hit þæt . . . cing* of lines 18, 19 to the *þa gelamp þæt . . . cyng* of lines 20, 21. It is rather improbable that the scribe would have made such a mistake as this if he had been making a clean copy from a draft for transmission to the king, and the mistake is even more improbable in the original letter if that was not cleancopied from a draft.

[3] With this letter may be compared that of Archbishop Wulfstan to King Cnut (*CD.* vi. 177), and the report in *CS.* ii. 236. These are also written in English.

CHAPTER VII.   103

lands in Cornwall, which had been held at one time by the Bishop of Crediton, and he advises that the lands shall be delivered to 'this bishop' of Cornwall. He states that they had been delivered to Daniel, bishop of that see, by King Eadred with the advice of his *witan*, and that afterwards, when Wulfsige was consecrated to the see by the writer of this letter, King Edgar and the bishops decided that Wulfsige was entitled to these lands. The question, apparently, again arose upon the consecration of Wulfsige's successor, who is only mentioned in the letter as 'this bishop.' This was evidently the time when the archbishop wrote the letter, for the history of the estates is not carried down later than the time of Bishop Wulfsige, as it would have been had 'this bishop' been other than his immediate successor. We have, therefore, dated the letter between 980, the date of Wulfsige's last signature[1], and 988, the date of the death of Dunstan, Archbishop of Canterbury. There can be, we think, no doubt that Dunstan is the archbishop in question, as the bishoprics concerned in the matter were in the province of Canterbury, and it must have been Dunstan whom King Edgar, according to this letter, ordered to consecrate Bishop Wulfsige, since the archbishop who consecrated him survived, as this letter proves, until the time of King Æðelred. It is true that Oswald, Archbishop of York, occupied his see during part of both reigns, but he could not have consecrated Wulfsige, as the consecration occurred at least five years before Oswald was translated to York. On other grounds it is unlikely that the writer of the letter was the northern archbishop. The evidence, therefore, seems conclusive that the archbishop who wrote this letter was Dunstan of Canterbury.

The chief interest of this letter lies in its connexion with what Bishop Stubbs calls 'one of the most vexed questions of Anglo-Saxon History'[2]—that is the division of the western bishoprics. It is evident that Dunstan was acquainted with the remarkable statement that purports to record the division of the two West-Saxon bishoprics into five. As Bishop Stubbs points out[3], the statement is found in the ancient records of at least three cathedrals, to wit 'in the Missal of Leofric of Exeter, now in the Bodleian Library, in the Codex Wintoniensis, now in the British Museum, and in the Register of John Cranbourne at Canterbury, which contains transcripts of the early documents of the metropolitan see as they existed in the fourteenth century[4].' Of these MSS. the oldest is the Leofric Missal, which is probably of the eleventh century. The Statement, which is dated 905, was copied

---

[1] As the date of Wulfsige's death is not recorded, he may have lived a few years after the date of his last signature. The first signature of Ealdred, his successor (?), does not occur until 993.

[2] William of Malmesbury, *Gesta Regum*, i. 140, note 3.   [3] *Ibid.*, ii. p. lv.

[4] These texts are printed in *CS.* ii. 276, 277. For convenience we refer hereafter to this document as the 'Statement.'

104   *NOTES.*

by William of Malmesbury into his *Gesta Regum*, and he uses it in his *Gesta Pontificum*, pp. 177, 178, and Florence of Worcester (i. p. 236) partly repeats it. Bishop Stubbs was of opinion that the statement 'acquired its present form soon after the middle of the eleventh century[1].' It is evident from the present letter that, at all events, the substance of the Statement is somewhat older than the date thus assigned. The Statement does not include the references to Ecgbriht and Sherborne (lines 2 to 5 of letter), but it gives more details regarding the division of the bishoprics. The chronological difficulties contained in the Statement appear in the letter—that Formosus, whose pontificate ended in 896, four years before King Edward's accession, wrote to that king and Plegmund in 905; that Wessex was without bishops seven years; and that the two bishoprics into which the see of Winchester was divided in 908[2], were divided into five bishoprics by Edward and Plegmund (in 905, according to the Statement). These difficulties have been frequently discussed, most recently and most ably by Bishop Stubbs.

After the account of the division of the bishoprics, the letter gives us matter of considerable interest that is peculiar to itself. It affords us almost contemporary evidence of the correctness of Leland's statement, based upon a charter of Æðelstan's that is now lost, that Æðelstan bestowed on Conan the bishopric of Cornwall[3]. It also enables us to add another name to the list of the bishops of that see, namely Daniel, who, we learn, was ordained at the command of King Eadred (946–955). This is, no doubt, the Bishop Daniel who signs from 955 to 959, who, Bishop Stubbs suggested, was bishop of Rochester or Selsey[4]. Daniel, bishop of Cornwall, is probably the Bishop Daniel who is named in an Exeter manumission of King Eadwig's (Thorpe, *Dipl. Angl.* 623)[5]. As he was appointed under Eadred (line 20) and signs through Eadwig's reign, he must have preceded Comoere, who subscribes in the time of King Edgar. Bishop Stubbs was unable to fix the date of the latter's consecration nearer than between 931 and 967 (*Registrum Sacrum*, p. 15)[6].

[1] Malmesbury, *G. R.* ii. p. lvi.   [2] Stubbs, l. c., ii. pp. lvi, lvii.
[3] The hand in which this statement is written in the letter (line 19) is contemporary with the hand of the body of the letter.
[4] See above, page 81, note to line 33.
[5] We are indebted to Bishop Stubbs for the note that William of Malmesbury knew of Daniel's existence, calls him a monk of Glastonbury, and dates his death in 956; *De Antiq. Glastoniensis Ecclesiae*, ed. Gale, p. 325, ed. Hearne, *Adam de Domerham*, i. 93. The day of his obit is given as 'viii. idus Oct.'
[6] The first four bishops of the West-Saxon see of Cornwall are therefore: (1) *Conan*, consecrated under Æðelstan (A.D. 926? Cf. Haddan and Stubbs, *Councils*, i. 676); signatures 931–934, and in a dubious charter of Æðelstan's with the impossible date 943 (*CS.* ii. 528[11]), and in another with the date of 843 (*CS.* ii. 454[5]), for which Birch suggests 939, the correct date being evidently 934; (2) *Daniel*, consecrated under Eadred, signs 955 to 959, dies, according to

CHARTER VII.

It is evident from this letter that Bishop Wulfsige's successor was consecrated before Dunstan's death in 988. The first signature of Ealdred, Wulfsige's successor, occurs in 993, but he must, unless there was an unrecorded bishop between him and Wulfsige, have been consecrated at least five years earlier. Bishop Stubbs informs us that he does not think it necessary to assume an intermediate bishop, and suggests that old age, or the infrequency of courts, or distance from the capital may explain the absence of Wulfsige's signatures after 980, assuming that he lived after that year.

Malmesbury, *Gesta Pontiff.*, p. 204, states that the see of Cornwall was at St. Petrocks (Padstowe), but adds that, according to some, it was at St. Germans. It is clear from line 21 of the present letter that the 'bishop-stool' was at St. Germans at the time of Daniel's consecration. As the writer of the letter makes no mention of the removal of the see, we may perhaps infer that he supposed it to have been there in Conan's time, which agrees with Leland's statement (cf. Haddan and Stubbs, i. 703). Bishop Stubbs remarks, in a communication to us, that he thinks Comoere may have sat at St. Petrocks, and that this would account for his name not appearing amongst the bishops' signatures. He remarks that the West Saxon 'shire-bishops' were moveable people, and that, at all events, the Ramsbury and Sunning line of bishops moved about, as they had no cathedral establishment[1]. Wynne and Powel, in their Welsh history, record that the Cornish see was transferred to St. Germans in 981 in consequence of the Danish destruction of St. Petrocks, but Haddan and Stubbs (i. 683) were unable to find the authority for this statement. It does not seem probable that this transference from St. Petrocks to St. Germans was the cause of this letter being written, although the date would be suitable, unless the transference was synchronous with the creation of a new bishop. There was evidently a question as to the ownership of the lands, though it is difficult to suggest any claimant except Crediton or Sherborne, to the latter of which they are said in this letter to have been given by

---

Malmesbury, in 956; (3) *Comoere*, who appears in the Bodmin manumissions as 'Comuyre presbyter' under Eadred (946-955) and as bishop under Eadgar (959-975); (4) *Wulfsige*, consecrated under Eadgar; signatures 963 (cf. *CS.* lii. 355) to 980. The *Æðelgea...biscop* mentioned in the Bodmin manumissions as contemporary with King Eadred must be *Æðelgar*, bishop of the neighbouring see of Crediton (934-953). That Comoere preceded Wulfsige is evident from the fact, proved by this letter, that the latter survived King Eadgar, in whose reign he was consecrated; hence Comoere, who is mentioned as bishop in the time of this king, must have been bishop during the earlier years of the reign. Some confusion has been introduced into the history of the early Cornish bishops by Malmesbury's unfortunate misreading of the *Coruinensis* of the Statement as *Cornubiensis*, so that Æþelstan of Ramsbury has figured as bishop of Cornwall; *Gesta Regum*, i. 141; *Gesta Pontiff.*, p. 178.

[1] The charter of Æðelred to Bishop Ealdred, A. D. 994 (*CD.* iii. 277) seems to intend making St. Petrocks the seat of the bishopric.

(IV. 7)   P

King Ecgbriht. If the see was transferred from St. Germans to St. Petrocks some time after Daniel's consecration, and was brought back again in 981, there is no obvious reason why any question as to the ownership of the land should have arisen, especially as the lands had been assigned to Daniel and to Wulfsige. The cause of the letter being written was clearly something more than a restitution of temporalities, if we may borrow a later phrase. If the lands were claimed on behalf of the bishop of Crediton, such claim would most likely arise at a time when that bishopric and that of Cornwall were vacant. Both bishoprics may have been vacant at the same time for anything we know to the contrary, as Ælfric, bishop of Crediton, died between 985 and 988, and therefore may have died in the same year as Wulfsige of Cornwall, who died, as we have seen, between 980 and 988.

Translation.

This writing the Archbishop sends to his lord, Æþelred, the king. It happened that the West Welsh (the inhabitants of Cornwall) rose against King Ecgbriht. The king then went thither and subdued them, and gave a tenth part of the land [to God] and disposed of it as it seemed fit to him. He gave to Sherborne three estates, Polltun, Cællwic, Landwiþan. And that remained so for many years until heathen hordes overran this country and occupied it. Then there came another time after that, when the teachers fell away and departed from England on account of the unbelief that had then assailed it; and all the kingdom of the West Saxons stood for seven years without a bishop. Then Formosus, the Pope, sent from Rome, and admonished King Edward and Archbishop Plegmund to amend this. And they did so; with the counsel of the Pope and all the witan of the English nation, they appointed five bishops where there were formerly two: one at Winchester, that was Fryþestan, a second at Ramsbury, that was Æþelstan, a third at Sherborne, that was Wærstan, a fourth at Wells, that was Æþelm, a fifth at Crediton, that was Eadulf. And to him (Eadulf) were assigned the three estates in Wales (Cornwall), to be under the authority of the people of Devon, because they (the people of Cornwall) had formerly been disobedient, without awe of the West Saxons. And Bishop Eadulf enjoyed these lands during his life, Bishop Æþelgar after him in like manner. Then it happened that King Æþelstan gave to Cunun the bishopric as far as the Tamar flowed (i. e. Cornwall). Then it happened that King Eadred commanded Daniel to be consecrated, and gave the estates, as the witan advised him, to the bishop-stool at St. Germans. Afterwards, when King Edgar bade me consecrate Wulfsige, he and all our bishops said that they did not know who could possess the estates with greater right than the bishop of the diocese, seeing that he was loyal and preached

CHARTER VII.

the belief of God aright and loved his lord (the king). If then this bishop does so now, I know not why he should not be worthy of the estates, if God and our lord (the king) grant them to him. For it does not seem to us that any man can possess them more rightfully than he, and if any (other) man take them to himself, may he have them without God's blessing or ours.

2. **Westwealas.** The 'West Welsh' are the people of Cornwall. They are so called in the Chronicle in 813, 835, and 926. In 823 they are called *Wealas* without qualification. Cf. the tract on the Saints of England: *þonne resteð sanctus Petrocus on West Wealum be þære sǽ neah þam fleote þe man clypað Hægelmuða* (at Padstow)[1].

Þá ferde se cyng þyder. Probably referring to 813, as the Chronicle says in this year: *þy geare gehergade Ecgbriht cyning on Westwalas from easteweardum oþ westewearde.*

3. **geteoþude.** In one of the documents connected with King Æðelwulf's famous 'Donation,' the verb *geteoþian* is used in the sense of to give a tenth of the land, not a tenth of its yearly product, and this meaning seems to be supported by the other deeds relating to the Donation. The Chronicle, A.D. 855, states clearly that he 'booked' or conveyed a tenth of his land: *gebocude Æþelwulf cyning teoþan dǽl his londes ofer al his rice, Gode to lofe.* It is in this sense that *geteoþian* is used in the present letter.

4. **Polltún.** The same spelling occurs in the Statement (*CS.* ii. 277 [14]). It is called *Pautone* in DB. i. 120 b, col. 1, where it is held by the Bishop of Exeter. In the Exon Domesday, p. 181, it appears as *Pautona*. Mr. Warren identifies it with the manor of Pawton, in the parish of St. Breock, a few miles east of Padstowe.

Cællwic. This is called *Cælling* in the Statement. It is probably the *Calwetone* of DB. i. 120 a, col. 2, held by the king. It is called *Caluuitona* in the Exon Domesday, p. 94. Mr. Warren has identified *Cælling* with Callington, a small market town lying between Launceston and St. Ives.

5. **Landwiþan.** The spelling agrees with that of the Statement. It is called *Longvitetone* in DB. i. 120 b, col. 2, and was held by the Bishop of Exeter. In the Exon Domesday, p. 183, it is spelt *Languitetona*. This is, as Mr. Warren states, the modern Lawhitton, a parish in the borough of Launceston. Lawhitton is the only one of these estates that has not severed its connexion with the bishopric of Exeter, being now the property of the Ecclesiastical Commissioners.

6. **Iariowas afeollun and ut gewitun of Angla lande.** In writing this passage the Archbishop seems to have had in his mind King Ælfred's preface to

[1] Liebermann, *Die Heiligen Englands*, Hanover, 1889, p. 18; *Liber Vitae of Hyde Abbey*, ed. Birch, 1892, p. 93.

the translation of Gregory's *Cura Pastoralis*, where the king laments the decay of learning in England: it had so fallen away (*swæ clæne hio wæs oðfeallenu on Angelcynne, Cura Past.*, ed. Sweet, 3[13]; *hus io lar Lædengeðiodes ær ðissum afeallen wæs giond Angelcynn, Ibid.* 7[15]) that there were few south of the Humber who could understand their services or translate a Latin letter into English.

7. **him** refers to **Angla lande**, 'the unbelief that had come upon it.'

9. **se papa of Rome byrig** can scarcely be taken to mean 'the pope of Rome,' as the genitive is almost invariably used with words denoting a dignity or office, cf. *Rome papa, Cura Past.*, ed. Sweet, 9[9]; *Gregorius pære Romaniscan burge biscop, OE. Beda*, ed. Miller, p. 106; *ærcebiscop Contwarena burge, Ibid.*, &c. It was not until later, as in the Peterborough Chronicle, that the construction with *of* became usual. Cf., however, *Genesis* xiv. 10, *ða ciningas ... of Sodoman and Gomorran = rex Sodomorum et Gomorrhae*.

11. **eall.** Uninflected for *ealra*.

14. **Wærstan.** No signatures of this bishop occur, and so little is known of him that Stubbs, *Regist. Sacrum*, p. 13, believed that Werstan was merely a corrupt reading for Æthelstan, the name of the bishop of Ramsbury. The present letter shows this belief to be untenable, and Wærstan is mentioned in the list of bishops of Sherborne in the Hyde *Liber Vitae*, p. 20. Malmesbury, *Gesta Pontiff.*, p. 178, gives Wærstan as the name of the bishop who was slain in Anlaf's night attack upon Æðelstan's camp before the battle of Brunanburh. But, as Stubbs points out, Alfred was bishop of Sherborne when this battle was fought. In the *Gesta Regum*, p. 143, Malmesbury relates the same account of an *episcopum quendam*. There are several bishoprics which were vacated about the time of this battle, but the tale cannot be true of the Bishop of Sherborne, as Alfred signs before and after the date of that event.

16. The reason here alleged for giving the estates to the Bishop of Crediton and assigning the jurisdiction thereof to Devon, because the people of Cornwall had previously been disobedient without fear of the West Saxons, is not very intelligible. The possession of three scattered estates in Cornwall would not materially assist the Bishop of Crediton or the people of Devon in converting the Cornish people into peaceful subjects of Wessex. The Statement gives a more plausible reason, that the object was that the bishop should visit the Cornish people yearly *ad exprimendos* (*extirpandos*) *eorum errores ; nam antea, in quantum potuerunt, ueritati resistebat et non decretis apostolicis oboediebant* (*CS*. ii. 277). There seems to be a confusion between the motives that were supposed to actuate King Edward and those upon which the bishops acted.

17. **buton Westsexena ege.** So the Chronicle, A. D. 823, records that the East Anglians sought the protection of Ecgbryht *for Miercna ege*.

CHARTER VII.   109

18. **Æþestan.** This is written on an erasure, the original hand at line 13 having the more correct form *aþelstan*. The spelling *Æpestan* occurs in original charters of 955 and 961 (*CS.* iii. 64 [13], 298 [13]), but is probably to be explained as a scribal error. The forms *Æpestan* of 949 (*CS.* iii. 41 [34]) and 956 (*Ib.* iii. 106 [29]) are from late MSS. The *l* seems to be frequently omitted in this name after the beginning of the eleventh century. Thus we have, in contemporary charters, *Æpestan* twice in 1001 (*CD.* iii. 317 [14], [20]), in 1015 (Earle, *Land Charters*, 224 [3], normalized by Kemble, *CD.* iii. 361 [19]), in 1021–1023 (*Ib.* iv. 20 [26]), and 1042 (Brit. Mus. *Facsimiles*, part iv. pl. 24). The Abingdon Chartulary, i. 54, has *Æthestan*, which is also normalized by Kemble, *CD.* iv. 75 [13]. Thus there is clear evidence of the dropping of the *l* in writing in the eleventh century. This usage accounts for the Domesday form of this name *Adestan* (i. 286 b, col. 2, 291 a, col. 1, &c.), a form that also occurs in the Exon Domesday, pp. 404, 409, and in Wace, *Roman de Rou*, i. p. 47, line 283, &c. The forms *Aeðeuulf* and *Aeðered* occur in original Kentish charters dated as early as 839 (*CS.* i. 598 [12], [19], [30], 599 [7], Sweet, *O.E.T.*, charter No. 24), but this charter has *Aeðelstan, Aeðelhard, Aeðeluulf,* and *Aeðelric*, besides *Aeðelm*. The writing of this charter is, however, the same as that of an addition, which dates between 871 and 889. In the endorsement the spelling *Æpewalde* occurs (599 [9]). The form *Æðerred* occurs in a Kentish charter of 862 (*CS.* ii. 114 [33]), which has also *Æðelred* (115 [3]). *Æðered* is met with in original charters in 875 (*Ib.* ii. 159 [1]), in 901 (ii. 230 [4], [34]), in 934 (ii. 404 [36]), and in later charters. The form *Æperic* occurs in 931 (*CS.* ii. 365 [39]), in 949 (*Ib.* iii. 30 [38]), in later charters, and in the Maldon Song, line 280. The *Cioberht* of 824 (*CS.* i. 520 [28]) is probably a graphic error, but the *l* has disappeared in the man's name *Ceobba* (*CS.* i. 332 [18]), which is, no doubt, a short form of the name *Ceol-berht* or *Ceol-beald*. *Ceored* occurs in a ninth century charter (*CS.* ii. 35 [78]), and *Ceorred* in a later copy of a charter of 841 (*Ib.* ii. 12 [2]).

In the case of forms like *Æðer(r)ed, Æðeric, Ceorred* and *Ceored* we seem to have assimilation of *lr* to *rr*, which would naturally tend to become *r* in unaccented syllables (as in *Æðered*). A similar change may be observed in the case of *nr*; cf. *Cyrred, Cyred* for *Cynred* (*CS.* i. 591 [13]; ii. 141 [27]), which are from original ninth and tenth century charters. It would perhaps be too hazardous to compare the loss of *n, l,* to that of *r* in *are, mire, þire* for *ānre, minre, þinre,* which are so frequently met with in late Old English and early Middle English, as with the exception of these words, which are often used enclitically, we find no trace elsewhere of assimilation of *n* or *l* to a following *r*. Moreover, the forms *mire*, &c., are paralleled by similar ones in the Germanic dialects of the Continent (cf. Sievers, *Anglia*, xiii. 328; xiv. 142).

19. **scæt**=*sceat*, preterite of *sceotan*. Cunun's bishopric extended 'as far as

the Tamar flowed,' i. e. reached to the Tamar, that river forming the limit. The bishopric was thus co-extensive with Cornwall.

23. rihtluour, a late West Saxon form for -*licur*, -*licor*.

scire = diocese. The word *scīr* is the natural OE. representative of 'diocese,' and it is no doubt used in this sense in the present case, although there were in Wessex bishops of certain shires.

25. gyf þonne þes bisceop nu swa deþ. 'If therefore this bishop now does the like.' The change from the preterite (*wæs, bodude, lufude*) should be noted. The bishop referred to in the present tense is obviously Wulfsige's successor, since Wulfsige is spoken of in the past tense.

26. The concluding words from *gyf him heora god ann* to the end, which are in another, but contemporary hand, are of course an addition, as the transition from the singular *ic* to the plural *ure, us* shows. The archbishop uses the singular throughout, and there is no apparent reason why he should use the ceremonious plural at the end. Can the plural pronouns refer to an assembly of the bishops or of the *witan*? Both appear in lines 20, 22 as having a consultative voice regarding the disposition of these lands.

VIII.

This is the original charter, which has never been printed before. A sixteenth century paper copy of the boundaries and endorsement, written in OE. letters, is preserved in Cott. MS. Claudius A 8, fo. 80 (old notation 74). This has escaped the attention of Kemble and Thorpe. The copy, which is provided with an interlinear Latin translation, is imperfect, a portion of the foot of each page having been cut away. According to Wanley, *Catalogus*, p. 226, it is in the handwriting of Joscelin, Archbishop Parker's well-known secretary. The charter is cited from this copy by Dugdale, *Antiquities of Warwickshire*, p. 225.

1. moderamina ... gubernat. Cf. the charter of Æþelstan in *CS*. ii. 398, *qui cunctum suo sancto moderamine ... gubernat*; this charter, however, uses *formulae* that belong to the times of Eadwig and Eadgar. The phrase *quadripertitus mundus* occurs in a charter of Æðelred's, A.D. 996 (*CD*. vi. 134). The charters of this king do not employ stereotyped proems, and hence they present great variety.

3. nihil intulimus ... quid possumus. Tim. vi. 7.

9. suum thesaurum thesaurizare in altis caelorum culminibus. Matt. vi. 20, *thesaurizate autem uobis thesauros in caelo*.

10. altithrono ... basileus. This phrase occurs in charters of King Edgar

CHARTER VIII. 111

(*CS*. iii. 491, 584, 594) and in one of King Æðelred's (*CD*. iii. 265), and, with numerous variations, in other charters of these kings and of King Eadwig. The stile is amplified from one that occurs in charters of King Æðelstan: —*fauente superno numine, basyleos Anglorum ceterarumque gentium in circuitu persistentium* (*CS*. ii. 351, 438, 442, 456). This was one of the numerous stiles used by Edmund and his successors. The charters of Æðelstan quoted above are preserved only in late copies, and there is no undoubted charter of this monarch wherein he calls himself *basileus*, although there are several of his charters depending upon late copies wherein he is so described (*CS*. ii. 373, 414, 417, 420, 459). But these charters, like several others ascribed to this king, use phraseology belonging to the chancery of his successors. It is possible that some of these charters have been remodelled upon the charters of Edmund and his successors, and, in some cases, Æðelstan's name may have been substituted for that of another king. This is clearly the case in *CS*. ii. 527, where a charter of Æðelstan's bearing the impossible date of 943 uses the stile of Edmund and his successors. The stiles of this latter king were employed continuously until the end of Æðelred's reign, and even occasionally in Cnut's time. The so-called Imperial stile of the English kings seems to have been introduced by Edmund. If this was so, Freeman's views (*N.C.* i. 554) require considerable modification.

11. **triuiatim.** This unexplained adverb is used in a charter of Eadwig's, A.D. 956: *Eaduuig, annuente altitroni moderatoris imperio, totius Albionis triuiatim potitus regimine* (*CS*. iii. 87). It occurs in the charters of Edgar's cited at the beginning of the preceding note, and also in other charters of this king, wherein his stile is slightly varied (*CS*. iii. 465, 605, 654). It is employed in Æðelred's charters (*CD*. iii. 74, 170, 265, 276) in like stiles. In one of this monarch's charters we read: *Æðelred Anglicae nationis, caeterarumque gentium triuiatim intra ambitum Britanniae insulae degentium . . . basileus* (*CD*. iii. 182). An examination of the royal stiles does not throw any light upon the meaning of *triuiatim*. The *undique secus, hinc inde circumquaque*, which occur occasionally (*CS*. ii. 398, 520, 599, 600; iii. 141, 188, 225, 345, 408), represent the *in circuitu*, not the *triuiatim*, of the present charter. Æðelred (*CD*. iii. 340) uses the phrase *ceterarumque gentium longe lateque per circuitum adiacentium*, but this can hardly be equated with *triuiatim*. Martianus Capella uses *triuiatim* in the sense of 'in the public streets,' from *triuium*, but the word cannot have this meaning in the preceding passages. In 1031 Cnut is *rex totius Albionis, ceterarumque gentium triuiatim persistentium basileus* (*CD*. iv. 35).

12. **Leofwino . . . duce.** Leofwine was the father of the well-known Ealdorman Leofric of Mercia (Flor. of Worcester, *an*. 1017, 1057). He was

Ealdorman of the Hwiccas in 997 (*Wicciarum prouinciarum dux*, *CD.* iii. 304 [5]). His name occurs as *dux* and *ealdorman* between 994 and 1023. Robertson (*Hist. Essays*, p. 184) holds that Leofwine became Ealdorman of the Hwiccii when the Mercian Ealdormanship was broken up, as he assumes, after the death of Ælfhere in 983 (Chron. C, D, E) and the exile of his son in 985 (*Ibid.*). Green, *Conquest*, p. 373, adopting these conclusions, states that Leofwine was created Ealdorman of the Hwiccas in 985.[1] Freeman thinks that he succeeded Eadric Streona as Ealdorman of Mercia in 1017 (*N. C.* i. 738), and this view is adopted by Green (*Conquest*, pp. 420, 426). The earliest preserved signature of his son Leofric, who seems to have succeeded him immediately, as *dux* occurs in 1032 (*CD.* iv. 39[34]). Florence records that, in 1017, Cnut made Leofric *dux* in place of his brother Norðman, who was slain at the same time as Eadric Streona. But this probably means that he was made Ealdorman of the Hwiccas or some other subordinate ealdormanry. Leofwine is probably the person of that name who is mentioned in the will of the Æðeling Æðelstan, the son of King Æðelred (*CD.* iii. 362, 363). If so, he had a brother named Leofstan (*Ibid.*). A royal huntsman named Leofwine is the recipient of a grant in 987 (*CD.* iii. 229).

13. **non tamen in uno loco**, &c. Cf. Edgar, A.D. 958 (*CS.* iii. 245[14]): *xvii. manentium non in uno tamen loco, sed in diuersis sparsim locis diuisos.*

14. **Suþham.** Southam, co. Warwick. It is called *Sucham* in DB. i. 238 b, col. 2, and was then the property of Coventry Abbey. Earl Leofric, the son of the grantee of the present charter, conferred it upon the abbey in 1043 [2] (*CD.* iv. 273), and his grant was confirmed by the king in the same year (*Ib.* iv. 253). In Æþelred's grant, A.D. 1001, to Clofig of land *æt Yceantune* (Itchington, co. Warwick), it is stated that half the land 'æt Suðham' belongs to Itchington (*CD.* iii. 317).

[1] The charter, dated by Kemble 990 (*CD.* iii. 251[3]), which Leofwine witnesses as *comes*, a frequent title of the minor Ealdormen, should clearly be dated 1005, which, indeed, seems to be the date expressed in the charter itself. He is also described as *dux* in 984 (*CD.* iii. 204[37]), but the other witnesses fix the date of this charter between 1005 and 1012. Leofwine witnesses once only as *dux* in 994 (*CD.* iii. 280[21]). He is probably one of the two *ministri* of this name who subscribe in 980 (*CD.* iii. 177[7]), and, no doubt, some of the signatures of *Leofwine minister* between 981 and 990 (*CD.* iii. 184[36], 198[32], 203[3]; vi. 119[31]) belong to him. The second *minister* of this name appears in 995 (*CD.* iii. 284[11]) in addition to the *dux*. A presumably earlier *minister* of the same name signs in 956 (*CS.* iii. 119[19], 130[30], 166[1]); he is, in all probability, the *Leofwine propinquus regis*, *minister* of 955 (*CS.* iii. 86[1]). Was this a relative of the Ealdorman? A Leofwine, a kinsman of Æðelmær, son of Ealdorman Æðelweard (see above, page 87, and below, notes to lines 68, 73), bequeathed lands at Shifford, co. Oxford, to Æðelmær before 1005 (*CD.* iii. 341).

[2] This date is derived from the *Inspeximus* of this charter on the Charter Roll, 19 Edward II, mem. 3, which gives a much better text of this charter than Kemble's.

CHARTER VIII. 113

14. Hlodbroce. Ladbrooke, adjoining Southam, called *Lodbroc* in DB. i. 240 b, col. 1; 241 a, coll. 1, 2; 242 a. Part of it then belonged to Godgifu, the daughter-in-law of Earl Leofwine, to whom it is granted by the present charter.

Hreodburnan. Radbourn (Upper and Lower), now a parish, but formerly extra-parochial, adjoining Ladbrooke. In DB. it appears as *Redborne* (i. 241 a, col. 1), and is linked with Ladbrooke as the estate of 'Turchil' of Warwick.

19–26. si quis . . . humilis penituerit. The same phrase occurs in charters of Eadwig's with the continuation *quod contra sanctam Dei ecclesiam rebellis agere presumpserit, nec in uita hac practica ueniam, nec in theorica requiem apostata obtineat ullam, set, eternis baratri incendiis trusus, cum Anania et Saphira iugiter miserrimus crucietur* (*CS.* iii. 255, 257). It is also used by Edgar with the same continuation (*Ib.* iii. 451, 585, 595) and with slight changes (iii. 492, 654). It is used with the same continuation by Æðelred (*CD.* iii. 183, 269, 277; cf. *CD.* iii. 179), and by Cnut (*CD.* iv. 5). Cf. *CS.* iii. 45[32].

20. epylempticus occurs in the passages cited in the preceding note. Cf. Corpus Gl. (*OET.*) 754: 'epilenticus, *woda*'; Epinal, 383: 'ephilenticus, *uuoda.*' In Corpus, 1044, *wodan* glosses *inergumenos* (= ἐνεργουμένους). This shows that ἐπιληπτικός is used in the sense of '*wood*, mad.' Ἐπιληπτικός, which is used by Hippokrates, is the late (Alexandrian?) form. Cf. ἐπιλημπτεύομαι, ἐπιλημπτός in the Septuagint (E. A. Sophokles), and the seventh cent. ἐπιλημψία, ἐπιλήμψιμος in Götz u. Gundermann, *Corpus Glossariorum Latinorum*, ii. 309.

26. syn for *synd*. Again in l. 36. Cf. *longemæra* for *lond-*.

27. forworhte. The reasons for the forfeiture of land are occasionally given in the charters, no doubt with the intention of precluding claims on the part of the former owner's kin. Thus we have records of forfeiture for theft (*CS.* i. 228[14]; ii. 436[13]; iii. 474[24], 612[13]; *CD.* iii. 291[6]), for treason (*CS.* ii. 243[23]; *CD.* vi. 160[16], 165[2], 170[13], 174[12]), for attempted murder by witchcraft (*CS.* iii. 372[24]), and for fornication (*CD.* vi. 141[17]). Cf. also *CD.* iii. 306[32], 341[29], 356[33], 357[2]; *CD.* vi. 128. See also No. XI, line 20.

30. Hlodbroc, meaning the brook, not the village.

31. on Ycænan. The River Itchen. It is called *in, on ycenan* in 1001 (*CD.* iii. 316[20], [21]), in a grant of land *æt Yceantune*, now Itchington. The form should, no doubt, be *Icenan*, the *y* being a common late West Saxon representative of *i*. The Hampshire river Itching is written *Icenan* in the oblique cases in *CS.* i. 555[4]; ii. 71[5], 135[27], 284[26], 288[4], 386[24], 456[28]; iii. 273[26], [31], 303[32], and *Ycenan, Ycænan* in *CS.* i. 540[9]; ii. 163[22], [28], 247[20]. These forms are principally derived from the twelfth century *Codex Wintoniensis*.

æfter streame þæt to þæm hyærde wycan. This use of *þæt*, apparently as an adverb, is very common in the charters. In the present instance it

(IV. 7) Q

seems to stand for *þæt hit cymð*, with which formula we frequently find it interchanging in one and the same charter (cf. *CD.* iii. 215[25] *andlang gemære ðæt on sceorfes mor* . . . ; *andlang broc ðæt on wæte leahe,* . . . . *æfter ðære stige ðæt on geaggan treow, of ðam treowe on ða bradan stræte ðæt* hit cymð *on medwe, ðonne æfter medwe sice ðæt* hit cymð *on Tresel. CD.* iii. 220[6] *ondlong weges ðæt on ða aldan stræte, ondlong ðære aldan stræte ðæt* hit cymeð *to Heortlaforda, of Heortlaforda ðæt eft on Sture.* Cf. also *CD.* vi. 144[9-11], 150[23-26], &c.). In another series of instances this explanation does not seem to be admissible; the *þæt* there appears to mean 'then,' 'thence,' or 'thus,' and is equivalent to '*ðonne*,' '*ðanon*,' or '*swa*,' with which it is interchangeably used (cf. *CD.* iii. 176[3], ðonne *andlang hærpaðes to dunneburnan* . . . . ðæt *andlang hagan*, &c., and *CD.* iii. 252, where *ðæt andlang* interchanges with *swa andlang*). Cf. also *CS.* ii. 541(=Sweet, *A. S. Reader*, pp. 57-8) þonne *of ðam beorge* . . . . þæt *fram ðam geate* . . . . þonne *suð* . . . . þonne *west* . . . . þæt *west* . . . . þæt *east*, &c.

A *Heordewuyca* was included in Earl Leofric's grant of Southam to Coventry in 1043 (see note to line 14), but this is probably Prior's Hardwick, a few miles to the south-east of Southam.

32. **ællenstubb.** This is probably the *ælrenan stob* (*CD.* iii. 316[19, 22, 26, 29]) that is mentioned, in the vicinity of the Itchen, in the boundaries of Long Itchington, the adjoining parish.

mærstan. Prior's Marston adjoins Prior's Hardwick, but, like the latter, it lies in the wrong direction from Southam. The word *mǣre*, 'a meer, boundary,' seems to occur in compounds in the form *mær*. Cf. *CS.* iii. 150[20]: *on mær broc* . . . *on mærstan* . . . *on ðone mær pyt*; and 152[30]: *á be gemære þæt on ða heafod stoccas, of ðan stoccan on ðone mær stan, of ðan stane á be gemære*. These are the boundaries of Tadmarton, co. Oxford, near the boundary of Warwickshire.

33. **gemyþan.** This word generally denotes the point where two rivers meet. Here it perhaps means the junction of the two brooks a mile to the east of Southam village. In *CS.* i. 308[4] the word is applied to the junction of the Teme with the Severn at Powick, co. Worcester. Other instances of the word are *CS.* i. 496[17]; ii. 41[9], 354[34], 575[24]; iii. 85[9], 157[11, 19], 224[11], 520[7]; *O.E. Beda*, ed. Smith, 618 (Miller, p. 398[17], has *gemyndum*). It is applied to the junction of two roads in the boundaries of Farnborough, co. Berks (*to þæra wega gemyþum, CS.* ii. 308[27], 371[12]; *CD.* iv. 66[18]). In *CS.* iii. 47[6] it is employed in connexion with *haga* a 'haw' or enclosure (*to hagena gemyþan*). The word is probably preserved in 'The Mythe' at Tewkesbury, the name of the point of land at the junction of the Severn and the Avon. It is questionable if it meant merely the mouth of a river, as it is said to do in Bosworth-Toller.

The word is almost invariably found in the dative plural. It is probably a neuter *ja*-stem corresponding to the OHG. *gimundi*[1], OS. *gimūthi*, and the nom. sing., if it occurred, would therefore be written *gemyþe*. In one instance, however, it is used as a fem. sing. (*CD*. iv. 157[10] *into ðere gemyðe*), so that it may have possibly been feminine in OE.

34. **coccebyle**, 43. **coogebyll**. Cf. *CS*. ii. 490[14]: *of dyrnan grafan to weg cocce; thonne of weg cocce to Godan þearruce; CS*. ii. 169[8] *æt scite cocce*. Cf. also *coccinge pol* (*CS*. iii.·634[23]); *to cocggan hylle* (*CS*. ii. 354[25]); *coggan beam* (*Ib*. iii. 478[13]); *coc rodæ* (*Ib*. iii. 157[18]); *cogan mere* (*Ib*. iii. 309[13]). Possibly Upper *Cock*, near Stockland, Bristol, co. Somerset, and *Cockercombe*, near Asholt, in the same county, may be connected with this unexplained word. Cockbury near Bishop's Cleeve, co. Gloucester, occurs as *coccan burh* (*CS*. i. 342[1]). *Cock* is not uncommon as the first part of local names, generally on or near hills. Some of the above may be from personal names, but the first three are certainly not so derived.

37. **hlandgemære.** For *land-*. Cf. 34, *beanhlande* for *-lande*, l. 40 *hlangan.*

Wylman forda. This is, no doubt, the *wilman ford* mentioned in the boundaries of *Wilmanlehtun* (*CS*. iii. 125[27], 126[18]), or Wormleighton[2], which adjoins Ladbrooke and Radbourn. In this case the boundaries proceed in the opposite direction to those in our charter: *of ðæn hlawe to þære sealt stræt, 7 æfter stræte to wilman forda*. This ford was on the *wylman broc*, according to line 39 of our charter. It is not impossible that *Will's* Pasture, formerly an extra-parochial place, but now in the modern parish of Radbourn, may derive its name from *wylman ford* or *broc*, as part of the glebe of Wormleighton is in Will's Pasture.

38. **sealtstret.** This is, no doubt, the 'salt-street' mentioned in the boundaries of Wormleighton (see preceding note), and is probably the road from Banbury to Southam. Salt-streets are mentioned at Evenlode, in *CS*. iii. 529[28], *CD*. vi. 215[14], 216[14], at Broadway, in *CS*. iii. 590[15], at Wolverton, in *CD*. iii. 160[13], 206[26], at Bredicot, in *CD*. iii. 263[32]. All these are in Worcestershire, and the salt-street at Bisceopesdun was, no doubt, in the same

---

[1] Also to the ON. *minni, mynne* (<*munþjo-*). Mr. H. Bradley has drawn our attention to the existence of this ON. *minni* in the name of the Yorkshire village of Armin, at the confluence of the rivers Ayre and Ouse. It was still written *Ayermynne* in the fourteenth century.

[2] Kemble, Joseph Stevenson, and Birch have failed to identify *Wilmanleahtun*, which is also mentioned in *CD*. vi. 174[2]. Dugdale, *Warwickshire*, p. 514, identifies Wormleighton with the *Wimerestone, Wimenestone*, of DB., and states that it occurs as *Wilmelathtune* [read *Wilmelachtune*] in the twelfth century, and as *Wylmelechtune* in 13 Edward I. It is called *Wilmeleghton* in 1316; *Cal. of Close Rolls*, 9 Ed. II, pp. 318, 319, 325, 337.

county (*CD*. iii. 367⁴). Salt Way is the name of the road between Droitwich and the Icknield Way.

39. hreodbroc. This seems clearly to be equivalent to *hreodburna*, and is therefore no doubt, the stream flowing between Upper and Lower Radbourn.

43. wætergefeal 'a waterfall.' Neither this word nor the uncompounded *gefeall* is recorded in the dictionaries. We have, however, met with the latter in *Wulfstan*, ed. Napier, 186³ *tungla gefeall* 'the falling of stars,' an expression which also occurs in the Vercelli MS., foll. 10ᵇ and 115ᵇ. Cook, *Glossary to the Old Northumbrian Gospels*, has *gefǣll* (with umlaut) 'fall, ruin.' In *gefeall*, *gefǣll* we probably have an old *os-*, *es-* stem (cf. Sievers, §§ 267 and 288, and *PBB*. ix. 254). On the absence of the inflexional *e* (-*gefeal* instead of -*gefealle*), cf. *PBB*. ix. 252.

44. stanhemeford. The *Stānhām* here recorded has vanished from the map. The second part of the name *heme* is a word that occurs frequently in the charters, although it finds no place in the dictionaries. Sweet, *Oldest English Texts*, p. 597, gives the nom. as *hǣm*, but it must be noted that the word seems only to occur in the plural (generally the genitive *hǣma*). (*Stān*)-*hǣme* (this would be the nominative plural) is, no doubt, a plural *i*-stem like *Engle*, *Norðhymbre*, *Mierce*; it denotes 'the inhabitants of (*Stān*)*hām*,' just as *Mierce* means 'the people of the *mearc*.' Similar formations occur in the other Germanic dialects: e.g. ON. *Sygnir*, *Vestfyldir*, 'the people of *Sogn*, *Vestfold*' (cf. Kluge, *Nominale Stammbildungslehre*, § 5). In Sweet's *O.E.T.* we have *Liofshema mearc*, *Modingahema mearc*, *Wichǣma* (-*hema*) *mearc*, and *Biohhahema mearc* (charter 29, *CS*. ii. 114), referring to Lewisham, Mottingham, Wickham Breux, and Beckenham, co. Kent. See also *CD*. iii. 227. In a later charter (*CS*. iii. 610) three of these boundaries are described as *Wíchammes gemǣru*, *Beohhahammes gemǣru*, and *Modingahammes gemǣru*. The word occurs in the following names, most of which still exist as -*ham* or *hampton*[1]: *Æschǣma* (*CD*. iv. 70 ²⁶); *Bealdanhema*, *Bealddunheama* (*CD*. iv. 124 ¹⁹; 134 ²⁶); *Brochematune* (DB. i. 43 a, col. 1); *Buchǣmatun* (*CD*. iii. 327 ⁷; *Burhhǣma*, *Burham* (*CD*. iii. 283³, ⁴⁹); *Bydenhǣma* (*CS*. iii. 52⁹); *Cethǣma* (*CD*. iii. 283², ³); *Cinghǣma* (*CS*. iii. 228⁸⁵); *Crohhǣma* (*CS*. iii. 341²⁰); *Dichǣmatun* (*CD*. iv. 98²); *Dodhǣma pull* (*CS*. i. 326²⁰): *Easthǣma* (*CS*. iii. 240³); *Hinhǣma* (*CD*. iv. 70²², ²³); *Incghǣma* (*CS*. ii. 167¹⁷); *Middelhǣma* (*CD*. iii. 211²³); *Micghǣma* (*CD*. iii. 193¹², 196¹⁴); *Monninghǣma dic* (*CD*. iii. 206²⁵); *Niwanhǣma* (*CD*. iv. 124²¹, 134²⁶); *Neoðere-hǣma* (*CD*. iv. 70¹⁹); *Orhǣma* (*CS*. iii. 52¹⁰); *Polhǣmatun*, *Polhamatun*, &c. (*CS*. ii. 492¹; iii. 164⁸; *CD*. iii. 203²⁶; iv. 48²⁰, ³³); *Segchǣma* (*CD*. iv. 70²⁵); *Stifingehǣme* (*CS*. iii. 392¹⁷);

[1] We omit the word *gemære* or *mearc*, one of which generally follows this word.

CHARTER VIII.

Stochæma land (*CS.* iii. 85⁶); *Swæchæme* (*CD.* iii. 263²³); *þornhæma dic* (*CS.* ii. 343¹⁶); *Uppinghæma* (*CS.* iii. 650¹⁵, ¹⁷). The word is, no doubt, equivalent to *hǣminga*, which is sometimes used.

46. **munificentiᶒ singrapha.** The dating clause is modelled upon that of King Edgar: *scripta est huius donationis singrapha, his testibus consentientibus quorum inferius nomina caraxantur*[1] (*CS.* iii. 454²², 506¹⁶, 508²⁹, 518⁶). Cf. also the variants at pp. 473²⁹, 309³⁵. Edgar also uses an expanded form of this clause, with the substitution of *munificentiae* or *priuilegii* for *donationis* (*CS.* iii. 258²⁹, 463²⁵, 590¹⁹, 595³¹). This latter form is also used by Cnut (*CD.* iv. 5²⁹; cf. 36¹²). The word *syngrapha* is frequently used as a more pretentious term than *charta*. The same clause as in the present charter is given word for word in Eadwig's charter to Abingdon (*CS.* iii. 255¹⁶). This charter has many phrases agreeing with those of the present one, and it seems to have been remodelled upon a charter of Æðelred's. The same phraseology from *huius* to *caraxantur* occurs in a charter of Æðelred's (*CD.* iii. 179²⁹), and portions of it are met with very frequently in this monarch's dating clauses.

48. **Britanniᶒ ... roboraui.** A similar phrase occurs in the attestation clauses of Eadred and Eadwig: *hoc donum agie crucis taumate confirmaui* or *roboraui* (*CS.* iii. 68³⁵, 129³⁷), and, with the insertion of *tripudians*, in 97¹⁰, 118²⁹, 131²². This is not, however, Eadred's usual attestation. In a few of Edgar's charters the clause *Britanniae Anglorum monarchus hoc taumate agiae crucis roboraui* (*CS.* iii. 259¹, 289¹⁶, 291³, 310³, 590²³, 595³⁶, 656¹) is used. It occurs with the omission of *Britanniae* (*Ib.* 431¹⁹), and with the simple title of *Anglorum Basileus* (325²⁹). The attestation at 616³⁰ stands alone amongst Edgar's charters. *Tauma* is frequently used in the charters of this period in the same sense as above. King Æðelbald, in his charter to Abingdon, A.D. 726–737 (*CS.* i. 224³¹), attests as follows: *Æðelbaldus, Brittanniae Anglorum monarchus, praeformatas propinquorum sed et regum donationes hoc signo firmauit*. This must be borrowed from a charter of Æðelred's.

50. **eiusdem regis beniuolentiam.** The same phrase is used by Archbishop Odo in 959 (*CS.* iii. 255²²), but this charter seems to have been remodelled upon one of Æðelred's. Archbishop Dunstan uses the phrase occasionally, with a different verb (*CS.* iii. 289¹², 291⁵, 310⁵, 590²⁵, 595³⁸).

52. **primas ... taumate confirmaui.** There are few instances prior to the reign of Æðelred of the use of varying synonyms for *episcopus* and the diversity of the bishops' confirmatory phrases. The great majority of the charters from Eadred to Edgar, and even in Æðelred's time, are much simpler in their phraseo-

---

[1] This clause, with the substitution of *munificentiae* for *donationis*, is used by Cnut (*CD.* iv. 2³¹). King Eadred speaks of a charter as *nostrae munificentiae singrafa* (*CS.* iii. 67³¹).

logy in this particular. Exceptions may be found at *CS.* iii. 66, 255, 259, 289, 291, 310, 325, 590, 596, 621. Some of these charters beget strong suspicions of later origin [1].

54. **tropheum.** The words *trophaeum agiae crucis* are used in attestation clauses in *CS.* iii. 50[31], 247[14], 306[4], 419[15], 435[17], 440[18], 446[30], 454[31], 466[26] (wrongly copied *caumate*), 504[24], 506[23], 509[1], 511[20], 580[41], and *trophaeum sanctae crucis* at 111[27], 160[6]. Most of these are charters of Edgar. The words also occur in Æðelstan's time.

58. **testudinem sanctae crucis.** This phrase is used in charters of Eadred, Eadwig, and Edgar in *CS.* iii. 17[17], 27[16], 30[27], 47[22], 53[10], 73[17], 85[34], 106[24], 127[36], 153[11], 307[31], 627[24]. Most of the subscriptions are those of bishops of Winchester.

60. **catascopus.** Used in bishops' subscriptions at *CS.* iii. 259[15], 291[17], 310[17], 596[11], 656[13]. *Speculator*, the Latin equivalent of κατάσκοπος, is used in *CS.* iii. 148[1], 174[21], 259[17], 596[15], and *superspeculator* in *CD.* iii. 240[31].

63. **depinxi.** This phrase *hoc eulogium manu propria apicibus depinxi* is used in Eadwig's charter to Abingdon (*CS.* iii. 255[35]), referred to in the note to line 46. With the omission of *apicibus*, the phrase occasionally occurs in Edgar's charters (*CS.* iii. 259[16], 289[25], 291[17], 310[17]). *Depingere* is used in subscriptions of this period in *CS.* iii. 33[20], 35[11], 45[14], 346[33], 385[22], 596[4], 627[32]. It, of course, merely means 'sign' or 'witness.'

68. **Æþelweard dux.** This is probably Ealdorman Æþelweard, 'Patricius Consul Fabius Quaestor Ethelwerdus,' as he delights to call himself in his chronicle, which terminates with the death of King Edgar in 975. There are so many Æðelweards about this period that it is difficult to distinguish one from another. Charters are witnessed by Æðelweard *minister* from 956 to 996 and in 1002 and 1005 (*CD.* vi. 144[32]; iii. 345[29]). Two *ministri* of the name witness in 959 (*CS.* iii. 256[17, 28], 260[10, 18]), in 964 (*Ib.* 394[38], 395[4], 397[18, 26]), in 965 (428[18, 20], 429[16, 23], 430[17, 23]), in 966 (455[13, 5]), in 968 (503[7, 13], 505[13, 5], 507[3, 10], 509[26, 17], 511[32, 39]), in 969 (522[23, 20]), in 970 (546[13, 19]), in 972 (598[21, 19]), in 974 (625[5, 10], 635[4, 19]), in 975 (647[4, 5]), in 977, 978 (*CD.* iv. 159[10, 13]; vi. 106[22, 25], 110[18, 21]). In 972 three appear (*CS.* iii. 591[24, 36]). Some of these signatures, no doubt, are those of the subsequent Ealdorman. One of these *ministri* had a brother Ælfwerd (*CS.* iii. 622[10]), who witnesses in 974. There is probably another Æðelweard [2], the *minister* or *miles* of Bishop Oswald of Worcester (*CS.* 484[6], 527[29]; *CD.* iii. 207[23], 244[4]). The great Ealdorman Æðelwine, 'Dei Amicus,' who died in 992, had a son

---

[1] Archbishop Dunstan (*CS.* iii. 393[3]) is once made to call himself *policrates*.
[2] This Æðelweard can scarcely be the Ealdorman, although his heir (his son?) bore the same name as the Ealdorman's son—viz. Æðelmær (see page 87 above).

CHARTER VIII. 119

named Æðelweard[1]. Then there is Æðelweard, the grandson of Ealdorman Æðelweard, who was slain by Cnut's order in 1017 (Chron.), and Æðelweard, the son-in-law of Æðelmær (see above, page 79, note to line 128). But these three Æðelweards probably do not enter our field of view until the beginning of the eleventh century. There may, however, be confusion with Æðelweard, the king's high-reeve (of Hampshire?)[2], who was slain in 1001 (Chron. A), since *hēah-gerēfa* is frequently rendered *dux*[3]. An Æðelweard signs, without description, between the *duces* and the *ministri* in Edgar's charter to Winchester (*CS*. iii. 397[26]) which is dated 922 (for 972?). He is described as *dux* in a charter dated 967, but this is obviously a mistake for 973[4] (*CS*. iii. 480[27]). He signs as *dux* after Brihtnoð, as in the preceding charter, in 975 (*CS*. iii. 645[23], 652[2]). The signature occurs once in 977 (*CD*. iii. 159[11]), and in 979 (*Ib*. iii. 171[12]), and after that date fairly regularly until 998, the date of our present charter. These signatures, there can be little doubt, belong to the *dux* of the present charter, and there is every reason to believe that he is the chronicler and the friend of Ælfric, the great prose-writer. Mr. Robertson (*Hist. Essays*, p. 184) suggests that the title *Patricius Consul* and *Patricius*, which Æðelweard uses in his chronicle, may have been applied to the senior Ealdorman, the one who signs first of all the *duces*. If this suggestion could be proved, there would remain no doubt as to the identity of the chronicler with the witness to the present charter[5]. There is certainly no other *dux* Æðelweard whose claims to be identified with the historian will bear examination. The identity of the historian and the Ealdorman whose signatures disappear after 998 is accepted by Freeman, Robertson, Green, and Hunt. Ealdorman Æðelweard appears to have negotiated the treaty whereby the Northmen, the victors of Maldon, were bought off in 991, as the Chronicle records that peace was bought at the instance of Archbishop Sigeric, and the treaty with

---

[1] Slain at Assandun in 1016 (Chron. C, D, E).
[2] This is, no doubt, the Æðelweard who is addressed, together with Ealdorman Ælfric (see note to line 69), Wulmær, *and ealle þa þegenas on Hamtunscire*, by the King, *circ.* 984 (*CD*. iii. 203[8]). He was evidently subordinate to Ælfric.
[3] Thus the three *hēah-gerēfan* of Chron. D, E, *an*. 778, are called *duces* in Simeon of Durham (ed. Hynde, p. 25). Upon *hēah-gerēfa*, see Freeman, *English Historical Review*, ii. 780, Robertson, *Hist. Essays*, p. 179.
[4] It is dated in the thirteenth year of King Edgar, who became king of Mercia in 958 and of England in 959, and it is witnessed by Archbishop Oswald (972–992), Bishops Sideman (973–977), and Cyneweard (973–975).
[5] It is noteworthy that Florence, *an*. 912, calls Æðelred, the great Ealdorman of Mercia, Ælfred's son-in-law, *dux et patricius, dominus et subregulus Merciorum*. But Æðelweard never wielded anything like the power of Æðelred of Mercia, and the *consul* is applied to Ealdorman Ælfgar (see above, page 86, note 2) in 930 (= 950?) and 961 (*CS*. ii. 348[10]; iii. 301[22]), and, at the last reference, to Byrhtferð, who both sign at the end of the *duces*.

(King) Olaf, Justin (ON. *Josteinn*), and Guðmund, son of Stegitain, was concluded by Sigeric, Æðelweard, and Ealdorman Ælfric [1]. Florence of Worcester (991) records that Justin and Guthmund, son of Steitan, were the leaders of the Danish army with whom Brihtnoð fought at Maldon [2]. The treaty can scarcely belong to 994, as the peace with Olaf in that year was made through the instrumentality of Ealdorman Æðelweard and Bishop Ælfeah (Chron. C, D, E). This Æðelweard cannot well be the high-reeve mentioned above, although the events occurred in Hampshire, his district. The Æðelweard *Occidentalium Prouinciarum Dux* of 997 (*CD*. iii. 304 [1]) must be the witness of this charter, and not the high-reeve. He was thus Ealdorman of part (or the whole?) of Wessex, and such a position would fitly be held by the historian, who records his descent from King Æðelred I, brother of Alfred the Great. For Æðelweard's possible relationship with Brihtnoð, see pages 87, 88, and for his son's son-in-law Æðelweard see page 79, note to line 128. The charter of Æðelmær, his son (see above, pages 87, 88), in *CD*. iii. 224, is spurious or wrongly dated, as it makes Æðelweard die before 987. Æðelmær, it may be noted, is called the king's kinsman in 993 (*CD*. iii. 267 [26]; cf. vi. 174 [29]).

69. **Ælfric dux.** Ælfhere, Ealdorman of Mercia (see above, page 84, note to line 36), died in 983, and was succeeded by Ælfric (Chron. C, D, E), his son (Florence of Worcester). An Ælfric *dux* witnesses a charter [3] dating between 975 and 978 (*CD*. iv. 108 [24]), which is also attested by a *minister* of this name. This *dux* is probably Ælfric, Ealdorman of Hampshire, who is described in 997 as *Wentanensium Prouinciarum dux* (*CD*. iii. 304 [2]). Freeman does not make out the identity of the Ealdorman of this name whose traitorous actions are so notorious. But Robertson (*Hist. Essays*, p. 182) seems to be right in maintaining that it is the Ealdorman of Hampshire who is the traitor. Ælfric of Mercia, called Ælfric Puer (*CD*. vi. 174 [3]), was outlawed in 985 (Chron. C, D, E), and Robertson maintains that no successor was appointed to his office. The charter of 999 in *CD*. iii. 312 seems to prove that his forfeiture was not reversed. This view is also supported by the fact that although two *duces* of this name subscribe in 983

---

[1] *Leges Ethelwerdi*, II (Schmid, *Gesetze der Angelsachsen*, p. 204). Concerning Ælfric, see the following note. Florence adds, in 991, the names of Æðelweard and Ælfric to the archbishop's as the advisers of this peace. This looks like an addition derived from the text of the treaty. See, however, page 144 below, note 1.

[2] Their names are also given (from Florence?) in the *Historia Eliensis*, p. 81.

[3] If this charter is to be trusted, it would seem that Ælfric was Ealdorman before 982, the date of Æðelmær's death, who, Mr. Robertson alleges, was his predecessor. But there is a grant of land at Wiley, co. Wilts, to a *minister* Ælfric in 977 (*CD*. iii. 158 [3]), and this *minister* is, no doubt, the same person as the Ealdorman, whose connexion with Wiltshire is well established.

and 984 (*CD.* vi. 113 [16], [19], 115 [8], 116 [26], 118 [24]; iii. 202 [31], [39]), only one subscribes after that date. Ælfhere's son is described as *comes* and *dux Merciorum* in 984 and 985 (*CD.* iii. 207 [16], 216 [27]). The charter of 989 (*CD.* iii. 246 [1]), granted with the licence of Ælfric *dux Merciorum*, seems to have the date copied wrongly. Robertson is, however, wrong in identifying Ælfric, brother of Eadwine, (who became abbot of Abingdon in 985, Chron. B, the Abingdon MS.), with Ælfric of Mercia. In this chronicle the exile of Ælfric (of Mercia) and the appointment of Eadwine are mentioned together, but the exile comes first. The Lambeth MS. of Florence, which formerly belonged to Abingdon, substitutes for the translation of the 985 annal : *Erat tunc maior domus* [1] *regiae Ælfricus quidam praepotens, fratrem habens Edwinum institutione monachum ; hic apud regem pretio exegit, ut frater eius Abbendoniae abbas praeficeretur, quod et factum est.* The Abingdon *Historia Monasterii*, p. 357, copies this passage, altering *Ælfricus* to *Edricus*, calling him *filius ducis Merciorum*, and adding that he was shortly afterwards exiled. The additional matter is clearly derived from the entries in the Chronicle for 983 and 985, and is, we hold, of no value against the silence of the Lambeth MS. [2] In Æðelred's charter of 993, wherein he renounces this sale of the abbacy, this *dux Ælfric* is spoken of as still living [3], and a *dux Ælfric* is one of the witnesses (*CD.* iii. 264; *BM. Facs.* iii. pl. 36; *Hist. Abendond.*, i. 358). This mention of *dux Ælfricus, qui adhuc superstes est*, cannot be meant for the exile of 985. Mr. Robertson urges with justice that the connexion of the traitorous Ælfric with the central provinces of Wessex is established by the entry in the Chronicle in 1003, where he leads and betrays the *fyrd* of Wiltshire and Hampshire. The Ealdorman of Mercia would not lead the *fyrd* of these West-Saxon shires. Mr. Hunt says it is uncertain whether the Ealdorman Ælfric, who fell at Assandun in 1016 (Chron.), was the traitor; but as there is no notice of any other Ealdorman of this name, we may infer that it was he. The signatures of Ælfric *dux* appear regularly until 999, and afterwards from 1001 to 1009, in 1012, 1013, 1014, and 1016. Of the missing year 1015 we possess no charters, but the 1016 signature is in about the position in which Ælfric's signatures occur.

70. **Ælfelm dux.** Signs from 993 to 1006 [4]. In 997 he is called *Norðan-*

---

[1] The words *maior domus* are proof that this passage was written after the Conquest.

[2] Robertson does not quote the Abingdon History as his authority for identifying Eadwine's brother with Ælfric of Mercia. He, however, states that 'Eadwine is omitted from the list of Abbots in the Book of Abingdon,' which is not compatible with the above quotation.

[3] Kemble, who stars this charter, which is obviously authentic, has obscured this point by unfortunately replacing the illegible letters at 266 [13] with [*abbati*]*s Ælfrici* instead of [*duci*]*s*, although *dux praefatus Ælfric* is mentioned at 267 [10]. The illegible word is recorded as *ducis* in the copy in the Abingdon History.

[4] The signature at *CD.* iii. 251 [3], ascribed by Kemble to 990, seems to belong to 1005, which

humbrensium Prouinciarum dux (*CD.* iii. 304³). Freeman, *N. C.*, i. 660, identifies him with the *minister* who signs in 985 [1], but this is rendered doubtful by the signatures of the *dux* and a *minister* of the same name in 995 (*CD.* iii. 284 [7], [16]). This Ealdorman was murdered in 1006 (Chron.); according to Florence of Worcester, by Eadric Streona at Shrewsbury. He was the father of Ælfgifu, of Hampton, the wife or concubine of Cnut, and mother of Harald Harefoot (Chron. E) and of Swain, King of Norway (Flor. Wig., *an.* 1035). His wife was Wulfrun (*Ibid.*) probably the foundress of the college of Wolverhampton (*Wulfrūnehamtun*; *Monasticon*, vi. 1443).

72. **Ordulf minister.** Signs from 980 to 1006. As he is described by Æðelred as his *auunculus* (*CD.* iii. 182 [10], 267 [26]), he was the brother of Ælfþryð, the wife of King Edgar (see above, pages 84, 85, note to lines 36, 41), and therefore the son of Ealdorman Ordgar, who died in 971 (Flor. Wig.). Ordulf is described by Florence, *an.* 997, as *Domnaniae primas*, which probably means *hēah-gerēfa*. He founded Tavistock Abbey (*CD.* iii. 182).

73. **Æþelmær minister.** Probably the son of Ealdorman Æðelweard (see above, note to line 68). He is described as *consanguineus* of the king in 993 (*CD.* iii. 267 [26]; cf. vi. 174 [29]), and is probably the Ealdorman Æðelmær who submitted to Swain with the western thanes in 1013 (Chron.). See page 87 above.

74. **Wulfheah minister.** Signs from 986 to 1005. He was blinded in 1006 (Chron.). According to Florence of Worcester he and Ufegeat, who was blinded at the same time, were the sons of Ealdorman Ælfhelm (see note to line 70).

75. **Wulfgeat minister.** Signs from 986 to 1005 [2]. He was deprived of his possessions in 1006 (Chron.), according to Florence for unjust judgements (cf., however, *CD.* vi. 170). Florence calls him *filius Leovecae*, which, no doubt, represents the masc. name *Lēofeca*, and says that he was the king's special favourite. For the political aspects of his forfeiture, see Freeman, *N. C.*, i. 657.

IX.

This is one of the two parts of the original indented will. It is printed in Madox, *Formulare Anglicanum*, 1702, p. 421, '*ex autogr. in arch. S. Petri Westm.*' Madox's text is a very accurate copy of the present counterpart, in which the punctuation is faithfully reproduced. It is printed in Kemble, *CD.* vi. 138, and in Thorpe, *Diplomatarium Anglicum*, p. 541. Both refer to Madox and to

is probably meant by the complex date given in the charter. Freeman, *N. C.* i. 660, says the signature is doubtful.

[1] He also signs in 982 (*CD.* iii. 188 [5]).
[2] It is, presumably, another Wulfgeat who signs prior to 978.

'Autog. in arch. S. Petri Westm.' The latter reference seems to be intended for Madox's authority, and not to mean that the original was at Westminster when Kemble and Thorpe wrote. The endorsement of the present counterpart shows that it came into Peter Le Neve's possession in 1727. The agreement of the endorsements with those given by Madox makes it fairly certain that this is the Westminster part of the indenture. Moreover, the endorsements read like monastic notes.

Although this will has been printed thrice, its chief interest has not, we believe, been pointed out. It is the will of Leofwine, son of Wulfstan, an Essex landowner, and it is dated nearly seven years later than the battle of Maldon. Now one of the heroes of this battle, the man who guarded the bridge, and who seemingly struck the first blow, was Wulfstan the son of Ceola.

> Hēt þā hæleða hlēo healdan þā bricge
> wigan wīgheardne, se wæs hāten Wulfstān
> cāfne mid his cynne, þæt wæs Cēolan sunu,
> þe ðone forman man mid his francan ofscēat,
> þe þær baldlīcost on þā bricge stōp.
> Þǣr stōdon mid Wulfstāne, wigan unforhte,
> Ælfere and Maccus, mōdige twēgen;
> þā noldon æt þām forda flēam gewyrcan,
> ac hī fæstlīce wið ðā fȳnd weredon
> þā hwīle þe hī wǣpna wealdan mōston.—*Song of Maldon*, 74 *sqq.*

The last line seems to imply that the 'bitter bridgewards' fell fighting at their posts. In lines 152 sqq. Wulfmær the young, Wulfstan's ungrown son, distinguishes himself at Brihtnoð's side. It is highly probable that the testator was the son of the Wulfstan of the song, and the brother of Wulfmær, because Brihtnoð's force must have consisted principally of the local levies, and the testator's possessions were close to Maldon. It was probably this local connexion of Wulfstan's that caused Brihtnoð to select him to guard the bridge[1].

Translation:—'This is the will of Leofwine, son of Wulfstan. That then is first, that I give into Westminster, to Christ and to St. Peter, for the sake of my soul, all the things that Christ will help me to on the estate at Kelvedon and at Mearcyncg seollan, in wood and in field. And I give from Purleigh into (at?) Notley, to God's servants, half a hide of land on the east side of the street, for the sake of my soul. And to my paternal aunt, Leofwaru, the chief building in Purleigh, and all that belongs to me there. And if Eadwold, her son, live longer than she, let him succeed thereto. But if she live longer,

---

[1] It is possible that the testator was the father of Wulfric, son of Leofwine, who fell in the great battle in East Anglia in 1010. There is little reason for holding with Freeman, *N. C.* i. 347, 671, that Wulfric, son of Leofwine, was the great Mercian noble Wulfric.

and God will it, let her give it to whomsoever obeys her best amongst the kindred of us both. And I give to my lord, Bishop Wulfstan, the land at Barling. This was done in the year 998 from our Lord's birth,' &c.

4. **Cynlaue dyne.** This is evidently Kelvedon, in Witham Hundred, co. Essex, and not Kelvedon Hatch, in Ongar Hundred, in the same county. The former is eight miles north-east of Maldon. In Domesday (ii. 14) the abbey of Westminster is returned as having five hides in *Chelleuedana* (ch=k), in Witham Hundred, and in the spurious charter of Edward the Confessor (*circa* 1100?), five hides in *Kinleuedene* are confirmed to the abbey (*Chart. Antiq.*, CC. No. I.; *CD.* iv. 177 [26])[1]. The church of Kelvedon was appropriated to the abbey in 1331 (*Calendar of Patent Rolls*, p. 180). Domesday (ii. 14 b) records that *Keluenduna*, or Kelvedon Hatch, in the Hundred of Ongar, was given to Westminster by Ailric (=Æðelric) after his return from the *navale prelium contra Willelmum regem*, and *Kilewendun* is confirmed in the aforesaid charter of Edward the Confessor as the gift of Ægelric (=Æðelric). In the *Inquisitiones Nonarum*, A.D. 1341, Kelvedon is entered as *Kellevedene* (p. 323), and Kelvedon Hatch is called *Kelwedone* (p. 315). It is probably the latter that occurs as *Chaluedene, Chaluedon* (ch=k) in the Pipe Rolls, 11, 12, 13, 14, and 15 Henry II. In 967 King Edgar granted land in *Cealua dun* to Archbishop Dunstan (*CS.* iii. 474), by whom it was evidently bestowed upon Westminster. The endorsements of the charter are *Kelweduncæ, Chelewedune,* and *Keleuedone*. These may mean either Kelvedon or Kelvedon Hatch, but the form in the charter is not reconcileable with the *Cynlaue dyn* of this will, so that the gift probably relates to Kelvedon Hatch. The form *Cealua*[2] appears to stand for *Cealfa,* the late form of the genit. plural of *cealf* ' calf.'

Mearcyncg seollan. This name is not mentioned in the Westminster charters cited in the previous notes, so that it is perhaps included in Kelvedon. Markshall (*Mercheshala,* DB. ii. 53 b), some four miles north of Kelvedon, can only be identified with *Mearcyng seollan* by assuming that *Mearcyng* is the equivalent of *Mearces,* and that *seollan* represents the dat. pl. of *sele* ' hall,' and that there is an interchange between *sele* and *heall* (or *heale*) in the name. The first assumption presents no difficulty, but the second is insuperable.

5. **of Purlea into Hnutlea.** This is a curious expression. Unless it means

---

[1] The abbey also receives confirmation of lands in *Kenleuedene, Ræine,* and *Lacedune,* which Guðmund had granted to it. In Domesday, i. 52 b, Hugh de Montfort is the tenant of Guðmund's lands in *Chellevadana, Lachentuna,* and *Raines,* that is Kelvedon, in the Hundred of Witham, and Latchingdon and Rayne.

[2] Sanders and Birch identify *Cealua dun* with Chaldon, co. Surrey, but Chaldon (*Cealfa dun, CD.* iv. 152[23]; *CS.* i. 64[21], iii. 470[19]) was the property of Chertsey Abbey.

that *Purlea* is an appurtenant to Hnutlea, it seems to prove that there was a religious establishment at the latter place[1]. But of this we have no record. There is a Purleigh, three miles south of Maldon, and *Hnutlea* is, apparently, Notley (White and Black Notley), about ten miles north of Maldon and about five miles west of Kelvedon. Neither of these belonged to Westminster at the time of Domesday. Notley is called *Nutlea* in Domesday (ii. 26, 55 a, 59 b, 84, 92 b, 94 a). If the meaning is that Purlea is a member of Hnutlea, and is not the modern Purleigh, then the reference to the 'east side of the street' would have some point, as it would mean the Roman road to Braintree.

7. **heafod-botl.** Evidently the OE. equivalent for the 'chief messuage' of later times. Cf. *CS*. iii. 630[8]: *ic gean hire þæs heauod-botles æt Gyrstlingaþorpe, 7 ealra þara æhta þe þæron standað, mid mete and mid mannum;* *CD*. iii. 294[16]: *dælon hi þæt heafodbotl him betweonan swa rihte swa hi rihtlicost magon.*

9. **hand,** denoting the person inheriting. Cf. *CS*. ii. 179[20],[23]: *þæt hit gange on þa nyhstan hand . . . þe ic syllan mot, swa wifhanda swa wæpned handa.*

gehyre. Cf. *CS*. ii. 367[3]: *Ic an þæs landes æt Denforda ofer minne dæg Æþelstane 7 Cynestane, gif hie me oþ þæt on ryht gehieraþ, 7 ic an þæs landes æt Butermere ofer minne dæg Byrhtsige twegea hida, 7 Ceolstanes sunum anes, gif hie me oð þæt on ryht gehieraþ, 7 ic cwepe on wordum be Æscmere on minum geongum magum swelce me betst gehieraþ.* Also *CD*. iv. 269[8]: *and Ælfric min hirdprest, and Ælric mine cnihtes ðæt lond at Lalleford ðe me best heren willen.*

10. **Wulfstane bisceope.** Wulfstan, bishop of London, consecrated in 996.

11. **æt Bærlingum.** Kemble identifies this with Birling, co. Kent, but it is obviously Barling in Essex, about twelve miles south-east of Maldon. At the time of Domesday (DB. ii. 13 b, 23 b) it was the property of the Canons of St. Paul's and of the bishop of Bayeux.

X.

This will, printed from the original, is now published for the first time, and is a valuable addition to this class of OE. records.

There were two bishops of Crediton named Ælfwold. The first was consecrated in 953 and died in 972, and the second was consecrated in 988 and subscribes until 1008. His successor Eadnoð subscribes in 1012, so that his death occurred between 1008 and 1012. This will is that of the second Alfwold, because he bequeaths land at Sandford (line 2), and King Æðelred in 997 granted

---

[1] *Into* is used with words of granting to signify the place upon which the grant is bestowed. Cf. *CS*. iii. 601 *passim*, 602 *passim*.

two hides of land there to him (*OS. Facs.* part iii, Ashburnham, No. 35). This charter is not in *CD.* or in Thorpe's *Diplomatarium.*

Translation:—This is the will of Alfwold, bishop. That is that he gives the land at Sandford to the monastery at Crediton for his soul-shot, with meat and with men as it stands, except penal slaves. And one hide thereof he gives to Godric, and one plough-team of oxen. And to his lord he gives four horses, two saddled and two unsaddled, and four shields and four spears and two helmets and two coats of mail, and the fifty mancuses of gold that Ælfnoð at Woodleigh owes him, and a ship sixty-four oared; it is quite complete, save alone[1] that he would have fully equipped it in a fitting manner for his lord, had God granted it. And to Ordulf two books, Hrabanus and a martyrology. And to the Æþeling forty mancuses of gold and the wild 'worf' on the land at Ashburn, and two tents. And to Alfwold, monk, twenty mancuses of gold and one horse and one tent. And to Byrhtmær, priest, twenty mancuses of gold and one horse. And to his three kinsmen, Eadwold and Æþelnoð and Grimkytel, to each of them twenty mancuses of gold, and to each of them one horse. And to Wulfgar, his kinsman, two wall-hangings and two seat-covers and three coats of mail. And to Godric, his brother-in-law, two coats of mail. And to Eadwine, mass-priest, five mancuses of gold and his cope. And to Leofsige, mass-priest, the man whom he had formerly granted him, whose name is Wunstan. And to Kenwold a helm and a coat of mail. And to Boia one horse. And to Mælpatrik five mancuses of gold. And to Leofwine Polga five mancuses of gold. And to Ælfgar, the scribe, one pound of pennies. He (Alfwold) had lent it to Tun and his brothers and sisters. Let them pay him (Ælfgar)[1]. And to Eadgyfu, his sister, one 'strichrægl' and one dorsal and one seat-cover. And to Ælflæd, 'offestre,' five mancuses of pennies. And to Spila three mancuses of gold and sixty pennies. And to Leofwine Polga and Mælpatrik and Byrhsige, to each of the three of them one horse. And to each retainer his steed, which he had lent him. And to all his household servants five pounds for distribution, to each according to what his due proportion might be. And to Crediton three service books: a mass-book, and a benedictional, and an Epistle-book, and one mass-vestment. And in each episcopal estate freedom to every man that is a penal slave, or whom he bought with his money. And to Wilton a chalice and paten of 120 mancuses of gold, less three mancuses. And to the chamber-attendants his bed-gear. And of this are to witness: Wulfgar, Ælfgar's son, and Godric of Crediton, and Eadwine, mass-priest, and Alfwold, monk, and Byrhtmær, priest.

3. **mid mete and mid mannum.** This alliterative phrase is of frequent occurrence in the bequests of land. The *mete* refers, no doubt, to the live-stock

[1] See note to line 20.

CHARTER X.

and to the corn in the barns, the *mannum* to the serfs. Cf. *ealswa hit stænt mid mæte 7 mid mannum* (*CS*. iii. 602 [32], 603 [15], [20] ; *CD*. vi. 148 [14]) ; *ealra þara æhta þe þæron standað, mid mete and mid mannum* (*CS*. iii. 630 [9]) ; *mid mete and mid mannum, and mid eallre tylðe swa ðærto getilod byð* (*CD*. iii. 294 [7]) ; *mid mete and mid mannum and mid eallre tilðe* (*Ib. saepe*) ; *swa gewered swa hit stande mid mete and mid mannum and mid ælcum þingan* (*CD*. iii. 181 [24]) ; *habban ðone bryce . . . ge on mete, ge on mannum, ge on yrfe, ge on ælcon þingon* (*CD*. vi. 149 [9]).

butan witeþeowum mannum. The *witeþeowe men* are excepted from the grant because the bishop directs (line 28) that they shall be freed on all the episcopal estates. *Witeþeow* is here an adjective as in Ine's Laws, cap. 24 and 54 § 2 ; Æthelst. ii, Pr. § 1 (Schmid, p. 130). Cf. also note to line 28.

4. **hiwscype**, 'hide of land.' Like *familia* in Medieval Latin, the OE. *hiwscipe*, which ordinarily meant 'family, household,' could be used to denote a measure of land, a hide. Cf. *OE. Beda*, ed. Miller, p. 332 : *þá onfeng heo anes heowscipes* (v. l. *hiwscipes*) *stowe* = 'accepit locum unius familiae.' Cf. also Schmid, p. 610, s. v. *híd*. Similarly *hiwisc* could mean either 'family' or 'hide of land ;' in the latter sense it is used in *Beda*, ed. Miller, p. 456, *tyn hiwisca landes . . . þritiges hiwisca* ; and in *CS*. ii. 69, 241 ; iii. 133, 139 ; *CD*. iv. 274 ; Schmid, p. 396, § 7.

an sylhðe oxna, 'a team of oxen.' Note the change of construction from the genitive, the case properly governed by *geann*, to the accusative : *sylhðe* (a neuter *ja*-stem) here standing in the accusative. Throughout the whole document the scribe hesitates between the two cases. The word *syhlðe* is not recorded in the dictionaries ; in Bosworth-Toller only *gesylhð* 'a plough' is given on the authority of Somner (Somner, by the way, has the correct form *gesylhðe*). An instance of the word occurs in a Worcester charter in *CS*. iii. 653 [16] (*II. gesylhðe oxna*). A similar formation is found in MHG. *pfluogide* 'a pair of plough-oxen' ; cf. also OHG. *juhhidi* 'team of oxen,' which has the same suffix (Kluge, *Nominale Stammbildungslehre*, § 70).

5. Alfwold's heriot corresponds almost exactly to that fixed in Cnut's laws for a king's thegn (cf. Schmid, p. 308 : *feower hors, twa gesadelode 7 twa ungesadelode, 7 twa swurd, 7 feower spera 7 swa feala scylda, 7 helm 7 byrnan, 7 fiftig mancus goldes*), except that, in addition, he leaves the king his ship. The heriot of Wulfric, founder of Burton Abbey (*CD*. vi. 147 [3]), is mentioned in his will as being : *twa hund mancessa goldes and twa seolforhilted sweord and feower hors, twa gesadelod and twa ungesadelode, and ða wæpna ða ðærto gebyriað*. That of the king's thegn, Ælfhelm (*CS*. iii. 629 [26]), is : *an hund mancosa goldes 7 twa swurd 7 feowur scyldas 7 feower speru 7 feower hors, twa gerædode, twa ungerædode*. Byrhtric similarly leaves to the king, amongst other things, *feower hors, twa*

gerædede, 7 twa sweord gefetelsode (*CS.* iii. 373 ¹³). For further instances of heriots, cf. Kemble, *Saxons in England*, ii. 99.

7. **æt Wudeleage.** Probably Woodleigh, South Devon.

8. **scegð** (from the Old Norse *skeið*) clearly denoted a vessel of considerable size, not a small, light boat, as is generally assumed. The one here mentioned has sixty-four oars. Alfred's 'long ships' had sixty oars and upwards (Chron. A.D. 897). Cf. also Chronicle, A.D. 1008, MS. F, *unam magnam nauem, quæ Anglice nominatur scegþ*. In Wright-Wülker, 181 ¹⁶, 289 ¹³, it glosses *trieris*. In 165 ⁴⁰ *scapha uel trieris = litel scip oððe sceigð*, the *litel scip* probably glosses *scapha*, and *sceigð* glosses *trieris*. The word used by Florence of Worcester, in describing the assessment of 1008, is *unam trierem*¹. The ON. *skeið* is applied to the very large ships of Olaf Tryggvason in the 'Passing of the Ships' before the battle of Svoldr (*Fagrskinna*, c. 76; *Flateyjarbók*, i. 477). In *CS.* iii. 630 ²⁵ Ælfhelm bequeaths his *scæð* to the abbots and monks of Ramsey, and another well-known instance of the bequest of ships is in the will of Archbishop Ælfric (*CD.* iii. 351), who leaves his best ship, with the sailing-gear thereto, to the king, another vessel to the people of Kent, and a third to Wiltshire (cf. Freeman, *N. C.* i. 662). A *ðinsig stægðman* is mentioned in Hickes, *Diss. Epist.*, pp. 2, 3. Kemble (*CD.* iv. 54 ²⁴), in reprinting Hickes, has substituted *Winsig scægðman*. Cf. Wright-Wülker, 111 ²⁶, *pirata = wicing oððe scegðman*.

lxtiiiǣre, 'sixty-four-oared,' is an adjective (*ja*-stem) formed from *ār* 'an oar,' like *seofonwintre*, &c., from *winter*.

hanon. One would expect this to denote some part or fitting of the ship which the bishop had not had time to supply, and which, therefore, was wanting. The word *hān*, fem., which occurs in the charters (*CS.* ii. 458 ¹⁴, 481 ¹⁶, &c.) and appears to denote a 'stone' (NE. *hone*), is, on account of its meaning, out of the question. A possible explanation is that we have here a Scandinavian loanword, viz. ONorse *hār* 'a thole-pin,' which occurs in MS. C ² of the Chronicle, A.D. 1040, *æt hā* 'for each thole-pin,' hence 'for each man.' As regards the form, we should have to assume that the word was declined in English as a weak substantive, in which case *hānon* (= *hānum*) would be quite parallel to *tānum* from *tā* 'a toe' (cf. Sievers, *Angelsächs. Gram.* § 278, Anm. 2). But were 'thole-pins' of sufficient importance to deserve special mention? Another possibility is that *hānon* is miswritten for *hāron* (n for p) = *āron*, from *ār* 'an oar'; but as our document seems to be the original will, the confusion between p and n, natural enough in a copy, is difficult to account for ³.

---

¹ Freeman's censure of Florence for thus translating *scegð* (*N. C.* i. 663) is therefore unfounded.
² MSS. D and E have *hamelan* = ON. *hamla* 'oar-loop.'
³ The same objection stands in the way of the assumption that *hanon* is miswritten for

CHARTER X.

It is also conceivable that *hanon* stands (with an inorganic *h*) for *ānon* = *ānum ; būtan þām ānum* meaning 'except alone that, with the one exception that.' Taking it in this way, we must assign to *gearwian* some technical sense; perhaps it refers to the moveable fittings or decorations of the boat and could be translated by 'fully equip,' or some such expression: 'it is quite complete, save alone that he would have fully equipped it in a fitting manner for his lord, had God granted it.'

10. **Hrabanum and martyrlogium.** A *martyrlogium* is mentioned amongst the books given by Bishop Leofric to Exeter, as are also *mæsseboc, bletsungboc, pistelboc* (cf. the present text, line 27), *CD.* iv. 275. A *masseboc* is bequeathed by Bishop Theodred (cf. *CS.* iii. 269 [22], 211 [9]).

The *Hrabanum* here mentioned is some work or works[1] of Hrabanus Maurus (born about 776, died 856), a pupil of Alcuin's, then teacher and, later, abbot at Fulda, whose school owed its greatness to him, and finally, from 847, archbishop of Mainz. He was the author of a considerable number of Latin works, chiefly of a didactic character, grammatical treatises, commentaries to St. Matthew and other portions of the Bible, homilies, &c. (cf. Ebert, *Allgemeine Geschichte der Literatur des Mittelalters im Abendlande*, ii. 120 ff.).

11. **þæra wildra worfa.** In the OE. laws (Schmid, p. 362) we find a mention of *wilde weorf*, and the word also occurs in the glosses, Wright-Wülker, 357 [3], *asellus = weorf*, and in the *Zeitschrift für deutsches Alterthum*, ix. 458, *subiugales = weorf, nyte*[*nu*], *hors.* Cf. also Wright-Wülker, 119 [39], *iumentum = hwyorif*[2], for which, however, Sievers (*Anglia*, xiii. 319) suggests as a possible emendation *hryðr, orf.* In the OE. metrical translation of the *Psalms* (Paris MS.), *Ps.* 112, verse 6, *of woruftorde* renders *de stercore.* In the above-mentioned passage from the Laws, Lye translates *wilde weorf* by *onager*, being led to this, no doubt, by the gloss *weorf = asellus.* But although asses were not unknown in England at this time[3], they can scarcely have been frequent enough for any one to have had numbers of broken and unbroken ones to bequeath, and 'wild asses' are, of course, quite out of the question. All that we are justified in inferring from the glosses cited is that *weorf* denoted some kind of beast of burden; probably it was a general name for animals thus used, applicable alike to horses, oxen, &c. In the Laws the most probable interpretation of *wilde weorf* seems to

hunon (from *hūn* = ON. *hūnn*, 'knob at the top of the mast-head'; cf. Wright-Wülker 288 [15] *hunþyrlu = carceria*) or for *h*[:::] *ānon*, 'except the h[:::] alone' (the scribe having run two words together).

[1] Possibly an English version. Cf. Giraldus Cambrensis, *Descriptio Cambriae*, II. c. 6 (*Opera*, vi. 177).
[2] Printed *hryorif* in Wright-Wülker. The MS. has *hwyorif*; cf. E. M. Thompson, *Brit. Archaeol. Assoc.*, 1885, p. 148, and Kluge, *Anglia*, viii. p. 450.
[3] *Assan dun* is explained by Florence of Worcester as *Mons Asini.*

be an untamed or unbroken horse or colt[1]. It cannot have meant 'wild cattle,' as the value there assigned to it is higher than that of an ox or cow[2]. In the case of Alfwold's will, it is perhaps most reasonable to put the same interpretation on the expression as in the Laws. 'Wild horses' are elsewhere mentioned in wills: thus in *CD*. vi. 133[32] Wynflæd bequeaths *hyre dæl ðera wildera horsa ðe mid Eadmere synt*, and Wulfric leaves to the Abbey at Burton *an hundred wildra horsa and .xvi. tame hencgestas* (Earle, *L.C.*, 221[20]; *CD*. vi. 149[26]).

æt Æscburnan. One of the Devonshire hamlets of Ash (?). No place of this name occurs in DB. of Devonshire or in the Exon Domesday.

getelda. Bishop Ælfric, 996–1006, similarly bequeaths his *geteld* to St. Albans (*CD*. iii. 352[14]). Ælfric Modercop, 1037, bequeaths to Bishop Ælfric his tent and his bedclothes, the best that he had with him when journeying (*mine teld and min bedreaf þat ic best havede ut on mi fare mid me*; *CD*. iv. 302[23]; Thorpe, *Dipl.*, p. 566). Wynflæd, *cir.* 995 (*CD*. vi. 132[12]), bequeaths her red tent (*hyre reade geteld*).

15. **wahryft,** 'wall-hanging, curtain.' Cf. *CS*. iii. 366[18] (given by Aðelwold to Peterborough); *CD*. iv. 275[20] (given by Leofric to Exeter); *CD*. vi. 133[30] (bequeathed by Wynflæd). Cf. *heallwahrift*, *CD*. iii. 294[24]; vi. 133[16]; *bedwahrift*, *CD*. vi. 133[9].

setlhrægl, 'seat-covering.' See below, line 22, *sethrægl*. Cf. *CS*. iii. 366[18] (given by Aðelwold to Peterborough); *CD*. iv. 275[20] (given by Leofric to Exeter); iv. 107 (bequeathed by Wulfgyð); vi. 133[16] (bequeathed by Wynflæd).

17. **kæppan,** 'hood,' or 'cope.' Cf. *CS*. iii. 366[14] (given by Aðelwold to Peterborough).

18. **Wunstan.** Cf. *CD*. iv. 312[28], where the same form occurs in a manumission. It also appears as a moneyer's name on coins of Edgar, Æðelred II, and Cnut.

19. **Boian.** This name occurs several times, from the tenth century onwards (*CS*. iii. 369[18], [27] *Boia on Myletune*; 536[3] *Edwig Boga*; *CD*. iv. 261[19] *Boia ðe ealde*; Earle, *L. C.*, 273[20] *Boia decanus*; 274[2,3,6,8] *Boia*; *Hist. Eliensis*, pp. 138, 139, *Boga de Hemminggeford*; Calendar in Cot. Titus D. XXVII, fo. 3, Jan. 3, *Obitus fratris nostri Boia*[3]). It is of frequent occurrence as the name of moneyers, in the forms *Boga, Boia, Bogea, Boge, Boie, Boiga*, on coins from Ælfred

---

[1] This is much the same explanation as that given by Thorpe, to which, with an entire disregard of the High German sound-shifting, he adds the suggestion that it is connected with the German *werfen*.

[2] A horse is there valued at 30 shillings, a mare at 20, a *wilde weorf* at 12 shillings, whilst an ox is valued at only 30 pence, a cow at 24 pence, a swine at 8 pence, &c.

[3] Printed by Hampson, *Medii Ævi Kalendarium*, p. 435; Birch, *Transactions of the Royal Society of Literature*, xi. 496.

CHARTER X.

to Edward the Confessor[1]. The name *Maneboia* (*CS*. iii. 371[23]) also occurs. Förstemann, *Altdeutsches Namenbuch*, p. 273, has a few examples of the Old Saxon name *Boio* (cf. Müllenhoff, *Alterthumskunde*, ii. 120), and the same form is found as an East Gothic name (cf. Wrede, *Sprache der Ostgoten*, p. 111). If these latter, as seems probable, are identical with our *Boia*, Kögel's derivation of them from **Bawja-* (cf. *A fd A*, xviii. 56, and *Z fd A*, xxxvii. 273) is impossible[2].

Leofwine Polgan. This second name (?) is rare. An *Ælfhelm Polga* is mentioned in the spurious charter of Dunstan (*CS*. iii. 265[7]) as a benefactor to Westminster[3] (printed *Wolga* in *CD*. vi. 17[3]). The same (?) Ælfhelm [*cui*] *cognomentum erat Polga* is mentioned in the *Hist. Eliensis*, p. 120, and as *Ælfelmus cognomento Polcan* at p. 127, and as *Æthelmus Polga* at p. 144. Förstemann, p. 211, has a single example of the name *Polgan*.

20. **Ælfgare writere . . . gehealdon hi hine.** 'To Ælfgar, the scribe, one pound of pennies. He (Alfwold) had lent it to Tun and his brothers and sisters. Let them pay him (Ælfgar).' One would have expected a *hit* after *lænde*. It seems less likely that the scribe has accidentally omitted the relative particle *þe*[4], in which case the rendering would have to run: 'which he had lent to Tun' (cf. lines 7 and 18). *Gehealdan* seems to be used here in the sense of 'to have a person paid, to pay him, to satisfy him,' and is construed with the accusative. Cf. *CD*. iii. 363[26] *And gehealde man of minan golde Ælfric . . . and Godwine . . . æt swa myclan swa Eadmund min broðor wat ðæt ic heom mid rihte to geuldende ah*, 'And let them satisfy Ælfric and Godwine from my gold for as much as Edmund, my brother, knows that I ought justly to pay them.' Cf. also *OE*. *Boethius*, chap. 13. *ðeah þu hie swa smealice todæle swa dust, ne miht þu þeah ealle men emlice mid geheakdan*, 'Though thou divide them (i. e. thy riches) as finely as dust, yet thou canst not therewith satisfy all men equally.'

Tune. This is evidently the dat. sing. of the masc. name *Tūn*, a short form of a name beginning with this stem.

22. **hricghrægl,** 'a dorsal.' Cf. *CD*. iii. 294[3] (bequeathed by Wulfwaru); *CD*. iv. 275[20] (given by Leofric to Exeter).

offestran. This seems not to be a proper name, the ending *-estran* pointing rather to some kind of female occupation. Is this the same *-festran* as in the Laws of Ine, c. 63, *his cild-festran*, 'and his children's nurse'?

---

[1] B. E. Hildebrand, *Anglosachs. Mynt*, 1881; and *Brit. Mus. Cat., Anglo-Saxon Series*.

[2] The wide diffusion of this name amongst the Germans suggests that the Scotch or Pictish prince Boia (Rhys, *Celtic Britain*[2], p. 255), bore a Germanic name, if, indeed, he was not of that race.

[3] This is the Ælfhelm whose will is printed in *CS*. iii. 629.

[4] An intentional omission of the relative, as in later usage, cannot be assumed here, as it was avoided in OE. (cf. *Anglia*, xiii. 348; xiv. 122).

S 2

23. **Spilan.** We have been unable to find another instance of this name, and only in one case have we met with it as part of a compound name. *Spilemon* was one of the abbey tenants in Worcester in the latter part of the eleventh century (Heming's *Chartular.*, ed. Hearne, i. 291). The name of the Winchester moneyer (in the reigns of Æthelred II, Cnut, Harold I, and Edward Conf.), given in the *Brit. Mus. Cat.* and by Hildebrand as *Swileman*, should probably be read *Spileman*. This is, no doubt, the origin of the surname *Spelman*. Förstemann, p. 117, has the names *Spiligern, Spilihard, Spilahard*, and *Spilinger, Spilinhard*.

24. **hiredmen.** Cf. Wulfwaru's bequest *eallum minum hired-wifmannum* (*CD.* iii. 295³).

25. **onrid**, 'that on which one rides, a steed, or mount.' The word also occurs in the twelfth century *History of the Holy Rood-tree* (ed. Napier, Early Eng. Text Soc. 1894, p. 18²⁰; cf. also note on p. 38), *Dauid . . . bead heom þ heo of heoræ anride lihtæn sceoldon*, 'David bade them alight from their steeds.' The word is not recorded in the dictionaries. Cf. *CS.* iii. 630²⁷: *ic gean . . . . minan geferan healues [þæs stodes] þe me mid ridað.* See also *CD.* iv. 289¹⁶,¹⁷.

27. **mæssereaf**, 'mass vestment.' Cf. *CS.* iii. 660²⁶; *CD.* iii. 294²; iv. 275¹⁶.

28. **bisceophâme.** This rare compound seems to mean 'bishop's village' or 'bishop's estate.' The only instances of its use that we have found occur in the will of Æðelflæd, the second queen of Edmund : *ic gean þes landes æt Hædham . . . into Paulus byrig æt Lundænæ to bisceop hamæ* (*CS.* iii. 601¹⁰), and in that of her sister Ælflæd, widow of Ealdorman Brihtnoð : *into Paules mynstre into Lundene þes landes æt Hedham to biscop hame* (*CS.* iii. 602²⁷). Ælflæd distinguishes between this land and the land given to the *hired* of St. Paul's, so that the former is clearly a gift to the bishop of London. Much Hadham, co. Hertford, is an ancient possession of the bishops of London. Cf. also *mynsterham*, *CS.* ii. 196¹⁷: *þone ofcræcan mon gedæle gind mynsterhamas to Godes ciricum.* Also Schmid, p. 70. This, however, is not quite parallel to the meaning of *bisceop-hâm*.

witeþeow. Almost every OE. will contains a clause liberating serfs, but the *witeþeowe men* are not always manumitted specifically. Archbishop Ælfric, who died in 1006, orders the release of *ælcne witefæstne man ðe on his tyman forgylt wære* (*CD.* iii. 352³⁰). Similarly Queen Ælfgifu, A.D. 1012, desires the king to free *on ælcum tunæ æl[c]ne witæþæownæ mann ðæ undær hiræ geðeowuð wæs* (*Ib.* 360⁶). And the Æðeling Æðelstan frees *ælcne witefæstne man ðe ic on sprece ahte* (*Ib.* 361¹⁶). It is noticeable that in these three instances the men released are those who had forfeited their freedom during the testator's time, whereas Bishop Alfwold makes no such restriction, liberating also the serfs bought by him. In like manner Bishop Ælfsige directs the release of *ælcne witeþeowne mannan þe on þam biscoprice sie* (*CS.* ii. 329¹⁴).

CHARTER XI.

29. **calic,** 'chalice.' Cf. CS. iii. 209[22]; 211[9] (bequeathed by Bishop Theodred); 366[13] (given by Aðelwold to Peterborough); 660[25] (mentioned in inventory of church goods at Sherburn, co. York); CD. iv. 275[15] (given by Leofric to Exeter).

disc, 'dish, plate, paten.' Cf. CS. iii. 660[26] (mentioned in list of church goods at Sherburn, co. York).

30. **beddreaf,** 'bedding, bedclothes.' Cf. CS. iii. 366[19]; CD. iii. 294[4]; vi. 132[23].

XI.

The text of this charter, which is here printed from the original, is given in CD. vi. 157 and in Matthew of Paris, *Chronica Maiora*, vi. 124 ('Additamenta'), from Cott. MS. Nero, D. I, fo. 149 b. The boundaries, which are now published for the first time, are not given in this MS., 'which was written at St. Albans, the greater portion being executed under Paris's directions, and with corrections in his hand' (Luard, preface to vol. vi, p. xi).

12. **æt Norðtune.** Norton, co. Hertford, 4½ miles north-east of Hitchin. It was held in demesne by the abbey at the time of Domesday (i. 135 b, col. 2).

13. **æt Rodanhangron.** This name has entirely disappeared. Chauncey, *Hertfordshire*, 1700, p. 82 b, identifies it with 'Rode Green, tho' it is no manor,' on the strength of the two entries in DB. Bawdwen has copied this identification into his translation of the Domesday Survey for Hertfordshire, 1812. By Rode Green Chauncey means the hamlet of Roe Green, in the parish of Sandon, in Odsey Hundred. But in DB. i. 140, col. 2, 142 b, *Rodehangre* or *Rodenehangre* is described as lying in Broadwater Hundred, and it is not given amongst the abbey lands. The Hertfordshire Hundreds are broken up into so many scattered portions that they are of less value in fixing localities than in other counties. It is evident from the present charter (line 12) that the land at Rodanhangra adjoined that at Norton, but it is curious that the respective boundaries have no points in common. From these boundaries we learn that Rodanhangra abutted upon a water known as the Broadwater. There is a hamlet of Broadwater in the parish of Knebworth, in Broadwater Hundred, which, no doubt, derives its name from the neighbouring stream, an affluent of the River Beane. But this stream does not come near to Norton, and therefore cannot be the Broadwater of this charter. Perhaps this latter is the sheet of water at Radwell Mill. In this case Rodanhangra must have lain within the present parish of Radwell, as the boundaries impinge upon the *stræt*, probably the Roman road from Biggleswade to Baldock. There is no stream of any size in this neighbourhood near the Icknield Way, which crosses the above-named road to Baldock. The name of *Rodanhangra* had evidently

disappeared prior to the thirteenth century, as Matthew of Paris does not identify it. Its disappearance seems to have happened at about the time of the first appearance of Baldock, a parish containing only 158 acres. Baldock might, apart from the absence of any 'broad-water,' thus represent this hide at Rodanhangra, but Baldock was not in the possession of the abbey at the time of its gift to the Knight Templars in the twelfth century, when it is first mentioned.

The word *hangra* has been explained by Kemble (*CD*. iii. p. xxix) as 'a meadow or grassplot, usually by the side of a road; the village green.' The only ground for this definition is the unscientific connexion of the word with the German *Anger*. From Kemble the definition has been taken by Bosworth-Toller and by Clarke Hall, *Student's Anglo-Saxon Dictionary*. The latter adds the definition 'slope,' derived from Earle, *Land Charters*, who also glosses the word as 'hanger,' without explaining what 'hanger' means. *Hangra* occurs frequently in the OE. charters, but none of the instances throws any light upon its meaning. An 'aspen-hangra' (*æsphangra*) occurs in *CS*. ii. 295^{35} and a *þornhangra* in *CS*. iii. 107^{21}. These show that the word was applied to woods. We have further evidence of this in Timberhanger, the name of a hill near Bromsgrove, co. Worcester (*Timbrehangre*, DB. i. 172 a, col. 2); the Hertfordshire *Haslehangra* (*Ib.* i. 134 b, col. 2); Oakhanger, cos. Berks, Hants; Hanger Wood, near Bilsington, Kent; Great and Little Hanger, woods near West Keynton, co. Wilts; Birchanger, near Porlock, co. Somerset. In local names the word survives in the name of Hanger Hill, which occurs near Ockham, Surrey; near Ealing, Middlesex; and near Caversfield, co. Oxford, &c. The form Hunger[1] Hill occurs near Holton, Somerset; near Condover, Salop; near Bicester, co. Oxford; at Nottingham; near Eakring, co. Nottingham; at Aylesby, co. Lincoln; near Kirk Hallam, co. Derby; and at North Duffield, co. York (*Cartul. S. Germani de Seleby*, ii. 13). There is a Hunger Down, on Romford Common, co. Essex. Cf. also Hungry Hill, near Aldershot, co. Hants. 'Hanger' is connected with hills in the case of Duncombe Hanger, near East Meon, co. Hants; Western Hanger, near Sellinge, co. Kent; and Hangers Down, near Ditcheridge, co. Wilts. The word is frequently to be met with on the Ordnance Maps. We may safely conclude, from the obvious connexion of 'hanger' with woods and hills, that the OE. *hangra* meant a wood growing on the side or sides of a hill-top. This is the meaning still borne by 'hanger' in Hampshire, according to Kelly's *Hampshire Directory*, 1885, p. 563. In W. D. Parish's *Dictionary of the Sussex Dialect*, 1875, p. 53, 'hanger' is defined as 'a hanging wood on a hill side,' and the same definition is

---

[1] *Hunger* is a dialectal development from OE. *hangra*. The representation of OE. *ang* (*ong*) by *ung*, as in the pronunciation of N.E. *among*, &c., is common in the dialects.

given in Parish and Shaw's *Dict. of the Kentish Dialect*, 1887. Cf. also Halliwell's *Dictionary of Archaic and Provincial words*. The *sadol-hongra* of *CS*. iii. 589 ¹⁴ may thus be explained as a wood on a hill-side resembling a saddle on a horse's back.

14. æt Oxangehæge. Oxhey, a hamlet in the parish of Watford, co. Hertford.

20. Leof[s]ino duce. The missing letter is here supplied from the St. Albans copy. Leofsige, Ealdorman of Essex (*CD*. iii. 304⁴), probably succeeded Brihtnoð. He signs as *dux* from 994 to 1001¹. He was banished in 1002 (Chron.) for the murder of Æfic, a high reeve (Chron.; *CD*. iii. 356).

41. Readan wylles heafod. This name is recorded in Radwell, a parish adjoining Norton on the east, on the River Ivel. The well referred to in the charter is evidently the source of the River Ivel, a spring on the south-eastern boundary of Norton parish, now known as Clerkenwell.

42. Wiligbyrig. Evidently the camp on *Willbury* Hill, south-west of Norton.

Stodfald dices. Stotfold, the adjoining parish, in Bedfordshire. The parish and county boundary runs along the road from Willbury Hill to Radwell Mill.

44. þære ea. The River Ivel at Radwell Mill.

46. æt bradan wætere. See note to line 13.

stræt. The Roman road crossing the Icknield Way at Baldock. The name of this road is preserved in Hare Street (*here-stræt*, see above, page 46, note to line 2) in the parishes of Ardeley and Cottered.

51. to Bæcces wyrðe. Batchworth, a hamlet of Rickmansworth, co. Hertford, adjoining Oxhey.

of Watforda. The ford that gives its name to Watford.

54. cyrstelmæle. Probably a cross marking the boundary of the Liberty of St. Albans.

55. þære defe. We have been unable to find another instance of the use of this word, which seems to be a common noun. It is not the name of a stream, since stream and river names do not occur in the boundaries with the demonstrative pronoun. Names that had no meaning to the English and that were, presumably, of Celtic origin are usually uninflected in the charters and are used without the demonstrative pronoun (Sievers, *Paul u. Braune's Beiträge*, ix. 251).

58. on colen : : : ge. Probably *on Colen[bryc]ge*, evidently a bridge over the River Colne near Watford.

¹ The charter in *CD*. iii. 348²⁰, 351¹¹, which is dated 1006, must belong to 1001 or 1002, as it is witnessed by Leofsige.

XII.

This charter is written in reddish-brown ink in a twelfth-century hand. It has no OE. characteristics, but, as it is entirely in Latin, these are not to be expected. Three other exemplars are in existence. Of these *fac-similes* are given in *OS. Facs.*, Part i, Canterbury Charters, Nos. 20, 21; Part iii, Stowe (Ashburnham) Charters, No. 40. In addition to these, there is an OE. version, of which a *fac-simile* is given in the Canterbury volume, No. 19. Nos. 19 and 20 are written in an OE. hand of the eleventh century, and may possibly be older than the Norman Conquest. The others (Nos. 21 and 40) are later. Extracts from the English grant are given in OE. in Chron. A (Winchester) under 1031 and in Latin and OE. in Chron. F (Canterbury) under 1029. The substance of the charter is given at the end of St. Matthew in the Gospel of Mæil Brith Mac Durnan at Lambeth (Westwood, *Palaeographia Sacra Pictoria*, p. 12); this is printed in *CD.* vi. 191. The Latin and OE. versions are printed in *CD.* iv. 21 from the Canterbury copies, and in Thorpe, *Diplomatarium*, p. 314, from the Canterbury and Stowe copies. A notice of the grant occurs in *Textus Roffensis*, ed. Hearne, p. 37.

Kemble has marked this charter as spurious, whilst Thorpe appears to consider it genuine. The principal objection to it, apart from the lateness of the copies, is that there is no exact parallel in OE. charters for the grant of such privileges and immunities. The reason of this is, no doubt, that such privileges in OE. times needed no other sanction than that of local usage. It is, therefore, difficult to resist the conclusion that this is a post-Conquest forgery or, at all events, an expansion of a simpler OE. charter, manufactured for the purpose of obtaining charter-evidence for the exercise of jurisdictions and privileges that were, probably, enjoyed by ancient custom. The charter is, however, a very skilful imitation of a genuine OE. one; so skilful, indeed, that we must conclude that it is founded upon a genuine charter of Cnut's. This supposititious original may have been a grant of the port of Sandwich, or may have been the vehicle of some entirely different donation. The language of the charter is free from the influence of Frankish *formulae*, by which the post-Conquest forgeries are usually betrayed, and the witnesses are such as might occur in a genuine charter of this date. Moreover, the thegns Æðelric and Godwine, who occur amongst the witnesses, were apparently Kentish landowners, and four other thegns, Ælfwine, Byrhtric, Sired, and Eadmær, were probably connected with the same county. These facts can only be explained by the theory that the charter is a copy of a genuine document of Cnut's, or that its *formulae*, witnesses, and date have been

CHARTER XII.

copied from a lost charter of this king's. The interesting OE. account of the deputation of monks from Christ Church, Canterbury, to Harold Harefoot at Oxford (*CD.* iv. 56; *BM. Facs.*, iv. pl. 20), which resulted in a confirmation of their rights in Sandwich, makes no mention of a grant by Cnut, and seems to imply that their privileges were older.

1. **certis adstipulationibus.** It has been stated in our notes to the preceding charters that Cnut's charters use the *formulae* of his more immediate predecessors on the English throne. In the brief list of this monarch's charters there is none in which the proem of the present charter is used, but we should not therefore brand it as a forgery, since the proem is one that was used by his predecessors, and may hence have been employed by him. It occurs word for word down to the end of line 9 of our text in a Somersetshire charter of King Edmund (*CS.* ii. 497), and in a Wiltshire charter of Edward the Martyr (*CD.* iii. 157), preceded by the invocation *In nomine dei summi et altissimi*[1]. With the slight change of *quam ob causam* for *quapropter* in line 9, it also appears in an Abingdon charter of King Edmund (*CS.* ii. 513). The first section of the proem, from *certis* to *amemus*, line 4, is used in a Kentish charter of King Eadwig (*CS.* iii. 233). The proem of King Eadred, *subtilissima mentis certatione Deum, quem diligimus, intima mentis affectione timeamus et amemus* (*CS.* ii. 595; iii. 9) may be compared. Cf. also Edmund (*CS.* ii. 549), and Eadred (*CS.* ii. 597).

2. **ortationibus.** Read *hortationibus*, as in most of the above-cited instances.

10. **Anglorum ... basileus.** The stile here used does not occur in genuine OE. charters, but stiles quite as brief were occasionally used. The *ceterarumque adiacentium insularum* may be compared with Æðelred's *coregulus Britannicae et caeterarum insularum in circuitu adiacentium* (*CD.* iii. 323).

14. **Piperneasse ... Mearcesfleote.** The former of these is the modern *Pepper Ness*, which is the name given on the 6-inch Ordnance map to the point of the coast exactly to the east of Halfway House (on the road from Sandwich to Ramsgate), close to the estuary of the Stour. The name *Mearcesfleot* appears to have been lost; Chron. F. ann. 1029, substitutes *Nortmute* for it. In *CD.* vi. 191 it is called *Northuuicha*, no doubt a misreading of *Northmutha*[2]. It appears to be

[1] The proem also occurs in two sister-charters of Æðelstan's, dated 931, to Bath and Malmesbury respectively (*CS.* ii. 351, 355). These charters, which cannot be genuine in their present form, must be dated by the witnesses in 941, and hence would have to be ascribed to Edmund. This would involve the excision of the passages regarding Ælfred's perjury, death, and forfeiture. It may be noted that Æðelstan's Malmesbury charters of 937 (*CS.* ii. 423, 425), which appear to be genuine, do not include these passages, which are, however, inserted in the composite charter given by William of Malmesbury (*CS.* ii. 426), wherein these two charters are embodied. The Bath charter is probably founded upon a charter of Edmund's, A.D. 941 (*CS.* ii. 497), which is preserved in the Bath chartulary.

[2] This is from an eighteenth century copy of the entry in Mac Durnan's Gospel.

identical with the stream which flows into the Stour just outside the north-east corner of Sandwich, close to the point where the Stour leaves the town, which is now known as the 'North Stream.' From *Piperneasse* to *Mearcesfleot* therefore embraces the whole stretch of the river from Sandwich to the sea.

16. **quam longius ... potest securis ... proici.** Cf. *CS.* iii. 189 [20] *ealswa feor swa an man mæi mid anen bille gewurpen.* Cf. also the means of fixing the west boundary of Sawtrey Fen: *debet homo ad hoc electus super pedes, quo profundius poterit, intrare, et dum ultra ire nequiuerit, auirunatum [= remum] unum octo pedibus longum introrsus de deuerso lanceando propellere, et a loco, quo auirunatus ille transnatare desierit, spatium quadraginta pedum per cordam debet mensurari, ibique signum in aqua infigi* (Cott. chart. vii. 3, *circa* A.D. 1147; *Monasticon*, v. 522. Cf. *Cartul. Mon. de Rameseia*, i. 161). These methods of measuring are thoroughly Germanic. See Grimm, *Deutsche Rechtsalterthümer*, p. 55, where many similar instances are collected.

tapereax. There is no other mention of this weapon than in the versions of this charter and in the notices of it in Chronn. A. and F. ON. *tapar-øx* is supposed by Vigfusson to be borrowed from English, though the converse would seem more probable. Mr. Mayhew (*Notes and Queries*, 6th Series, viii. 143) has suggested that the word is adopted from the Russian *topor*, 'axe.'

27. **quod si alter,** &c. Similar condemnations of charters militating against the particular grant are met with occasionally in late charters. See Brunner, *Zur Rechtsgeschichte der römischen u. germanischen Urkunde*, Berlin, 1880, i. 181. In none of these instances, however, does the imposing *formula* here used occur. Yet its stile is decidedly like that of the tenth and eleventh century OE. charters, and is so different from that of the twelfth century forgeries that we are inclined to think that it rests upon, at all events, the basis of an OE. *formula*.

29. **siricum.** For *soricum*. This Romanic use of *sorex* in the sense of mouse might possibly occur before the Conquest.

39. **si ... aliquis,** &c. The anathema clause reads like a genuine OE. one. If not genuine, it is pieced together out of several set phrases that are met with in the anathemas of genuine charters. A somewhat similar anathema is used by Cnut (*CD.* iv. 19).

tumulo supercilio inflatus. Cf. Æðelred's *supercilio inflatus* (*CD.* iii. 196 [8]), and Edward's *typho turgentis supercilii inflatus* (*CD.* iv. 77 [81]).

42. **scripta est,** &c. The dating-clause appears to be a genuine OE. one, and, indeed, very similar clauses are used by Cnut.

45. **indeclinabiliter.** This word is used frequently in the attestations of King Eadred and his successors.

46. The bishops may all have attested in the year of this grant.

CHARTER XII.   139

uexillo sancto. The word *uexillum* is frequently used in subscriptions to genuine charters as a synonym of *signum*.

54. Godwine dux. This is the celebrated Earl Godwine, whose first signature as *dux* occurs in 1018 (*CD*. iv. 3 ³). He signs after Eglaf and Iric, the two next witnesses, upon three occasions (*CD*. iv. 3 ¹³, 6 ¹¹, 14 ³⁵), and before them as many times (*CD*. iv. 9 ¹³, 20 ²⁷, 27 ³¹). He precedes Iric in *CD*. vi. 179 ³⁷.

[Eg]laf dux. The second and greater Danish fleet that followed that of Thorkell to England in 1009 was, according to Florence of Worcester, under the leadership of *Hemingus* and *Eglafus*. Thorkell the Tall was the brother of Sigvaldi, the chief of the famous vikings or *condottieri* of Jōmsborg, and the Jomsvikinga Saga and other Norse sources enable us to identify *Hemingus* with Jarl Hemingr, Thorkell's brother, and his companion with Eilífr, son of Thorgils Sprakaleggr ¹ (Steenstrup, iii. 259). The equivalence of the OE. *Eglāf* and ON. *Eilīfr* seems to admit of no doubt, since *eg, æg, ege* are used in OE. to represent the sound of ON. *ei* (*Swegen* = *Sveinn*, *scægd* = *skeid*, &c.), and *lāf* is the OE. form of the Germanic name-stem **laiboz*, which occurs in ON. names, as *leifr, lǣfr*, or *lafr*, accordingly as it bears chief, secondary, or no accent ². According to Munch ³, it was shortened in Denmark and Norway to *lifr* in this particular name, now usually written *Ellev* in Norway ⁴. In the form *līfr* we have apparently a different ablaut-grade, or it may have arisen from association with the adj. *ei-līfr*, 'everlasting.' The name *Eilīfr* is a common one in the sagas, and seems to have entirely displaced the **Ei-leifr* or **Ei-lāfr* represented by the OE. *Eg-lāf* ⁵. Thus there seems to be no reason to doubt the identity of Florence's *Eglavus* with the *Eilīfr* of the sagas. He is probably the *Eglaf* of the present charter, since many of the Jomsvik chiefs remained in Cnut's service ⁶. As Earl Godwine married Gyða, the daughter of Thorgils Sprakaleggr (called *Spraclingus* by Florence, *an.* 1049), he was brother-in-law of Eilīfr as well as of Jarl Ulfr. This important relationship was unknown to Freeman, who states

---

¹ Munch, *N.F.H.* II. ii. 101, holds that this Thorgils, the ancestor of the younger Danish royal family, was the son of Styr-Bjǫrn of Jōmsborg and of Thyri, daughter of Harald Gormsson, King of Denmark, the father of our King Swain.

² Cf. Noreen, *Altnord. Grammatik*, § 57, 4 b and § 121, 1.

³ *Om Betydningen af vore nationale Navne* (*Samlede Afhandlinger*, iv. 133).

⁴ It is also spelt *Eiliv, Eilef, Elef, Ellef* (Ivar Aasen, *Norsk Navnebog*, Christiania, 1878, p. 13). See also O. Nielsen, *Olddanske Personnavne*, Copenhagen, 1883, p. 19.

⁵ To be carefully distinguished from the native OE. *Ecg-lāf*. The ON. **Ei-leifr* is recorded in the Rønninge runic inscription as *Ailaif* (Nielsen).

⁶ The Jōmsvīkinga Saga (*Fornmanna Sögur*, xi. p. 161; *Flateyjarbók*, i. p. 205) says that, after the death of King Swain (A.D. 1014), Eilífr became chief of the Varangians at Constantinople, and there fell in the end. This, however, must have happened ten years later, when Eglaf disappears from English history.

T 2

(*N.C.* i. 447) that Eglaf was, 'according to some accounts,' a brother of Earl Thorkell. This must arise from some confusion with Eglaf's companion Heming, who was Thorkell's brother, or from an erroneous identification of Thorgils Sprakaleggr, Eglaf's father, with Thorkell[1]. The Jōmsvíkinga Saga[2] (*Flateyjarbōk*, i. 203; *Fornmanna Sögur*, xi. 159) records that Swain established a body of housecarls or a standing army, the famous *Þingamanna-lið*[3], in England, and that Eilífr Þorgilsson commanded the body in London, and had sixty ships in the Thames. The other body, consisting of the men of sixty ships, was established at Slessvik, in the north of England[4], under the command of Jarl Hemingr, brother of Thorkell the Tall. This Slessvik has been identified by Suhm with the hamlet of Sloswick, in the parish of Worksop, co. Nottingham, and Munch (*N.F.H.* II. ii. 473) and Sir George Dasent (*Jest and Earnest*, i. 218) have tacitly accepted this identification. But, notwithstanding the similarity of the two names, it is very improbable that Sloswick was the northern quarters of the þingamenn, since it possesses no advantages for a military station, and has no access for ships[5]. As the southern station was at London, we should expect to find the other at or near York. The village of Hemingborough (*Hamiburg*, DB. i. 299 a, col. 2), on the Ouse, near Selby, co. York, may possibly derive its name from the commander of the þingamenn of Slessvik[6]. After Swain's death the English plotted to massacre the þingamenn in both stations by a stratagem,

---

[1] The two names are confused by the saga-writers, since *Fagrskinna*, p. 134, on one occasion speaks of this Thorgils as Thorkell. The father of Thorkell the Tall was Strutharaldr, jarl or king in either Skån or Sjælland (Munch, *N. F. H.* I. ii. pp. 100, 109).

[2] Or rather a separate *þáttr* inserted in the Flatey Book, since it does not appear in the Arna-Magnaean MSS. of the Jomsvíkinga Saga, No. 510, 4to (ed. Carl af Petersens, Lund, 1879), and No. 291, 4to (ed. Carl af Petersens, Copenhagen, 1882), or in the Stockholm codex, No. 7, 4to of this saga (ed. Gustaf Cederschiöld, Lund, 1875), or in Arngrim Jonsson's Latin translation of the saga.

[3] Munch, *N. F. H.* II. ii. p. 109; Steenstrup, iv. 131. Regarding the derivation of *þingamenn*, see Kaufmann, *PBB.* xvi. 209, note 1.

[4] This is also stated in the Saga of St. Olaf (*Fornmanna Sögur*, v. 154; cf. *Flateyjarbōk*, i. 205, ii. 22). The number of sixty ships is merely a round number (cf. the Latin use of *sexaginta* for an indefinite number, Johannes Schmidt, *Die Urheimat der Indogermanen*, Berlin, 1890, p. 41), and is the number usually given in the sagas in reference to fleets.

[5] It cannot be affirmed with certainty that Slessvik was within reach of ships, but London, the other station, certainly was, and the language of the saga, *annat þingamannalið var nordr í Slessvik; þar red firir Hemingr jall, brodir þorkels hafua: þar voru enn lx. skipa* (*Flatey.*, i. 203), seems to imply that the *þingamenn* retained their ships by them.

[6] Hemingborough is clearly the *Hemingaborg* of the skald Ottar the Black (*Knytlinga Saga*, *Fornm. Sögur*, xl. 189), which was captured by Cnut, as the Ouse (*Usa*) is mentioned. The editors of the *Corpus Poeticum Boreale*, ii. 156, have needlessly emended *Hemingaborg* to *Snotungaborg*, a purely supposititious form of the name of Nottingham (OE. *Snotungaham*).

for which Ulfkill Snillingr[1] is made responsible. Hemingr and all his men in Slessvik fell victims to the plot, but Eilífr, being warned by Þorðr[2], one of the þingamenn, who was informed of the plot by his mistress, escaped with three ships, and fled to Denmark. Steenstrup (iii. 279, note 2) refers this massacre to 1015. Although some of the statements in the sagas are in conflict with the higher authority of our own chroniclers, there yet remains a considerable number of events that harmonize so well with the English records that they cannot be set down as mere inventions, or ascribed to later borrowings from English sources. Distortions and anachronisms were inevitable in these traditions, which were entirely untrammelled by chronological data. We cannot, of course, here argue the question of the authenticity of the sagas, but we may point out, regarding the preceding episode, that Heming's name does not appear in English history after the assumed date of his death at Slessvik, whilst Eilífr, his fellow-commander of 1009, witnesses Cnut's charters as *dux*; that Heming's death at Slessvik would occur shortly before the defection of his brother, Thorkell the Tall, from the English service; that this murder supplies a much more satisfactory reason for Thorkell's defection than Freeman's suggestion (*N.C.* i. 356); that, as a double obligation to avenge Heming's death lay upon Thorkell, first as his brother, secondly as a member of the Jomsvik confederacy, the sagas are probably right in ascribing Ulfkell's death to Thorkell's vengeance ; and that they probably do not much exaggerate the authority which Thorkell enjoyed in the early years of Cnut's reign, especially as they record that Cnut was his foster-son[3]. We are, therefore, inclined to think that this account of the fate of the Jömsborg þingamenn in England is based upon real events. Eilífr, like most of the vikings of Jömsborg, adhered to Swain and Cnut[4], and he witnesses Cnut's charters between 1018 and 1024. In 1022 he wasted West Wales (Demetia, Dyfed). His name is given under this year in the *Annales Cambriae* as *Eilaf.* See Freeman, *N.C.* i. 447; Steenstrup, iii. 392. The *Brut y Tywyssogion* (*Red Book of Hergest*, ed. J. G. Evans, p. 266) record that *Eilaf* fled to Germany at Cnut's death. But as he ceases to sign in 1024, it is probable that he accompanied his brother, Jarl Ulf, when he was made viceroy of Denmark by Cnut in 1025 or 1026[5]. He may therefore be the Eglaf who is mentioned in the Peterborough

[1] Ulfcytel of East Anglia, slain at Assington in 1016.
[2] See below, note to line 55, page 148.
[3] There is also the singular coincidence that Þorðr, who warned Eilífr of the plot, is the name of a witness with Eilífr to this and other charters of Cnut. See note to line 55, page 148.
[4] For the political reasons for this adhesion, see Munch, *N. F. H.* II. ii. 108.
[5] The Abingdon Chronicle (C), under 1023 (an error for 1025 or 1026), says that Thorkell was made viceroy. Munch, p. 672, note 3, holds, from Norse evidence, that this is a mistake for Ulf.

(A) and Canterbury (F) MSS. of the Chronicle in 1025 with Ulf as the opponents of Cnut at the battle *æt ea þære halgan* (the river Helge-Aa, near Christianstad, Munch, p. 732, note 1), since Saxo Grammaticus says that Ulf was fighting against Cnut in this battle. In this, however, he is opposed by the sagas. See Freeman, *N.C.* i. 765. The battle is more fully discussed by Munch, p. 732 sqq. Both these writers suggest that Ulf and Eglaf of this annal were the sons of Jarl Rǫgnvald of Gøtland[1]. The entry in the Chronicle is very puzzling, as its date should be, according to the Norse authorities, 1027, it does not mention the real leaders King Olaf of Norway and King Anund of Sweden, and says that the Swedes were victorious, whereas Cnut won the sea-fight, although he was worsted in the fight on land. The Chronicle is also noteworthy for its agreement with Saxo against the Saga of St. Olaf. Munch (pp. 726–7) thinks that the annalist derived his information from Danish or Norwegian sources. Perhaps, as Munch suggests (p. 734, note), the Chronicle and Saxo refer to an earlier battle (in 1025?) in the same neighbourhood between Cnut and Anund. As St. Olaf did not participate in this supposititious earlier battle, it is naturally not mentioned in his saga. It is possible that Jarl Ulf and Eglaf were fighting against Cnut in 1025, and that Ulf had made peace with Cnut again before 1027. Eglaf probably went to Constantinople and became a captain in the Warangian guard after these events, as the Jōmsvīkinga Saga says that he did after the death of Swain (see above, page 139, note 6). Eglaf's name is written *Eglaf* in contemporary charters of 1017–23 and 1024 (*CD*. iv. 31 [23]; *OS. Facs.*, part ii, Ilchester, pl. 2; *BM. Facs.* iv. 15), and this is the usual form in other charters. It also appears in original charters as *Eghlaf* (*CD*. iv. 20 [29]; *BM. Facs.* iv. 16); *Egillaf* (*CD*. iv. 3 [12]; *OS. Facs.*, part ii, Exeter, pl. 9); and *Elaf* (*OS. Facs.*, part ii, Winchester College, pl. 4). In copies it also occurs as *Eilaf* (*CD*. iv. 6 [11], 9 [14]), *Ælaf* (*Ib*. 27 [32]), and *Aglaf*, for *Æglaf* (*CD*. vi. 180 [12] = *Hist. et Chartul. S. Petri Gloucestriae*, i. 9 [2]). The last reference connects him with Gloucester, so that he was perhaps Ealdorman of the Hwiccas or of Mercia before Leofric (see above, p. 112). The name is written *Æilaf, Æillaf,* and *Eilaf* in the twelfth century portions of the Durham *Liber Vitae* (18a, 23b, 47b).

55. **Iric dux.** Signs from 1018 to 1023 [2]. In the OE. version of this charter

[1] It may be objected to this suggestion that the sagas do not record that Rǫgnvald's sons were engaged in the battle, so that, if they were, they must have been minor leaders. As they had no connexion with England, it is improbable that the English annalist should elevate them to the position of chief leaders. On the other hand, Jarl Ulf and Eglaf were well known in England, and an Englishman of this period would most naturally connect these two names, if given without qualification, with them.

[2] His name also occurs as a witness to a charter in *CD*. vi. 190 (*OS. Facs.* iii., pl. 41), which is assigned to 1032 by Thorpe, *Diplom.* p. 324. This is the only possible date for other witnesses, but as Yric and Eglaf (see preceding note), who are both named, do not witness after 1024, it is evident that the charter, which is written in a later hand, is untrustworthy.

CHARTER XII. 143

the name is spelt *Yric*, which is evidently the correct form, as it is found in two contemporary charters of 1019 and 1021–3 (*OS. Facs.* ii., Winchester, pl. 4, not in *CD.*; *BM. Facs.* iv., pl. 16; *CD.* iv. 20 [26]). It occurs as *Yrric* in a contemporary charter of 1018 (*OS. Facs.* ii., Exeter, pl. 9; *CD.* iv. 3 [12])[1]. The form *Yric* is preserved in several later copies of lost charters of Cnut (*CD.* iv. 6 [10], 14 [35], 25 [23]; vi. 179 [37], 191 [2]). The late copies also spell the name *Yrik* (*CD.* iv. 27 [32]) and *Yrc* (9 [13]). The blundered form *Huc* (29 [17]) is an easily explained misreading of *Iric*, the long down stroke of the OE. r (ꞃ) and the *I* having been read as *H*. The Abingdon, Worcester, and Peterborough copies of the Chronicle call him *Yric* in 1016, whilst in the following year the first of these writes *Irce*, dat., the second *Eiric*, and the third *Yrice*, which also appears in the Canterbury version. An earlier bearer of the name, the Norwegian king of Northumbria, is called *Yric* in 952, 954, in the Worcester, Peterborough, and Canterbury versions. The Worcester MS. has *Yryc*, *Hyryc* in 948. Florence of Worcester writes *Yrcus* in 949, 950, and 1017, but *Egricus* in 1016. Simeon of Durham speaks of the Northumbrian king as *Eiricus* (ed. Hynde, pp. 65, 90). As the Northumbrian king and the witness to the present charter bear the name *Eirikr* in the Norse sagas, and as ON. *ei* is represented in OE. by *eg*, *ei*, it is evident that the name should appear in OE. as *Egric* or *Eiric*. But the authority of Florence and Simeon cannot outweigh that of the contemporary charters and the Chronicle, which prove that the first syllable of the name was not the ON. *ei*. Moreover, the Northumbrian king's name is given as *Eric* on the coins ascribed to him [2]. It is possible that Simeon's spelling of the name is the result of acquaintance with the Norse poems and tales from which the sagas were subsequently compiled, or of familiarity with the name *Eiric* [3]. If the first be the true explanation, it is evident that *Eirikr* must have usurped the place of the Norse name represented by *Yric* [4] within less than a century after the death of the witness of this charter. The only other English instances where the name agrees with the Norse form are found in the Worcester MS. of the Chronicle and in Florence of Worcester. Scandinavian influence cannot be assumed so readily in Worcester as in Durham, but, rash as the suggestion may seem, there is a possibility that the monks of

[1] The other Exeter charter of 1018 (pl. 10), in which the name is also written *Yric*, is in a somewhat later, probably post-Conquest, hand.
[2] *British Museum Catalogue of Anglo-Saxon Coins*, i. p. 237.
[3] The name occurs under this spelling in an early thirteenth century entry in the Durham *Liber Vitae*, p. 53, col 2.
[4] The name was probably *$\bar{Y}r\bar{\imath}kr$, not *$Yr\bar{\imath}kr$, since the former is metrically equivalent to *Eirikr*. It may be explained as a name derived from *rīkr* and *ȳr*, 'bow,' or *'ȳr*,' which would be the ON. form of the primitive-Norse name *WiwaR*, which occurs on the Tune runic inscription (cf. *Wiwila* on the Veblungsnæs inscription. Cf. also ONorthumbrian *-wiu* in *Oswiu*, &c. and Sievers, in *PBB*. xviii. 413).

NOTES.

Worcester had some acquaintance with the Scandinavian accounts of the history of the subject of this note. Yric is a prominent figure in the sagas relating to King Cnut's family and to the vikings of Jōmsborg (see preceding note). These sagas relate that Toki or Palna-Toki (= Toki son of Palni), the chief of Jōmsborg[1] and the foster-father of King Swain, had a son named Āki, the father of Vagn, whose life was spared by Yric in Norway. Steenstrup, *Normannerne*, ii. 227, note 4, has remarked upon the strange coincidence that an Aki son of Toki (both powerful royal *ministri*) sold an estate in Worcestershire to Ealdred, bishop of Worcester, 1046-1060 (*CD.* iv. 138), and that the bishop's gift thereof to the church of Worcester is witnessed by a *Wagen minister* (= ON. *Vagn*) and by an *Atsor minister* (= ON. *Qzurr*), which latter name occurs amongst the descendants of Vagn son of Aki[2]. The occurrence of these names renders it probable that a branch of the house of Palna-Toki was settled in Worcestershire in the eleventh century, and the monks of Worcester may have derived from this family information concerning the actors in the sagas of the Jōmsborg cycle. Florence of Worcester has in several instances information found in no other English writer that may well have reached him or the monks of Worcester from a Danish source[3]. This may have been Hakon, the son of the subject of this note, or his retainers, as he was Ealdorman of Worcestershire.

Whatever may be the explanation of the discrepancy between the OE. *Yric* and the ON. *Eirīkr*, it is certain that the *dux Iric* who witnesses this charter is the son of Jarl Hakon[4] of Norway, whose dramatic murder by his thrall has been

---

[1] Munch, *N.F.H.* I. ii. 72, note 2, 100, note 5, rejects the statement that Palna-Toki was the chief of Jōmsborg. Attention may be drawn to Munch's suggestion (73 note) that the Danish Ealdorman Pallig or Palling, the brother-in-law of King Swain, was a *Palni* (reading *Palling* as *Palnig*), a member of Palna-Toki's family, perhaps his son.

[2] Wagen is described in a (post-Conquest) Latin version of a deed of 1049-1052 as one of the *barones* of Earl Leofric, and Atsor is called *Asserus filius Tolrii* (= Toki?); *CD.* iv. 285; Matt. Paris, *Chron.* vi. 29 (Additamenta).

[3] Thus he records in 1049 that Jarl Ulf was the son of *Spraclingus* = Sprakaleggr, the Norse nickname of Thorgils, the father of Ulfr, Hemingr, and Eilifr (see preceding note); that the second Danish fleet of 1009 was commanded by *Hemingus* and *Eglafus*, the aforesaid Hemingr and Eilifr; the names of the father, mother, and sons (Thorkell and Hemming) of the wife of Hakon, the son of Yric, the witness of this charter (under 1029, 1044); the information regarding Hakon's exile in 1029; the name of the Dane *Thrum* who slew Archbishop Ælfheah (see below, note to line 55). Moreover, Florence is the only English writer who records the name of the battle of *Ringmere*, the *Hringmaraheiðr* of the sagas, and that the Danish leaders of 991 were Justin and Guthmund (see, however, page 120, note 1, above).

[4] It may be noted that, as Hakon was the son of Bergliót, daughter of Þórir þegiandi (= the Silent), jarl of Mœri, the elder brother of Hrolfr (Rollo), and was therefore second-cousin to Richard I of Normandy, Eirīkr was third-cousin of Richard II and of his sister Emma, the wife of King Æðelred and of King Cnut.

CHARTER XII.

rendered familiar to English readers by Longfellow's *Saga of King Olaf*. This son, who is called *Eirikr* in the sagas, is a well-known figure in the historical sagas, and might well stand as a type of the noblest of the Vikings. As Yric has not found a place in the *Dictionary of National Biography*, and as Freeman has failed to grasp his importance, little excuse is required for giving a brief sketch of his life. He has, of course, been fully dealt with by the great Norwegian historian Munch, and we shall therefore content ourselves with a general reference to his *Norske Folks Historie*, where the authorities are duly cited. Eirik's achievements were celebrated by seven skalds, fragments of whose poems are preserved in the sagas[1]. The chief were Eyiulfr Daðaskald, whose 'Banda-Drápa' relates to the early part of Eirik's life (Munch, *N.F.H.* i. ii. 484, note 2), and Þórðr Kolbeinsson, whose 'Belgskaga Drápa' apparently dealt with the middle portion of Eirik's life, and whose 'Eiríks Drápa' probably treated of his life in England, whither Þórðr accompanied him (*Ib.* 485, note 1). According to the *Fagrskinna*, the most trustworthy compilation of the Norwegian kings' sagas (*Ib.* 99), Eirik was the son of Jarl Hakon by a woman of lowly origin, and was born when his father was only fifteen years old, that is, in 952. But Munch (p. 61, note 4) holds that fifteen is a mistake for twenty-five, so that Eirik was born in 962. In this case he would be about the same age as Swain (born about 960, p. 73), and slightly older than his famous and brilliant rival, King Olaf Tryggvason (born in 963, pp. 20, 401). Eirik grew up with his foster-father, Þorleifr Spaki in Meldal, and is described as fair, strong, and tall. In his eleventh or twelfth year he attempted to occupy the position by his father's ship always assigned to Tíðendi-Skopti ('the teller of tidings'), the brother of Þóra, his father's wife, but he was obliged by his father to give way. This slight he avenged in the following year by attacking Skopti's ship and slaying him. After this, the first of his sea-fights, he fled to Denmark, probably to Swain (Munch, 64, 74), with whom he contracted a life-long friendship. He was made tributary king of Raumarike and Vingulmark in Norway by Swain's father, King Harald Gormsson. Here he received tidings of the expedition of the Jomsviking pirates against Norway, under the leadership of Sigvaldi and Thorkell the Tall (see preceding note). Although this expedition was probably instigated by the Danish king, his over-lord, Eirik made common cause with his father in withstanding the invasion, and the credit of the great victory in 986 at Hjǫrungavágr (now Lidvaag in Söndmöre, Munch, 115, note 1), one of the greatest sea-fights of the north, was mainly due to him. The sagas preserve circumstantial accounts of his achievements during the fight. The scene on land after the fight, when Eirik, to his father's annoyance, pardons the captured Vagn and the remnant of his men

[1] They are collected in Vigfusson and Powell's *Corpus Poeticum Boreale*, ii. 98 sqq.

who had not been executed, is one of the best-known incidents in the sagas. In 995, after his father's death and the conquest of Norway by Olaf Tryggvason, Eirik fled to Sweden, and went in the same year on a viking expedition in the Baltic. Every year of his exile he harried Garðariki (Russia), because Vladimir, its prince, was a friend of Olaf's. He married, in 996, Gyða, the daughter of King Swain (Munch, pp. 315, 410), thus cementing his friendship with that terrible monarch. The next important event in Eirik's life was the great sea-fight at Svoldr (near Greifswald), which ended with the defeat and death of Olaf Tryggvason (Sept. 9, 1000). Eirik was the main instrument in winning this victory, and consequently the great prize of Olaf's famous ship the 'Long Serpent' fell to him. The sagas preserve interesting details of the fighting, and record Eirik's two narrow escapes from the deadly arrows of the famous archer, Einarr Þambarskelfr, who afterwards became his brother-in-law and most trusted friend. Eirik is also a prominent figure in the dramatic scene on the shore before the fight, when he names the passing Norwegian ships to the King of Sweden and Swain, who are impatiently looking out for Olaf's celebrated ship. It is noteworthy that Eirik was advised in this fight by Thorkell the Tall, who was on his ship. It is related that Eirik, in the stress of the fight, vowed, like the Merowingian Chlodwig, to become a Christian if he won the victory, and that he substituted a crucifix for the image of Thor on his ship. His courtesy and consideration after the victory to Olaf's widow and the prisoners read like an episode from a romance of chivalry, and justify Munch's remark (p. 409) that there are few nobler characters than Eirik in the early history of Norway. After the fall of Olaf, Norway was divided amongst the confederated princes, and Eirik, as the most powerful of the Norwegian rulers, is generally regarded as Olaf's successor. He did not, however, assume the name of king, but, like his father, contented himself with the ancient title of the head of his race, Jarl of Hlaðir. Cnut, after his father's death in 1014, sent to Eirik, as a famous warrior and successful general, to help him in the conquest of England. Eirik resigned his rule in Norway to avoid quarrelling with his brother Swain, who was dissatisfied with the portion of Norway governed by him as a vassal of Sweden, and Eirik divided his share between his son Hakon and Swain. From this time (1015) Eirik disappears from Norwegian history (Munch, p. 480). He probably accompanied Cnut in his expedition against Uhtred of Northumberland, as Cnut made him earl of Northumbria in 1016 in Uhtred's place (Chron.). He was probably engaged in the siege of London in this year, as the Norse *Annalar* record that he came to England and won (*sic*) London, and that his son succeeded him in Norway[1]. According to

[1] *Flateyjarbók*, iii. 505, App. to Vigfusson's *Sturlunga Saga*, ii. 351, under the erroneous date of 1012.

CHARTER XII. 147

the *Knytlinga Saga*, c. 15, Eirik, with part of the þingamenn, beat Ulfkell in two battles in East Anglia[1]. Cnut, upon his accession to the rule of the whole of England in 1017, confirmed Eirik in his earldom. About this time St. Olaf gained possession of the Norwegian crown and drove out Hakon, Eirik's son, and Swain, Eirik's brother. Hakon came to England, and signs amongst Cnut's *duces* from 1019 to 1036, being, according to *CD*. iv. 56[4], ealdorman of Worcestershire. Eirik's attachment to Cnut was further strengthened by Hakon's marriage with Cnut's niece Gunhildr. Eirik's long friendship and service to Cnut and his father make us loath to believe that this great king rewarded him with exile. Freeman (*N.C.* i. 429), adopting the statements of Malmesbury and Huntingdon, fixes Eirik's exile in 1023, the date of his last signature. Huntingdon's statement seems to be founded upon Malmesbury (*G.R.*, p. 219), so that Malmesbury is the only authority for the exile. From what we know of Eirik's character it is very unlikely that the cause of his exile, as stated by Malmesbury, p. 215, was that he claimed half the kingdom from Cnut. The exile of Eirik certainly gives a rhetorical completeness to the passages in Malmesbury and Huntingdon, and it is difficult to avoid the suspicion that the striving after this completeness is the reason for the statement. Thorkell, whose outlawry in 1021 is recorded in the Chronicle, was restored to Cnut's favour in 1023, the earliest possible date for Eirik's exile, so that they cannot both have been exiled at the same time. Malmesbury says that Eirik returned to his *natale solum*, which is highly improbable, unless the expression means the Scandinavian north, for Norway was in 1023 in the possession of St. Olaf, who had expelled Eirik's son and brother[2]. The sagas, which know nothing of Eirik's exile, state that he bled to death shortly before, or after, a pilgrimage to Rome, either from natural causes or as the result of an operation upon his uvula (Munch, p. 483). Cnut's relations with Hakon, Eirik's son, do not favour the view that he had exiled Eirik, for Hakon continued in his favour for some years after Eirik's alleged exile, and was made viceroy of Norway when that kingdom was added to Cnut's possessions (1028). There is, however, reason to believe that Hakon eventually fell out of favour, for we have the statement of Florence of Worcester, in 1029, that Cnut sent Hakon *quasi legationis causa in exilium*. As Hakon had been ealdorman of Worcestershire, Florence's authority here is not lightly to be set aside. Freeman's suggestion (*N.C.* i. 430) that the

---

[1] Munch, p. 481, note 2, compares the *Encomium Emmae*, 169 A.
[2] Steenstrup, iii. 321, does not believe that Eirik was exiled. *Fagrskinna*, c. 88, says that he died in England, but fixes his death thirteen years after the death of Olaf Tryggvason, i.e. in 1013, thus agreeing with the *Annalar* (*Flatey.*, iii. 506 ; *Sturlunga Saga*, App. ii. 351). These dates are obviously wrong.

meaning of Florence's strange phrase is that Cnut sent Hakon to Norway 'to fill the post which his father had held as viceroy in Norway,' is opposed to the sagas (Munch, p. 766; Steenstrup, iii. 382), which say that Cnut recalled him to England from Norway shortly before he was drowned at sea. Eirik at the time of his death (or exile) was about 70, or, if Munch's correction (p. 484) of *Fagrskinna* be right, 60. He was, according to the Norwegian historian, a brave and honourable warrior, of noble and chivalrous mind. The weakness that marked his government of Norway arose from his good nature and complacent disposition, qualities little suitable to the restless times in which his life was cast.

55. Þorð. ON. *Þórðr*, from **þórwǫrðr* (Noreen, *Altnord. Gram.*², § 240, 2). This name appears amongst the *ministri* witnessing royal charters from 1018 throughout Cnut's reign, and into that of Edward the Confessor. There were two *ministri* of the name in Cnut's time. They witness an original charter of 1024 as *ðorð* and *þorð* (*CD.* iv. 31²⁵, ²⁷, *OS. Facs.* i, Ilchester, pl. 2). They also, as *þureð* and *þoreð*, witness a charter of 1023 (*CD.* iv. 27³⁵, ³⁶), preserved in the twelfth century *Codex Wintoniensis*. One of them witnesses, as *þored*, an Exeter charter of 1018 (*CD.* iv. 3¹⁶; *OS. Facs.*, Pt. ii, Exeter, pl. 9), and another of the same date, but in later hand, as *þoryd* (Exeter, pl. 10), and a Hyde charter of 1019 (*OS. Facs.*, Pt. ii, Winchester College, pl. 4) as *þured*. The name of a moneyer appears on Cnut's London coins as *ðoræð* and *ðoreð*[1]. Kluge, in Paul's *Grundriss*, i. 789, states that OE. *þored* represents ON. *þóroddr*, but it is evident that it is an adaptation of *þorðr*. The forms *þored, þoryd* suggest connexion with ON. *þorrǫðr*, but, as we have seen (p. 75, note to line 93), this name appears in OE. as *þurferð*.

Þorðr was the name of the þingman who warned Eilífr of the plot to murder the þingamenn at London (see preceding note on Eglaf), and, as many of these men entered Cnut's service, he may be the same person as the present witness[2]. In the saga of St. Olaf, Earl Thorkell and Þorðr the Viking are appointed to lead the attack on one side of London, whilst Cnut attacks it on the other (*Flateyjarbók*, ii. 23; *Fornm. Sögur*, v. 154). This Þorðr the Viking is perhaps the Þorðr who was second in command of the six viking ships attacked by Olaf under Sotasker, when Þorðr submitted to Olaf and followed him (*Flatey.* ii. 15). This was Olaf's

---
[1] B. E. Hildebrand, *Anglosachs. Mynt.*, p. 279. In the *Brit. Mus. Catal. of AS. Coins* the name is impossibly regarded as equivalent to OE. *þeodred*. Earlier instances of the name are: A.D. 940, *þered* (= þored) *minister* (*CS.* ii. 489²⁹); A.D. 969, *þuredus presbiter* (*CD.* iii. 46²⁵); A.D. 971, *ðureð* (*CD.* iii. 72¹⁴); A.D. 983–88, *þorod, þoreð, þured*, &c., *dux*, perhaps Ealdorman of Deira, Freeman, *N.C.* i. 661 (*CD.* iii. 198²⁴, 237¹¹; vi. 113¹⁹, 115⁸, 118²⁵, 121⁶). These forms are all derived from post-Conquest copies, in which *o* and *e* are frequently confused.

[2] *Þorðr* was, however, not an uncommon Norse name.

CHARTER XII. 149

first battle. If the witness to the present charter is this viking, it is evident that he must have left Olaf to follow Cnut.

One of Cnut's ministers of this name is described as 'Steallere' in 1035 (*CD*. vi. 191²). A Kentish charter of 1032 (*CD*. iv. 38⁸) is witnessed by *þorð*, *þurcylles*¹ *nefa*.· This may be the witness to the present charter. An *optimas regis* named Ðored sold land to Peterborough before 1022 (*CD*. iv. 11). The name occurs in DB. i. 286, col. 1; 289 b, col. 2, as *Tored* or *Toret*.

55. Þrym. ON. *þrymr*, originally, no doubt, a nickname. This witness subscribes in 1020-3 as *Ðrim* (*CD*. iv. 17¹⁸), in 1022 as *Ðrumm* (15⁸). In the version of the present charter printed by Kemble (*CD*. iv. 23⁷) Ðrym's name is inserted as a *dux* between those of Eglaf and Yric. In the OE. version (25²³) he appears in the same position as *eorl*. Our text is here more correct than Kemble's. It is not impossible that þrym is the *Thrum* who, *impia motus pietate*, put an end to the sufferings of Archbishop Ælfheah (Flor. Wig. 1012; *Vita S. Elphegi* apud Wharton, *Anglia Sacra*, ii. 141), as this Thrum, being in the army of Thorkell the Tall, must have been one of the Jómsborg vikings, some of whom remained in Cnut's service after the exile of Thorkell.

55. Agmund. ON. *Qgmundr*. It is noticeable that the ON. *u*-umlaut does not appear in the OE. loan-words (*lagu* = ON. *lǫg*, &c.)². Hence this name appears in OE. as *Agmund*, *Agemund*. Another instance is afforded by *Atsor* (*CD*. iv. 139⁸⁰) = ON. *Qzurr*. There is a grant to Agemund of land in Dorset by Cnut in 1019 (*CD*. iv. 7). He witnesses in 1024 (*CD*. iv. 31²⁶).

56. Æþelric. Æþelric was a Kentish thegn, and therefore fitly witnesses this charter. He is addressed by Cnut in 1013-20, together with the archbishop of Canterbury and the bishop of Rochester (*CD*. iv. 9²⁶), and he was sheriff of Kent towards the end of Cnut's reign (*CD*. vi. 187¹⁸; 189¹⁴). There is a grant by Cnut to a *minister* named Æþeric of land at *Mæwi* in 1031 (*CD*. iv. 35). Kemble has not identified this place, but as it seems to be on the River Meavy or Mew, co. Devon, it is doubtful whether the grantee is the Kentish Æþelric. The latter is, no doubt, the same person as *Æðelric bigenga* who witnesses a Kentish charter of Cnut in 1032 (*CD*. iv. 38⁹). As Kemble gives no MS. authority for this text, and Thorpe, *Diplom*. p. 328, simply gives 'MS. Cott. Aug. ii. 70' with a query³, we are unable to ascertain the age of the MS. Hence it may be that *Bigenga* (OE. *begenga*, 'cultivator') is a misreading of *Bicga*, the nickname of a Kentish thegn of the same name (*Ægelric Bigga*), who witnesses a charter

---

¹ Perhaps the *þurcyl hoga* of *CD*. iv. 31²⁹ (OE. *hoga* 'careful, prudent') or the 'þurcyl the white,' of iv. 54.
² Brate, *PBB*. x. 48 and 68; Kluge, *Grundriss*, i. 788.
³ Cott. Aug. ii. 70 is Æþelric's agreement of 1044, cited below.

of Cnut's (*CD*. vi. 191 [5]), and whose will (or a Latin version of it) is printed in *CD*. vi. 199 (A. D. 1050–4). Ægelric Bygga witnesses an original Kentish deed of 1047–8 [1] (*CD*. iv. 117 [22], *BM*. *Facs*. iv, pl. 28), and he is mentioned as witness in a Canterbury deed of 1038–50 as *Ægelric Bicga* (*OS*. *Facs*., Pt. iii, Canterbury, pl. 43). He is clearly the Ægelric who makes an agreement with the archbishop of Canterbury in 1044, the MS. of which is preserved (*CD*. iv. 86; *BM*. *Facs*. iv. pl. 17). That *Ægelric* [2] stands for *Æðelric* is proved by the reference to Ægelnoð, archbishop of Canterbury (=Æðelnoð, 1020–1038). Moreover, Ægelric is called *Æðelrich* in the late English version of this agreement in the Canterbury register (*CD*. iv. 87). Thus there is good ground for holding that Æðelric, the witness of the present charter, is Æðelric Bigenga, and that he and Ægelric Bygga [3] are one and the same person. Æðelric signs charters as late as 1044 (*CD*. iv. 80 [6]).

56. **Ælfwine**. Witnesses from 1019 to 1044. In 1022 (*CD*. iv. 15 [4]) he is described as *satrapa*, a title often given in King Æðelred's time to the minor Ealdormen [4], but here applied to all the *ministri*. He is probably the Ælfwine *dux* of 1032 (*CD*. iv. 44 [17]) and 1035 (vi. 186 [56]). The first of these is from the York *Registrum Album*, and may therefore be an error of transcription for *minister*. But in the second instance, from the Sherborne chartulary, his signature at the end of the *duces* is separated from those of the *ministri* by the abbots' signatures. He is probably the 'Ælfwine the Red' of the agreement of Æðelric in 1044 (*CD*. iv. 87 [7]), and, if so, was a Kentish landowner. Ælfwine the Red witnesses a Canterbury charter of 1038–50 (*OS*. *Facs*. III, Cant. pl. 43).

Byrhtric. Signs in 1019, 1024, and 1026 (*CD*. iv. 9 [23], [25], 31 [30], 35 [1]). He is perhaps (the Kentish?) Byrhtric whose daughter's marriage-agreement is printed in *CD*. iv. 10. It is probably another thegn of this name whose signature occurs from 1038 onwards into the reign of Edward the Confessor.

57. **Leofric**. Signs from 1019 to 1024.

---

[1] This charter is dated by Kemble '1038–1050,' that is the duration of the archiepiscopate of Eadsige, one of the witnesses, and in *BM*. *Facs*. '1044–48,' the date of Siward, bishop of Upsala, another witness. As it is witnessed by Wulfric, abbot of St. Augustine's, it cannot be earlier than 1047, when he became abbot (Thorne, *De Rebus gestis abbatum S. Augustini*, in Twysden, *Decem Scriptores*, col. 1784).

[2] The *Ægelric* of these writs arises from the late forms of the name in *Æðel* produced by the dropping of the intervocalic ð.

[3] A Kentish thegn of the time of Edward the Confessor named *Esber biga* (i. 1 a, col. 2 ; 2 a, col. 1) or *Sbern biga* (i. 2 a, col. 1 ; 7 b, col. 1; 8 a, col. 2 ; 12 a, col. 1 ; 13 a, col. 2) is recorded in Domesday. These probably represent an OE. *Ōsbeorn Bicga*. A Kentish Ælfred Bicga (*Aluredus biga*) occurs at i. 9 a, col. 2 ; 9 b, col. 1.

[4] Cf. *CD*. iii. 356, A.D. 1012 : *Leofsinum, quem de satrapis nomine tuli, ad celsioris apicem dignitatis dignum duxi promouere, ducem constituendo*. Florence of Worcester translates *se Defenisca þegen* of the Chron., 988, by *satrapa Domnaniae*.

Sired. Signs once only in 1023, apart from this charter, as *dux* (*CD.* iv. 27 ³⁵). Perhaps the Kentish Sired the Old of *CD.* iv. 10 ²⁶, A.D. 1016–20.

Godwine. Appears to have been a Kentish thegn, as he grants land in Kent about 1020 (*CD.* vi. 178) and he witnesses a Kentish charter, with an impossible list of witnesses, dated 1026 (*CD.* iv. 32 ²⁴). Freeman (*N.C.* i. 667) identifies the *Goduuinus þegen* of this document with Earl Godwine, but, if the deed have an authentic basis, it is more likely to be this Kentish Godwine. The latter is called *satrapa* in 1022 (*CD.* iv. 15 ⁵), but this probably means only 'thegn' (see note 4, page 150), as four other *ministri* are similarly described. He subscribes as *minister* in 1026 (*CD.* iv. 34 ³⁷), and in 1032 without description (*CD.* iv. 44 ²¹). He is, no doubt, one of the Godwine's of the Kentish marriage-agreement of a Godwine with Byrhtric's daughter (*CD.* iv. 10), and probably the *Godwine Brytæl, minister*, who witnesses in 1035 (*CD.* vi. 187 ¹⁹), and perhaps the Godwine who witnesses in 1044 (*CD.* iv. 80 ⁸).

Eadmær. Witnesses a charter of 1038–44 relating to Kent (*CD.* iv. 78 ⁷⁷). He is probably the Kentish 'Eadmær æt Burham,' who witnesses Godwine's marriage-agreement of 1016–20 (*CD.* iv. 10 ²⁷) and Æðelric's agreement of 1044 (*CD.* iv. 87 ⁶).

XIII.

This interesting confirmation of the liberties of the canons of Crediton is here published for the first time. There is no mention of it in the *Monasticon* or in Oliver's *Monasticon Dioceseos Exoniensis*. The *Magister Leowinus* is probably the *Leowine se canon* of the manumission in Earle, *L.C.*, p. 261 ⁶, and the *Osbertus Capellanus* may be *Osbern se Kapet*, since *-bern* and *-bert* in compound names were frequently confused at and after this period.

XIV.

This very early grant to the Hospital of Burton Lazars, co. Leicester, is not mentioned in Tanner's *Notitia Monastica* or in the *Monasticon*, vi. 632.

XV.

The date of this charter, which has been hitherto unknown, is probably 1165 or shortly after. The donor, Nigel de Moubrai, received the manor of Banstead upon his marriage with Mabel, daughter of William Fitz Patrick, earl of Salisbury (Manning and Bray, *History of Surrey*, ii. 582). He was in possession in 1170 (*Ib.*). His confirmation of the grant of Banstead church to Southwark priory is printed in the *Monasticon*, vi. 171. As this confirmation is witnessed by

Hamelin de Warenna, it cannot be dated earlier than 1164, when Hamelin, the half-brother of Henry II, married the daughter and heiress of the earl of Surrey and Warenne (Robert de Torigni, *Chron.*, ed. Howlett, iv. 221). Nigel de Moubrai was one of the witnesses to the Constitutions of Clarendon in 1164 (Stubbs, *Select Charters*³, p. 138). There is a grant in the *Monasticon*, vi. 172, by Nigel's wife to Southwark priory of one of the virgates of land in Banstead that Ralph Vineton held—no doubt the Ralph *Vinator* of our charter. A Walter *Vinitor* is mentioned in a Reigate fine of 5 John (Feet of Fines, co. Surrey, 5 John, No. 56).

XVI.

An inaccurate text of this charter is printed in the *Monasticon*, v. 63, from the register of Castleacre priory. The deed has a note at the top: 'This deed is printed very faulty by and curtail'd in 1 vol. Dug. Mon. Ang. fo. 632, 633. Francis Blomfield, 1740.' For Bromholm priory, see *Monasticon*, v. 59.

17. delegaū = *delegauit*, referring, like *habuit* in the following line, to the donor's father.

XVII.

This deed is not noticed in the *Monasticon*, vi. 99.

XVIII.

This important charter has been hitherto unknown. It proves that the assumption that the donor, Bernard de Baliol I, was the eldest son of Guy de Baliol (Dugdale; Surtees, *Hist. of Durham*, iv. 51) is unfounded. He was, we learn, Bernard's *auunculus*, probably meaning a paternal uncle. Guy's grant, hereby confirmed, is noticed in the charter of Henry II (*Monasticon*, iii. 549 a). The grant has, however, been known principally through the confirmation of Bernard's son (*Ib.* 551 a). Bernard was one of the leaders at the Battle of the Standard, and was captured with Stephen at Lincoln in 1141. He died before 1167. Our charter should probably be dated fifteen or twenty years earlier than the date we have assigned, since it would, no doubt, be granted very soon after Bernard's succession.

XIX.

There is no notice of this deed in the *Monasticon*, iv. 206.

INDEX.

NOTE.—The adjectives in compound local names, which occur in the text in the oblique cases, are indexed under the weak nominative singular form. Vowel length is only occasionally marked.

Abbevill', Walter de, xviii. 9.
Acra, Herbert de, xix. 17.
Adelaid, wife of Henry I, xiv. 7.
Adulf, bishop. *See* Aþulf.
Æc, eahta, i. 39.
Ædric the Palmer, xvi. 35.
Ægelric=Æþelric, p. 149.
Ældred, abbot (A.D. 969), vi. 179.
Ælfeag, bishop. *See* Ælfheah.
Ælfeg, ealdorman. *See* Ælfheah.
Ælfelm, ealdorman of Northumbria (993-1006), viii. 70 ; p. 121.
Ælfere, ealdorman. *See* Ælfhere.
Ælfgar, x. 31.
— bishop of Elmham (A.D. 1007), xi. 78.
— ealdorman (A.D. 946-951), p. 86.
— — kinsman of King Eadwig (*ob.* 962), p. 86.
— minister (A.D. 957), v. 48.
— — (A.D. 1007), xi. 93.
— — (A.D. 1007), xi. 102.
— writere, x. 20 ; p. 131.
Ælfgifu, wife of King Æðelred, xi. 66.
— of Hampton, p. 122.
Ælfheah, archbishop of Canterbury (A.D. 1007), xi. 64 ; p. 149.
— bishop of Wells (A.D. 930), iv. 78.
— bishop of Lichfield (A.D. 969), vi. 158.
— — — (A.D. 998), viii. 54.
— — of Winchester (A.D. 998), viii. 56.
— ealdorman (A.D. 956-972), vi. 190 ; p. 84.
— minister (A.D. 930), iv. 101.

Ælfheah, minister (A.D. 957), v. 40.
Ælfhere, ealdorman of Mercia (A.D. 956-983), v. 36 ; vi. 182 ; pp. 84, 101, 120.
— abbot (A.D. 1007), xi. 85.
Ælfhun, bishop of —? (A.D. 1007), xi. 77.
Ælflæd, wife of Ealdorman Byrhtnoð, pp. 86, 87.
— offestre, x. 22 ; p. 131.
Ælfmær, Ælmær, bishop of Selsey (A.D. 1023), xii. 52.
— abbot (A.D. 1007), xi. 87.
— — (A.D. 1023), xii. 53.
Ælfnoþ æt Wudeleage, x. 7.
Ælfred, minister (A.D. 930), iv. 106.
— — (A.D. 930), iv. 112.
— — (A.D. 957), v. 42.
Ælfric, archbishop of Canterbury (A.D. 998), viii. 50 ; (A.D. 1007), xi. 21, 109.
— archbishop of York (A.D. 1023), xii. 47.
— abbot (A.D. 969), vi. 170 ; p. 101.
— ealdorman of Hampshire (A.D. 975-1016 ?), xi. 90 ; p. 120.
— of Mercia (A.D. 983-985), viii. 69 ; p. 120.
— minister (A.D. 957), v. 47.
Ælfsige, bishop of Winchester (A.D. 1023), xii. 49.
— abbot (A.D. 998), viii. 64.
— — (A.D. 1007), xi. 80.
— — (A.D. 1007), xi. 82.
— — (A.D. 1007), xi. 83.

(IV. 7)   x

Ælfsige, minister (A. D. 957), v. 41.
— — (A. D. 957), v. 44.
— — (A. D. 957), v. 55.
Ælfsinus, bishop of Winchester (A.D. 957), v. 23.
Ælfstan, bishop of Rochester (A. D. 969 !), vi. 156.
— ealdorman (A. D. 930-934), brother of Æðelstan ' Half-King ' ?, iv. 89 ; p. 74.
Ælfþryð, wife of King Edgar, pp. 84, 85, 85 *note* 3.
Ælfwald, dux (A. D. 925-944), iv. 87 ; p. 74.
— *See* Alfwold.
Ælfweard, abbot (A. D. 998), viii. 65.
— — (A. D. 1007), xi. 79.
— minister (A. D. 957), v. 52.
Ælfwig, bishop of London (A. D. 1023), xii. 48.
— minister (A. D. 1007), xi. 105.
Ælfwine, bishop of Lichfield (A. D. 930), iv. 75.
— ealdorman (A. D. 1032), p. 150.
— minister (A. D. 957), v. 46.
— — (A. D. 1023), xii. 56 ; p. 150.
— the Red (A. D. 1038-50), p. 150.
Ællenstubb, viii. 32 ; p. 114.
Ælmær. *See* Ælfmær.
Æluricus, bishop of Crediton (A. D. 969 !), vi. 164.
Ænlypa æcer, iv. 124.
Ænulf, dux (A. D. 969), vi. 189 ; p. 102.
-ǣre, ' oared,' x. 8 ; p. 128.
Æsc, brāde, i. 25 ; ii. 14.
Æscbriht, dux (A. D. 931-934), iv. 88 ; p. 74.
Æscburnan land, co. Devon?, x. 11 ; p.130.
Æsccumb, i. 29; ii. 20.
Æsculfes weorðig (in Sandford, co. Devon), iv. 49 ; p. 71.
Æscwi, bishop of Dorchester (A. D. 969 !), vi. 157.
Æþelbeald, priest (A. D. 969), vi. 195.
Æðelbert, king of Kent, vi. 28 ; p. 93.
Æþelferþ, minister (A.D. 957), v. 45.
Æðelflæd æt Domerhame, wife of King Edmund, pp. 84, 86, 87.

Æðelfrið, ealdorman (A. D. 883-915 ?), p. 83 *note* 2.
Æþelgar, bishop of Chichester (A. D. 969 !), vi. 162.
— — of Crediton, vii. 18.
— abbot (A. D. 969), vi. 173 ; p. 101.
Æþelgeard, minister (A. D. 957), v. 43.
Æðelhard, king of Wessex, i. 1, 51 ; p. 38.
Æt helig, v. 5, 58 ; p. 81.
Æþelhelm, minister, iv. 103.
— — iv. 111.
Æþelm, bishop of Wells (909?-914), vii. 14.
Æðelmær, ealdorman, (*ob.* 982), p. 88 ; p. 120 *note* 3.
— minister (A. D. 998), son of Ealdorman Æðelweard ?, viii. 73 ; p. 112 *note* 1 ; p. 122.
— the Fat, son of Ealdorman Æðelweard, p. 87.
— minister (A. D. 1007), xi. 94.
Æþelnoð, x. 14.
— archbishop of Canterbury (A. D. 1023), xii. 46.
Æðelred II, king, vi. 147 ; vii ; viii ; xi.
Æðelric bigenga (= Bicga ?), p. 149.
— Bygga (Ægelric), p. 149.
— minister (A. D. 1007), xi. 101.
— — (A. D. 1023), xii. 56 ; p. 149.
Æþelsige, ealdorman, son of Æðelstan 'Half-King' (A. D. 950-958), v. 37 ; p. 84.
— priest (A. D. 969), vi. 199.
Æþelsinus, bishop of Sherborne (A. D. 969 !), vi. 159.
Æðelstan, Æþestan, king, iv ; vii. 18.
— Æðeling, son of King Æðelred, xi. 69.
— ' Half-King,' ealdorman (A. D. 923-958), p. 82.
— (II.), ealdorman (A. D. 940-974), pp. 82, 84.
— bishop of Ramsbury, vii. 13.
— — of Hereford (A. D. 1023), xii. 52.
— minister, iv. 102.
— — iv. 105.
Æþelweard, Æðelwerd, ealdorman, the historian (973-998), viii. 68 ; p. 118.
— ealdorman (A. D. 1018), son in-law of

Æðelweard—*continued.*
Æðelweard the historian?, iv. 128;
p. 79.
— son of ealdorman Æðelwine (*ob.* 1016),
p. 119.
— high-reeve (of Hampshire?) (*ob.* 1001),
p. 119.
— minister (A. D. 930), iv. 108.
Æþelwine, 'Dei Amicus,' ealdorman, son
of Æþelstan 'Half-King,' pp. 85, 118.
— bishop of Wells (A. D. 1018), iv. 127.
— minister (A. D. 1007), xi. 98.
— — (A. D. 1007), xi. 106.
Æðelwold, Aðelwold, abbot of Exeter
(A. D. 1018), iv. 128; p. 79.
— bishop of Winchester (A. D. 969), vi.
19, 155.
— — — (A. D. 1007), xi. 71.
— ealdorman (*ob.* 946-947), p. 74.
— — son of Æðelstan ' Half-King ' (A. D.
956-962), pp. 83, 84, 85.
— minister (A. D. 1007), xi. 95.
— — (A. D. 1007), xi. 107.
Æþeric, bishop of Dorchester (A. D. 1023),
xii. 5 .
Æþestan, *for* Æþelstan, p. 109.
Æþestan. *See* Æðelstan.
Agmund, minister (A. D. 1023), xii. 55;
p. 149.
Ailward, Richard son of, xiv. 13.
Aki, son of Toki, p. 144.
Albineio, Roger de, xiv. 11.
Albini, William de, earl of Chichester,
xiv.
Aldehithe, xvi. 22.
Aldenham, co. Hertford, vi. 98; p. 96.
Aldewrþa (in Horton, co. York?), xvii. 6.
Aldulf, archbishop of York (A. D. 998),
viii. 52.
Alfred, sub-archdeacon, xiii. 40.
Alfwold, bishop of Crediton (A. D. 957),
v. 29; p. 125.
— — — (A. D. 988-1008?), viii. 63; will
of, x; p. 125.
— minister (A. D. 957), v. 57.
— monk, x. 11, 32.

Alr, i. 23; ii. 14; p. 54.
Alretun (Alderton, co. Suffolk), xvi. 8.
Alrscaga, 'alder-holt,' i. 26; ii. 17.
Alvers, Richard de, xv. 12.
Andlanges, i. 11, 29; ii. 21; p. 57.
Angelcynn, vii. 11.
Angla land, vii. 7.
Apple-trees mentioned in boundaries,
p. 52.
Apuldor, i. 20; ii. 11; p. 52.
Apuldre, p. 53.
Armin, co. York, p. 115 *note* 1.
Ashford, co. Middlesex. *See* Ecelesford.
Aþelwold. *See* Æðelwold.
Aþulf, bishop of Hereford (A. D. 951-
1012), v. 31; vi. 161; viii. 62; xi. 74
(Adulf); p. 81.
Atsor, minister, p. 144.
Augo, William de, xiii. 37.
Austen, Robert, F.S.A., pp. v, 89.

Bacton (Baketunia, co. Norfolk). *See*
Baketunia.
Bæcces wyrðe (Batchworth, co. Hert-
ford), xi. 51, 109; p. 135.
Bærlingum, æt (Barling, co. Essex), ix.
11; p. 125.
Baketunia (Bacton, co. Norfolk), xvi. 3,
6, 9, 16.
— Richard, the priest of, xvi. 26, 28.
Baldock, co. Hertford, p. 134.
Balliolo, Bernard (I) de, xviii.
— Guy de, xviii. 5.
— Ingelram de, xviii. 8.
Banstead, co. Surrey. *See* Benested.
Barat, Ralph, xix. 16.
Barling, co. Essex. *See* Bærlingum.
Barnard Castle, co. Durham, xviii. 4.
Barnstaple, co. Devon, O. E. mint at,
p. 79. *See* Beardastapol.
Basileus, pp. 110, 137.
Batchworth, co. Hertford. *See* Bæcces
wyrðe.
Beanhland, viii. 34.
Beardastapol (Barnstaple, co. Devon), iv.
131; p. 79.

Beckenham, co. Kent, p. 116.
Beddrēaf, x. 30; p. 133.
Benested (Banstead, co. Surrey), xv. 5.
Beonna, p. 64.
Beonnan ford, i. 41; ii. 34; p. 64.
Beorclēah, xi. 56.
Beorhtnoð (A. D. 1018), iv. 118.
— See Brihtnoð.
Beornewæaldes hlaw, viii. 33.
Beornnoð, p. 85 note 4.
Beornwynne trēow, i. 27; ii. 18; p. 56.
Beremund, priest (A. D. 969), vi. 197.
Bertune, co. Norfolk, xvi. 13.
Birhtwold, bishop of Ramsbury (A. D. 1018), iv. 126.
— abbot (A. D. 1007), xi. 86.
Birihtwine, bishop of Sherborne? (A. D. 1018), iv. 128.
Bisceophām, x. 28; p. 132.
Bishoprics, division of the western, vii; p. 103.
Blakeberge (Blackburgh, co. Norfolk), abbey of St. Katherine, grant to, xix.
Bleccenham (near Hendon, co. Middlesex), vi. 98; p. 96.
Bletsungbōc, x. 27.
Blomfield, Francis, pp. vii. 152.
Boia, x. 19; p. 130.
Bolling, William de, xvii. 12.
Boneboz, Robert de, xvi. 35.
Books, bequest of, x.
Bradan wætere, æt, co. Hertford, xi. 46; p. 135.
Brakeholm (in Bacton, co. Norfolk?), xvi. 24.
Briges, co. Norfolk?, xvi. 21.
— Toche de, xvi. 22.
Brihtmær, abbot (A. D. 1023), xii. 53.
Brihtwig, abbot (A. D. 1023), xii. 53.
Brihtwine, bishop of Sherborne (A. D. 1023), xii. 52.
Brimley, co. Devon, p. 70.
Broadwater, co. Hertford, p. 133.
Brōc. See Cyneferðes-, Lillan-, Risc-, Scip-, Wo-broc.
Brōc-heard, p. 70.

Brocheardes-hamm (in Sandford, co. Devon), iv. 46; p. 70.
Brocklesby, co. Lincoln, p. 70.
Bromholm (in Bacton, co. Norfolk), xvi. 5, 25.
— monastery of, xvi.
Bromlēah (in Sandford, co. Devon), iv. 47; p. 70.
Brooksby, co. Leicester, p. 70.
Broxtowe, co. Notts, p. 70.
Brunwoldes trēow, i. 29; ii. 20; p. 57.
Bucell', Ralph, xv. 13.
Bucgan ford, i. 28; ii. 20; p. 56.
Bucge, p. 56.
Buci, Robert de, xv. 12.
Buga, minister, iv. 97.
Burewold, bishop of Cornwall (A.D. 1018), iv. 127.
Burton Lazars, co. Leicester, grant to brethren of, xiv.
Byrccumb, i. 24; ii. 14; p. 55.
Byrhsige, x. 24.
— minister (A. D. 1007), xi. 99.
Byrhtelm, bishop of Winchester (960–963), p. 88.
— — of London (A. D. 957), v. 24.
— — of Wells (A. D. 957), v. 28.
Byrhtferþ, minister (A. D. 957), v. 49.
Byrhtmær, preost, x. 12, 32.
Byrhtnoð, ealdorman (A. D. 956–991), v. 39; vi. 185; pp. 85, 102.
Byrhtric, minister (A. D. 1023), xii. 56; p. 150.
Byrhtwold, bishop of Ramsbury (A. D. 1023), xii. 50.

Cæfcan græfa, i. 35; ii. 26; p. 61.
Cællwic (Callington, co. Cornwall), vii. 4; p. 107.
Cærswille, co. Devon, i. 36; ii. 28; p. 62.
Caines æcer, co. Devon, i. 35; ii. 27.
Calic, x. 29; p. 133.
Canterbury, Christ Church, xii.
Caresfeld (Charsfield, co. Suffolk), Baldwin, dean of, xvi. 28.
Casewic (Keswick, co. Norfolk), xvi. 4.

Catascopus = episcopus, viii. 60; p. 118.
Cealda hlinc, iv. 45; p. 68.
Cealua dūn, p. 124.
Cenwald, bishop of Worcester (A.D. 930), iv. 80; (A.D. 957), v. 25.
Cenwulf, king of Mercia, vi. 32; p. 93.
Charsfield, co. Suffolk. *See* Caresfeld.
Chenŀ, Ralph, chaplain of, xiv. 12.
Chichester, William de Albini, earl of, xiv.
Chiltington, West, co. Sussex. *See* Cillingtune.
Chippenham, co. Wilts, p. 73.
Ciddan, Cyddan ford, i. 34; ii. 26; p. 60.
Cillingtune (West Chiltington, co. Sussex?), vi. 104; p. 98.
Cnaresburc, William de, xix. 15.
Cnoll. *See* Cuddan cnoll.
Cnut, king, iv. 126; xii; pp. 141, 146.
Coccebyle, Cocgebyll (co. Devon), viii. 34, 43; p. 115.
Cock, Upper, co. Somerset, p. 115.
Cockbury, co. Gloucester, p. 115.
Cockercombe, co. Somerset, p. 115.
Cole, William, p. 80.
Colen[bryc]g (a bridge over the River Colne, co. Hertford), xi. 58; p. 135.
Comoere, bishop of Cornwall, p. 104 and *note* 6.
Conan, Cunun, bishop of Cornwall, vii. 19; p. 104 *note* 6.
Consul=Ealdorman, p. 118 *note* 5.
Cornh[ulle], Michael son of Ralph de, xv. 14.
Cornwall, site of see of, p. 105.
Coueh[am] (Cobham, co. Surrey), William de, xv. 13.
Coventry priory charters, pp. vii, 94, 100.
Crediton, co. Devon, canons of, liberties of, xiii.
— *See* Cridiantun, Cridie.
Cridian brycg (Creedy Bridge, co. Devon), i. 10, 43; ii. 1, 36.

Cridiantun, Crydianton (Crediton, co. Devon), iv. 29, 129; vii. 15; x. 2, 26; xiii. 8.
Cridie, Crydie, fem., the River Creedy, co. Devon, or Crediton, i. 6, 41, 43; ii. 1, 36; iv. 51, 119, 122; x. 31; pp. 45, 64.
Crydian tun. *See* Cridiantun.
Crydie. *See* Cridie.
Cuddan cnoll, iv. 42; p. 68.
Cumb. *See* Æsc-, Byrc-, Drosn-, Fox-, Francan-, Hafoc-, Holan-, Hrucgan-, Hurran-, Swin-, Wealdan-, Wulf-cumb.
Cunun. *See* Conan.
Cuðhelming bēam, xi. 56.
Cuðred, afterwards king of Wessex, i. 52; pp. 39, 45.
Cydda, p. 60 *note* 1.
Cyddan ford. *See* Ciddan.
Cyneferð, bishop of Rochester (A.D. 930), iv. 82.
Cyneferðes brōc, iv. 51.
Cynesige, bishop of Lichfield (A.D. 957), v. 32.
Cynlaue dyne (Kelvedon, co. Essex), ix. 4; p. 124.
Cyppan hamm (Chippenham, co. Wilts), iv. 64; p. 73.
Cyrstelmæl, xi. 54; p. 135.
Cyrtlan geat, i. 19; ii. 10; p. 52.

Dalch. *See* Doflisc.
Dalingeho (Dallinghoo, co. Suffolk), xvi. 8.
Danegeld, mortgages of land for payment of, p. 76.
Daniel, bishop of Winchester (A.D. 739), i. 54.
— bishop of Cornwall (A.D. 957), v. 33; vii. 20; pp. 81, 104.
— son of Walter, xviii. 10.
Datchworth, co. Hertford. *See* Dęcewrthe.
Dawlish, co. Devon, p. 63.
Dēade lacu, co. Devon, iv. 124; p. 79.
Dęcewrthe (Datchworth, co. Hertford) vi. 103; p. 98.

INDEX.

Defenas, the people of Devon, vii. 16.
Defu (?), xi. 55; p. 135.
Dēormere, i. 31; ii. 23; p. 58.
Depinxit, p. 118.
Devonshire, English conquest of, p. 44.
Dewlish, River, co. Dorset, p. 63.
Dicesget, i. 37; ii. 29; p. 62.
Dilham (co. Norfolk), xvi. 6.
Disc, 'paten,' x. 29; p. 133.
Dispensator, Turstan, xvi. 13.
Diðford. *See* Dyðford.
Divelish, River, co. Dorset, p. 63.
Dodda, p. 49.
Doddan hrycg, i. 14; ii. 5; p. 49.
Doflisc (the River Dalch, co. Devon), i. 39; ii. 32; p. 63.
Dovra, Herbert de, clerk of Bernard de Balliol, xviii. 8.
Dowlish, co. Somerset, p. 63.
Drosncumb (Drascomb, co. Devon), i. 31; ii. 22; p. 58.
Dudd, abbot (A. D. 739), i. 57; p. 45.
Dūn. *See* Grēne dūn.
Dunstan, archbishop of Canterbury, vi. 19, 148; vii.
Dyðford, diðford, i. 37; ii. 28; p. 62.

Eadgar, king, v. 20; vi.; vii 21.
Eadgær, bishop of Hereford (A. D. 930), iv. 81.
Eadgyfu, x. 21.
Eadmær, minister (A. D. 1023), xii. 57; p. 151.
Eadmund, dux (A. D. 937-963), v. 35; p. 84.
Eadnoð, abbot (A. D. 1007), xi. 88.
— bishop of Crediton (A. D. 1018), iv. 117, 127; p. 77.
Eadred, king, vii. 20.
Eadric, ealdorman, brother of Æðelstan 'Half King' (A. D. 942-949), p. 86.
— minister (A. D. 930), iv. 107.
— — (A. D. 930), iv. 114.
— — (A. D. 957), v. 56.
— — (A. D. 1007), xi. 92.

Eadulf, bishop of Crediton (A. D. 930), iv. 26, 76; vii. 15, 17.
Eadweard, bishop of —? (A. D. 930, 931), iv. 85; p. 73.
Eadwig, king, v.
Eadwine, mæsse prēost, x. 16, 31.
Eadwines gemǣre, xi. 49.
Eadwold, ix. 8.
— x. 13.
Ealdred, bishop of Cornwall, p. 105.
— — of Worcester (1046-1060), p. 144.
Ealhelm, ealdorman (A. D. 940-951), p. 88.
Earn, p. 50.
Earnes hrycg, i. 16; ii. 7; p. 50.
East healh, xi. 53.
Eaxe. *See* Exe.
Ecelesford (Ashford, co. Middlesex), vi. 106; p. 99.
Ecgbriht, king, vii. 2.
Ecgfrith, praefectus (A. D. 739), i. 58.
Eda, Richard son of, xvii. 7.
Edgar, king. *See* Eadgar.
Edward, son of King Edgar, vi. 38, 147.
— the Elder, vii. 9.
Efes, 'edge' (of a wood ?), iv. 50.
Egesan treow, i. 38; ii. 30; p. 62.
Eglaf, earl (A. D. 1023), xii. 54; p. 139.
— leader of Danish fleet in 1009, p. 139.
Einarr þambarskelfr, p. 146.
Eirikr, Jarl, son of Jarl Hakon of Norway, pp. 142, 144 sqq.
Elfstan, bishop of London (A. D. 969 !), vi. 154.
Eorþgeberst, i. 26; ii. 17; p. 55.
Eowe, the River Yeo, co. Devon, i. 26; ii. 16; p. 55.
Epylempticus, viii. 20; p. 113.
Ergasterium, 'monastery,' iv. 35; p. 67.
Ernaldus, xiii. 37.
Eðandun (Edington, co. Wilts), v. 11; p. 81.
Exanceaster, Exeter, iv. 129.
Exe, Eaxe, the River Exe, co. Devon, i. 11 *bis*; ii. 2.

Exeter, bishop of. *See* Osbert; Warelwast.

Fearnburg, i. 16; ii. 7.
Felixstowe, co. Suffolk, p. 71.
Feltham, co. Middlesex, vi. 106.
Fentune, co. Essex, vi. 98; p. 96.
Fileðlēah, iv. 49, 52; p. 70.
Filsham, co. Sussex, p. 71.
Fincheham (Fincham, co. Norfolk), Geoffrey, dean of, xix. 10.
Fintes lēah, iv. 41, 54; p. 67.
Florence of Worcester, p. 143.
Focgan igeðas, i. 12; ii. 3; p. 48.
Folcmær, abbot (A. D. 969), vi. 169.
Foldbriht, abbot (A. D. 969), vi. 175; p. 101.
Forceps = calamus, p. 73.
Ford. *See* Beonnan-, Bucgan-, Ciddan-, Hanan-, Herepað-, Hroces-, Hrucgancumbes-, Lilles-, Risc-, Stan-, Wealdancumbes-ford.
Fordwine, dux (A. D. 969), vi. 187.
Forfeiture of lands, viii. 28; pp. 67, 113.
Formosus, Pope, vii. 9.
Forðhere, bishop of Sherborne, i. 6, 55; pp. 39, 41.
Fox cumb, i. 25; ii. 15.
Fræna, dux (A. D. 930), iv. 94; p. 75.
Franca, p. 57.
Francan cumb, i. 30; ii. 22; p. 57.
Friðelaf, dux (A. D. 969), vi. 188.
Friþestan, bishop of Winchester (A. D. 930), iv. 83; vii. 12.
Friðugyð, queen, i. 53; pp. 39, 41.
Frobirig stocc, xi. 47.
Fryþestan. *See* Friþestan.
Furn', Philip de, xiii. 39.
Future case, use of, in OE. charters, p. 38.
Fyrd-stræt, p. 46 *note* 5.

Gainesford (Gainford, co. Durham), xviii. 3.
Gamel the sacristan, xvi. 35.
Gayton, co. Norfolk. *See* Geitun.

Geat. *See* Cyrtlan-, Dices-, Hagan-get.
Geclofa, 'counterpart of an indenture,' p. 80.
Gehealdan, 'pay, satisfy,' x. 21; p. 131.
Gehȳran, p. 125.
Geilholm, xvi. 17.
Geitun (Gayton, co. Norfolk), Alan de, xix. 15.
Gemȳþe, viii. 33; p. 114.
Gen-bōc, 'counterpart of an indenture,' p. 80.
Geoffrey, the priest of Honing (co. Norfolk), xvi. 13.
— the reeve, xix. 13.
Germanus, abbot (A. D. 1007), xi. 84.
Geteld, x. 11, 12; p. 130.
Getēoþian, vii. 3; p. 107.
Gewiht, p. 77.
Gilbert (de Grandgamp?), xvi. 36.
Gisnei, William de, xvi. 34.
Glanville, Bartholomew de, xvi.
— Basilia, mother of Bartholomew de, xvi. 37.
— Hervey de, xvi. 30.
— Leticia, daughter of Bartholomew de, xvi. 37.
— Matilda, wife of Bartholomew de, xvi. 37.
— Osbert de, xvi. 32.
— Randulph de, xvi. 30.
— Reginald de, xvi. 32.
— Robert de, xvi. 31.
— Roger de, xvi. 13, 30.
— William de, xvi. 2, 31.
Gocelin the priest, xvi. 29.
— the prior's nephew, xvi. 36.
Goc[elin] uinator, xv. 13.
Godeman, abbot (A. D. 1007), xi. 89.
Godric, x. 4, 16.
— be Crydian, x. 31.
— minister (A. D. 1007), xi. 97.
Godwine, bishop of Rochester (A. D. 1023), xii. 52.
— — Lichfield or Rochester (A. D. 1007), xi. 76.
— Brytæl, minister (A. D. 1035), p. 151.

Godwine—*continued.*
— earl (1018–1053), xii. 54 ; p. 139.
— minister (A.D. 1023), xii. 57 ; p. 151.
Godw[ine], abbot (A.D. 969), vi. 176;
 p. 101.
Græfa, -e, 'bush, thicket, grove,' i. 35 ;
 ii. 26 ; p. 61.
Grandgamp, William de, xvi. 36.
grēna hyll, viii. 42.
— weg, i. 20 ; ii. 11 ; viii. 38 ; p. 53.
Grendel, p. 50.
Grendeles pyt, i. 14 ; ii. 5 ; p. 50.
Grēne dūn, i. 27 ; ii. 17 ; p. 55.
Greneho (in Greenhow Hundred, co. Norfolk?), xvi. 21.
Grim, dux (A.D. 930), iv. 95 ; p. 75.
Grimkytel, x. 14.
Guþrum, dux (A.D. 930), iv. 92 ; p. 75.
Gyða, daughter of King Swain, wife of Jarl Eirikr, p. 146.
— wife of Earl Godwine, daughter of Thorgils Sprakaleggr, p. 139.

Hac[on], Richard, son of, xiv. 12.
Hæahhewelle, viii. 35.
-hǣme, names ending in, p. 116.
-hǣminga, in local names, p. 117.
Hafoccumb, i. 40, 42 ; ii. 33, 34.
Haga, iv. 47 ; p. 70.
Hagan ge(a)t, i. 13, 40, 42 ; ii. 4, 33, 35.
Hakon, earl, son of Eirikir, ealdorman of Worcestershire, pp. 144, 147, 148.
Halgeford (Halliford, co. Middlesex), vi. 106 ; p. 98.
Hamma (Ham, co. Surrey), xv. 7.
Hamme (Ham, co. Essex), vi. 97 ; p. 96.
Hamo, xix. 12.
Hanan ford, i. 24 ; ii. 15 ; p. 55.
Hand, a person inheriting, ix. 9 ; p. 125.
Hangra, p. 134.
Haninges (Honing, co. Norfolk), xvi. 7, 10, 13.
Hánon, dat. pl. ?, x. 8 ; p. 128.
Hāra þorn, xi. 55.
Hardwick, Prior's, co. Warwick, p. 114.
Hasting', Richard de, xv. 11.

Hēafod. *See* Byrccumbes-, Drosncumbes-, Foxcumbes-, Holancumbes-, Hurrancumbes-, Wulfcumbes-heafod.
Hēafod-botl, ix. 7 ; p. 125.
Healh, xi. 53.
Healre dūne, on, i. 33 ; ii. 25 ; p. 60.
Heding, Walter de, xviii. 8.
Helge-Aa, near Christianstad, battle of, 1025, p. 142.
Helig, æt, v. 5, 58 ; p. 81.
Heming, leader of Danish fleet in 1009, p. 139.
Hemingborough, co. York, p. 140.
Hemminus, xiii. 41.
Hendon, co. Middlesex, p. 97.
Hendred, co. Berks, p. 72.
Henne stigel (Henstill, co. Devon), iv. 53 ; p. 71.
Henstill, co. Devon. *See* Henne stigel.
Here, p. 47.
Herefrid, the priest, xvi. 11.
Herefryth, praefectus (A.D. 739), i. 56.
Herepaþ, herpað, i. 10, 27, 42 ; ii. 2, 18 ; iv. 41, 43, 44, 49, 123, 125 ; pp. 46, 56, 64, 68.
Herepaðford, i. 19 ; ii. 10 ; p. 52.
Herestrǣt, p. 46.
Hereweald, bishop of Sherborne, p. 41.
Heriot, p. 127.
Hīwscype, x. 4 ; p. 127.
Hjǫrunagavágr, battle of, p. 145.
Hlidaford (Lidford, co. Devon), iv. 131 ; p. 79.
Hlinc. *See* Cealda hlinc.
Hlodbroc (Ladbrooke, co. Warwick), viii. 14, 28, 30, 36, 37, 40, 77 ; p. 113.
Hlos, p. 70.
Hloslēah, iv. 48 ; p. 70.
Hlȳpe, i. 23, 41 ; ii. 14 ; p. 54.
Hnutlēa (Notley, co. Essex), ix. 5 ; p. 125.
Hola cumb, iv. 41 ; p. 68.
Holewelle (Holwell, co. Bedford), vi. 103 ; p. 98.
Honing (Haninges, co. Norfolk), xvi. 7.
Horham, co. Suffolk, xvi. 7, 16.

INDEX. 161

Horses, wild, p. 130.
Hortona, Thomas, son of Hugh de, xvii.
Housecarls, p. 140.
Hrabanus Maurus, x. 10; p. 129.
Hremnes burg (Ramsbury, co. Wilts), vii. 13.
Hrēodbrōc, viii. 39; p. 116.
Hrēodburna (Radbourn, co. Warwick), viii. 14, 29, 37, 77; p. 113.
Hrigchrægl, x. 22; p. 131.
Hroces ford (Ruxford, co. Devon), iv. 53; p. 72.
Hroðward, archbishop of York (A. D. 930), iv. 74.
Hrucgan cumb, i. 15; ii. 6; p. 50.
Hrycg. *See* landsceare-, doddan-, earnes-, middel-hrycg.
Hundred, p. 41.
Hunstanestun (Hunstanton, co. Norfolk), Randolph de, xix. 11.
Hurel, Richard, xvi. 14.
Hurran cumb, i. 32; ii. 24; p. 58.
Hyærde wyc, viii. 31; p. 114.

Idoua. *See* Geclofa.
Iduma, iv. 2; p. 65.
Ifigbearo, i. 15; ii. 6; p. 50.
Incarnation, era of the, p. 45.
Indentures, OE. terms for, p. 80.
Ine, king of Wessex, p. 39.
Ing', Herveo de, xiv. 13.
Ingolf, Geoffrey son of, xvii. 15.
Iric, earl of Northumbria (1018–1023), xii. 55; p. 142 sqq.
Itchen, River, co. Warwick. *See* Ycene.
Itching, River, co. Hants, p. 113.
Itchington, co. Warwick, pp. 112, 113, 114.
Ivel, River, co. Hertford, p. 135.

John XIII, Pope, vi. 42; p. 94.
Jómsborg, vikings of, p. 139 sqq., 149.
Jómsvikinga Saga, pp. 140, 144, 145.

Kæppe, x. 17; p. 130.
Kardinal, Geoffrey, xvii. 13.
— Thomas, xvii. 14.

(IV. 7)

Kelvedon, co. Essex. *See* Cynlaue dyne.
Kenulfus. *See* Cenwulf.
Kenwold, x. 18.
Keswick (co. Norfolk). *See* Casewick.
Ketel, Richard son of, xvi. 15.
Kineward, abbot (A. D. 969), vi. 171; p. 101.

Lacu, i. 21; ii. 12; p. 54.
Ladbrooke, co. Warwick. *See* Hlodbroc.
Landhredding, iv. 118; p. 76.
Landscearu, p. 48.
Landsceare hrycg, i. 12.
Landwiþa (Lawhitton, Launceston, Cornwall), vii. 5; p. 107.
Langa stān, i. 32; ii. 23; p. 58.
— þorn, viii. 40.
Lankeland, xvi. 22.
Lēadgewiht, iv. 118; p. 77.
Lēah. *See* Beorc-, Brom-, Fileð-, Fintes-, Hlos-, Pideres-, Wude-leah.
Leoffa, abbot (A. D. 969), vi. 193.
Leofl..., abbot (A. D. 969), vi. 177.
Leofric, abbot (A. D. 998), viii. 67.
— abbot (of St. Albans?, A. D. 1007), xi. 21, 110.
— ealdorman of Mercia (1032?–1057), p. 112.
— minister (A. D. 1023), xii. 57; p. 150.
Leofsige, ealdorman of East Anglia (994–1002), xi. 20; p. 135.
— mæssepreost, x. 17.
Leofwaru, ix. 6.
Leofwine, ealdorman of the Hwiccas (997–1023), viii. 12, 30, 71, 77; xi. 91; p. 111.
— minister (A. D. 1007), xi. 96.
— — (A. D. 1007), xi. 104.
— Polga, x. 19, 23; p. 131.
— son of Wulfstan, ix.; p. 123.
Leowinus, Magister, xiii. 37; p. 151.
Lesire, Edward, xix. 16.
Lestrange, Guy, xix. 14.
— John, xix. 17.
— Ralph, xix.

Y

Leu, Ralph de, sub-archdeacon, xiii. 40.
Lewisham, co. Kent, p. 116.
Lifing, archbishop. *See* Lyuing.
Lilla, p. 51.
Lillan, Lyllan brōc, i. 18 ; ii. 9 ; p. 51.
Lilles ford, iv. 44 ; p. 68.
Lotoringensis, William, xiii. 38.
Loþereslege (near Hendon, co. Middlesex), vi. 98 ; p. 97.
Lucan weorðig, iv. 50.
Luhan treow, i. 13 ; ii. 4 ; p. 49.
Lyllan brōc. *See* Lillan brōc.
Lytla gāra, iv. 123.
Lyuing, Lifing, bishop of Wells (A. D. 1007), xi. 75 ; archbishop of Canterbury (A. D. 1018), iv. 126.

Mælpatrik, x. 19, 23.
Mǣr=gemǣre, p. 114.
Mærstan, viii. 32 ; p. 114.
Mæsseboc,. x. 27.
Mæssereaf, x. 27 ; p. 132.
Mæwi (River Meavy or Mew, co. Devon), p. 149.
Maldon, battle of, p. 123 ; date of, p. 88.
Manumission of serfs, p. 132.
Mapuldorgeat, xi. 52.
Marchere, dux (A. D. 969), vi. 183.
Markshall, co. Essex, p. 124.
Marston, Prior's, co. Warwick, p. 114.
Martin, Thomas, p. vi.
Martyrlogium, x. 10.
Matilda, wife of King Stephen, xiv. 7.
Mearcesfleot, near Sandwich, xii. 15 ; p. 137.
Mearcyncg seollan, æt, ix. 4 ; p. 124.
Merl', Morel de, xiv. 12.
Mete and mannum, mid, x. 3 ; p. 127.
Middelhrycg, i. 19 ; ii. 10 ; p. 52.
Mideltun, Alan de, xix. 13.
— Godard de, xix. 16.
Monte Chan[isio], Hubert de, xiv. 11.
Morcere, p. 102.
Mordune (Morden, co. Surrey), vi. 97 ; p. 96.
Mottingham, co. Kent, p. 116.

Moubrai, Nigel de, xv.
— Roger de, xv. 11.
Mulesle (Mundesley, co. Norfolk), xvi. 10.

Narburgh, co. Norfolk. *See* Nereburg.
Nempnett, p. 59.
Nereburg (Narburgh, co. Norfolk), John de, knight, xix. 12.
Neutun', Elsi de, xviii. 9.
Neve, Peter le, ix. 18 ; pp. vi, 123.
Nimed. *See* Nymed.
Normanvile, William de, treasurer of Exeter, xiii. 38.
— Robert de, xiii. 41.
Norðtun (Norton, co. Hertford), xi. 12, 41, 108 ; p. 133.
Norwich, W. bishop of, xiv. 1.
Notley, co. Essex, p. 125.
Nuiers, Master Robert de, xix. 11.
Nymed, Nimed, i. 33, 39 ; ii. 25, 31 ; pp. 58, 63.
Nymet, p. 59.
Nymphsfield, co. Gloucester, p. 59.

Oda, archbishop of Canterbury (A. D. 957), v. 5, 21, 59.
— bishop of Ramsbury (A. D. 930), iv. 79.
Odda, minister (A. D. 930), iv. 96.
Odo, xiii. 37.
— the clerk, xix. 15.
— the priest, xix. 10.
Offa, king, vi. 32 ; xi. 15.
Offestre, x. 22 ; p. 131.
Onrid, x. 25 ; p. 132.
Ordbyrht, bishop of Selsey, xi. 73.
Ordgar, ealdorman (*ob*. 971), p. 122.
Ordulf, x. 9.
— minister (A. D. 980-1006), son of ealdorman Ordgar, viii. 72 ; pp. 87, 122.
Osbert, bishop of Exeter, xiii. 11.
— the chaplain, xiii. 39.
Oscytel, bishop of Dorchester (A. D. 957), v. 26.
Osferð, dux (A. D. 930), iv. 86.
Osgar, abbot (A. D. 969), vi. 172 ; p. 101.

INDEX.

Oslac, dux (A.D. 969), vi. 184; p. 102.
Osred, dux (A.D. 969), vi. 186.
Osulf, bishop of Ramsbury (A.D. 957), v. 27.
Osward, priest (A.D. 969), vi. 200.
Oswig, minister (A.D. 1007), xi. 103.
Oswold, archbishop of York (A.D. 969!), vi. 153.
Oustona, Roger de, xvii. 14.
Oxangehæge, æt, (to) (Oxhey, co. Hertford), ix. 14, 50, 109; p. 135.
Oxhey, co. Hertford. *See* Oxangehæge.

Palling, ealdorman, p. 144 *note* 1.
Palmer, Ædric the, xvi. 35.
Palna-Toki, p. 144.
Pantocrator, iv. 10; p. 66.
Paris, Matthew of, pp. vii, 133.
Paston, co. Norfolk, xvi. 20.
Paðford, i. 30; ii. 22; p. 57.
Patricius=Ealdorman, p. 118 *note* 5.
Paulinus medicus, xviii. 10.
Peter the Reeve, xv. 14.
— Humphrey son of, xvi. 33.
— William son of, xvi. 32.
Pideres leah (Pidsley, co. Devon), iv. 47; p. 70.
Pidsley, co. Devon. *See* Pideres leah.
Piperneass (Pepper Ness, near Sandwich), xii. 14; p. 137.
Pistelboc, x. 27.
Plegmund, archbishop, vii. 10.
Polltun (Pawton, in St. Breock, Cornwall), vii. 4; p. 107.
Powick, co. Worcester, p. 114.
Produme, Richard, xix. 15.
Puda wyrðe, xi. 51.
Purlea (Purleigh?, co. Essex), ix. 5, 7; p. 125.
Puttan stapul, i. 27; ii. 18; p. 56.
Puttoc, praefectus (A.D. 739), i. 59.
Pyt. *See* grendeles-, wulf-pyt.

R... ding[w]ylle, xi. 57.
Radbourn, co. Warwick. *See* Hrēodburna.

Radwell, co. Hertford, p. 133.
Ralph the chaplain, xvi. 29.
— medicus, xiii. 38.
— uinator, xv. 13.
Ramsbury, co. Wilts. *See* Hremnes burh.
Readan wylles heafod, the source of the River Ivel, co. Hertford, xi. 41, 44; p. 135.
Redemption of land from Danegeld, p. 76.
Richard the priest of Bacton, xvi. 26, 28.
— the Reeve, xvi. 33.
Riscbroc, ii. 30; p. 63.
Riscford, i. 33; ii. 24; p. 58.
Rodanhangra, co. Hertford, xi. 13, 45, 109; p. 133.
Roe Green, co. Hertford, p. 133.
Roger the chamberlain, xiv. 13.
— Robert son of, xv. 12.
Roland, Rodlandus, xix. 12.
Rome, pilgrimages to, p. 39.
Rothomago, Robert de, xiii. 40.
Ruxford, co. Devon. *See* Hrocesford.
Ruskevile, Robert de, xvi. 15.

Sachevil', Jordan de, xvi. 29.
Sæberht, subregulus of London, vi. 29; p. 93.
St. Albans, co. Hertford, xi; charters of, p. 99. Sče Albanes stow, xi. 111.
Sče Albanes stow. *See* St. Albans.
St. Denis (Ile-de-France), abbey of, p. 91.
St. Germans, co. Cornwall, vii. 21; p. 105.
St. Petrocks, co. Cornwall, p. 105.
Salt Street, p. 115.
Sancto Laudo, Geoffrey de, xiii. 39.
Sandford, co. Devon, iv. 27; x. 2.
Sandwic (Sandwich, co. Kent), xii. 13, 21, 25.
Satrapa=ealdorman, p. 150.
— =þegen, p. 150.
Sāulsceat, x. 2.
Scal', Robert de, xix. 13.
— Roger de, xix. 13.
Sceaftrihte, i. 23; ii. 14; iv. 42, 44, 47, 48, 53; p. 54.

INDEX.

Sceat, iv. 121 ; p. 78.
Sceg̃ð, x. 8 ; p. 128.
Sceocabroc (the River Shobrooke, co. Devon), iv. 122, 125 ; p. 79.
Scipbrōc, ii. 30 ; iv. 44 ; pp. 63, 68.
Scireburna (Sherborne, co. Dorset), vii. 4, 13.
Sealtstret, viii. 38 ; p. 115.
Serfs, manumission of, p. 132.
Setlhrægl, x. 15, 22 ; p. 130.
Ships, bequests of, p. 128.
Sicclinhala (Sicklinghall, co. York), William son of Robert de, xvii. 11.
Sideman, abbot (A. D. 969), vi. 174 ; p. 101.
Sigar, bishop of Elmham (A. D. 969!), vi. 165.
— bishop of Wells (A. D. 969 !), vi. 163.
Sigeræd, king of East Saxons, p. 40.
Sigered, minister (A. D. 930), iv. 99.
Sighelm, bishop of Sherborne (A. D. 930), iv. 77.
Sillintune (Sullington, co. Sussex ?), p. 98.
Silver weight, p. 77.
Singrapha, pp. 102, 117.
Sire, Edward le, xix. 16.
Sired, minister (A. D. 1023), xii. 57 ; p. 150.
Slessvik in England, p. 140.
Sloswick, co. Notts, p. 140.
Smale ac, xi. 54.
Smēðe hleaw, xi. 46, 50.
Southam, co. Warwick. *See* Suþham.
Southwark. *See* Sudwurch.
Spannie, Roger de, xix. 14.
— Roger, brother of Roger de, xix. 14.
— William, brother of Roger de, xix. 14.
Spila, x. 23 ; p. 131.
Sprēot, xii. 23.
Staines, co. Middlesex. *See* Stana.
Stana (Staines, co. Middlesex), vi. 105 ; p. 98.
Stanard, priest of Keswick, co. Norfolk, xvi. 4.
Stanbeorg, i. 36 ; ii. 27 ; p. 62.
Standan, special use of, p. 78.

Stanford, i. 25 ; ii. 16 ; iv. 52 ; p. 56.
Stānhēmeford, viii. 44 ; p. 116.
Stephen, king, xiv. 6.
Stigel, xi. 57. *See* Henne stigel.
Stocc gemǣre, xi. 43.
Stocchesl' (Stokesley, co. York), Rainer de, xviii. 9.
Stodfald (Stotfold, co. Bedford), xi. 42, 43 ; p. 135.
Strichrægl, x. 21.
Styrcær, dux (A. D. 930), iv. 91 ; p. 75.
Suathefeld (Swafield, co. Norfolk), xvi. 16.
Sudwurch (Southwark, co. Surrey), canons of St. Mary's, xv.
Suestlinges (Sweffling, co. Suffolk), xvi. 8.
Suildam, Roger, son of Reiner de, xix. 16.
Sulh, p. 47.
Sulhford, i. 11 ; ii. 2 ; p. 47.
Sūre apuldor, i. 20 ; ii. 11 ; p. 52.
Suþham (Southam, co. Warwick), viii. 14, 26, 77 ; p. 112.
Sūð ofer, p. 55.
Sutt[on], Vitalis de, xv. 6, 12.
Svoldr, battle of, p. 145.
Swain, king, pp. 140, 145.
Swincumb, i. 38 ; ii. 29.
Swinlentona (Swillington, co. York), xvii. 12.
Sylhče, x. 4 ; p. 127.

Tadmarton, co. Oxford, p. 114.
Talebot, William, xix. 17.
Talevaz, Michael, son of Roger, xvi. 33.
— Roger, xvi. 33.
Tamur (the River Tamer, cos. Cornwall and Devon), vii. 19.
Tankersley, co. York. *See* Thankerleia.
Tapereax, xii. 16 ; p. 138.
Tauma, viii. 49 ; p. 117.
Teddington. *See* Tudintun.
Teign. *See* Teng.
Telligraphus, vi. 97, 107.
Teng (=the River Teign, co. Devon), i. 30 ; ii. 21 ; p. 57.

INDEX. 165

Tents, bequests of, p. 130.
Testudo, viii. 58 ; p. 118.
Tettan burna, co. Devon, i. 17 ; ii. 8 ; p. 51.
Tewkesbury, co. Gloucester, p. 114.
Þæt = þæt hit cymð, p. 113.
— = þonne, þanon, p. 114.
Thankerleia (Tankersley, co. York), Henry, son of Nigel de, xvii. 14.
Ðelbrycg, iv. 49 ; p. 71.
Þeningboc, x. 27.
Þeodred, bishop of London (A. D. 930), iv. 84.
Þimer (= Wimer), abbot (A. D. 969), vi. 178.
Þingamanna-lið, p. 140.
Þoreð = Þorð, p. 148.
Thorkell the Tall, earl, pp. 139, 145, 146.
Þornisces weg, iv. 43 ; p. 68.
Thorrentona, Tlorrentona (Thornton, co. York), John de, xvii. 13.
— Roger de, xvii. 13.
— William de, xvii. 12.
Þorð, minister (A. D. 1023), xii. 55 ; p. 148.
Þorðr, pp. 141, 141 *note* 3.
Þrym, minister (A. D. 1023), xii. 55 ; p. 149.
Þurcyl Hoga, p. 149 *note* 1.
— the White, p. 149 *note* 1.
Þured, priest (A. D. 969), vi. 192.
Þureð = Þorð, p. 148.
Þurferð, dux (A. D. 930), iv. 93 ; p. 75.
Toche de Briges, xvi. 22.
Tochesgate (in Mundesley, co. Norfolk ?), xvi. 12.
Torneie = Westminster, vi. 26.
Torp, Warin de, xvi. 14.
Tottaness (Totness, co. Devon), iv. 130.
Trescs (Thirsk, co. York), William the clerk of, xvii. 11.
Treow. *See* Beornwynne-, Brunwoldes-, Egesan-, Luhan-treow.
Triuiatim, viii. 11 ; p. 111.
Trophaeum sanctae (*uel* agiae) crucis, p. 118.

Tudintun (Teddington, co. Middlesex), vi. 105 ; p. 98.
Tun, x. 20 ; p. 131.
Turstan the despenser, xvi. 13.

Uhtred, dux (A. D. 930), iv. 90 ; p. 74.
Ulf, earl, pp. 139, 142.
— William son of, xvi. 34.
Ulfcytel of East Anglia (*ob.* 1016), pp. 141, 147.
Ulfkytel, minister (A. D. 1007), xi. 100.
Underwedd, iv. 119.
Unna, mas., or Unne, fem., nom. prop. *See* Unnan beorg.
Unnan beorg, i. 37 ; ii. 29.
Utlage, Walter, xvi. 14.
Ual', William, xiv. 13.
Ualein[iis], Robert de, xvi. 29.
Uexillum = signum, p. 138.
Uitalis, Ralph, xiii. 39.
Uinator, Goc[elin], xv. 13.
— Ralph, xv. 13.

Wærnan fæsten, i. 34 ; ii. 25 ; p. 60.
Wærstan, bishop of Sherborne, vii. 14 ; p. 108.
wætergefeal, 'waterfall,' viii. 43 ; p. 116.
Wagen, minister, p. 144.
Wāhryft, x. 15 ; p. 130.
Walter, brother of Ralph medicus, xiii. 38.
— Daniel, son of, xviii. 10.
Waurælwast, Robert de, xiii. 36.
Warelwast, William of, bishop of Exeter (A. D. 1107-1137), xiii.
Warin, masc[ulus], xiv. 13.
Watford, co. Hertford, xi. 51 ; p. 135.
Wattune (Watton-at-Stone, co. Hertford), vi. 104 ; p. 98.
Wealas, the people of Cornwall, vii. 16.
Wealdan cumb, i. 17 ; ii. 8 ; p. 51.
Weardsetl, iv. 54 ; p. 72.
Weights, Old English, p. 77.
Well', Walter de, xv. 14.
Wennington, co. Essex. *See* Winintune.
Weorðig, p. 71.
— *See* Æsculfes-, Lucan-weorðig.

Westminster Abbey, vi; ix; pp. vii, 89 sqq., 123 sqq.
Westsexan, vii. 8, 17.
Westwealas, the people of Cornwall, vii. 2; p. 107.
Wickham Breux, co. Kent, p. 116.
Wihtgar, minister, iv. 113.
Wilde worf, x. 11; p. 129.
Wileford (Wilford, co. Suffolk), xvi. 9.
Wiligburg (Willbury Hill, co. Hertford), xi. 42; p. 135.
William, chaplain, xiv. 12; xv. 11.
Wilmanlehtun (Wormleighton, co. Warwick), p. 115.
Wiltun (Wilton, co. Wilts), x. 29.
Wimer, abbot (A. D. 969), vi. 179.
Wimundehamia (Wymondham, co. Norfolk), xiv. 5.
Wineman, priest (A. D. 969), vi. 199.
Winintune (Wennington, co. Essex), vi. 97; p. 96.
Wintancester (Winchester), vii. 12.
Wirmegeie (Wormgay, co. Norfolk), xix. 4.
Wistan, viii. 27.
— the mason, xvi. 17.
Witeþeow, *adj.*?, x. 3, 28; pp. 127, 132.
Wiþigho, xi. 49.
Wiþigslæd, i. 39; ii. 32; p. 63.
Wlfgeat, priest (A. D. 969), vi. 196.
Wlstan, priest, vi. 194.
Wō brōc (wōn brōc, *acc.*), i. 29; ii. 21; p. 57.
Woodkirk, co. York. *See* Wudekyrcæ.
Worcester, bishop of. *See* Ealdred.
Worf, x. 11; p. 129.
Wormgay, co. Norfolk. *See* Wirmegeie.
Wormleighton, co. Warwick. *See* Wilmanlehtun.
Wrinslesfordia, Sampson de, xvii. 11.
Wrthested, Alexander, son of Odo de, xvi. 34.
— Eberard, son of Odo de, xvi. 32.
— Odo de, xvi. 2.
— Reginald, son of Odo de, xvi. 35.
— Richard, son of Odo de, xvi. 31.

Wudekyrcæ (Woodkirk, par. of West Ardsley, co. York), St. Mary's, cell of St. Oswald's, Nostell, grant to, xvii.
Wudelēah (Woodleigh, South Devon?), x. 7; p. 128.
Wulf-, place names compounded with, p. 53.
Wulfcumb, i. 36; ii. 27.
Wulfgar, x. 15.
— Ælfgares sunu, x. 31.
— abbot (A. D. 998), viii. 66.
— — (A. D. 1007), xi. 81.
— bishop of Wilton (A. D. 969!), vi. 160.
— minister (A. D. 930), iv. 98 (Wulfgær).
— — (A. D. 930), iv. 104.
— — (A. D. 957), v. 50.
Wulfgeat, minister (A. D. 986-1005), son of Leofeca, viii. 75; p. 122.
Wulf-haga, p. 53.
Wulfheah, minister (A. D. 986-1005), son of Ealdorman Ælfhelm, viii. 74; p. 122.
Wulfhelm, archbishop of Canterbury (A. D. 930), iv. 73.
— minister, iv. 100.
Wulfmær, minister, iv. 109.
Wulfnoð, abbot (A. D. 1023), xii. 54.
— minister, iv. 110.
Wulfpyt, i. 21; ii. 12; p. 53.
Wulfred, archbishop, vi. 109; p. 99.
Wulfric, minister (A. D. 957), v. 54.
Wulfsige, bishop of Sherborne (A. D. 957), v. 30.
— — of Cornwall, vii. 22; p. 104 *note* 6.
— — of Sherborne (A. D. 998), viii. 60.
— minister, iv. 115.
Wulfstan, Wulstan, ix. 1.; p. 123.
— archbishop of York (A. D. 1007), xi. 67; (A.D. 1018), iv. 126.
— bishop of London (A. D. 998), viii. 58; ix. 10; p. 125.
— minister (A. D. 957), v. 51.
Wulstan. *See* Wulfstan.
-wunne for -wynne in personal names, p. 56.
Wunstan, x. 18; p. 130.

Wyllun, to (Wells), vii. 14.
Wylman broc, viii. 39.
Wylman ford, viii. 37, 44; p. 115.
Wymondham. *See* Wimundehamia.
Wynsige, minister (A.D. 957), v. 53.
Wyrtrum, iv. 45, 46, 50, 53, 54; p. 68.

Ycene (the River Itchen, co. Warwick), viii. 31, 36; p. 113.
York, St. Mary's Abbey, grant to, xviii. 3.
Yppescelf, viii. 35, 42.
Yric, earl. *See* Eirikr.

THE END.

www.ingramcontent.com/pod-product-compliance
Lightning Source LLC
Chambersburg PA
CBHW032155160426
43197CB00008B/925